At Home in the Kitchen

Mennonite, Hutterite & Amish-Style Cooking

Judy Walter

© Copyright 2009

ISBN 978-0-9812534-0-4

Published and distributed by:
At Home in the Kitchen
P.O. Box 22033
Lethbridge, Alberta
Canada T1K 6X5

Printed in the United States

Carlisle Printing
OF WALNUT CREEK LTD
2673 Township Road 421
Sugarcreek, OH 44681

Dedication

AT HOME IN THE KITCHEN, is lovingly dedicated to my daughters Beverly and Karen who wanted all of our favorite recipes under one cover. It was my distinct pleasure to spend time in my kitchen making appealing and nutritious meals they enjoyed. Now they are quite at home in their own kitchens preparing tasty meals for my sons-in-law and grandchildren.

A number of my recipes come from my mother who was a wonderful cook and inspired me to become creative in the kitchen.

My mentor and friend was a beloved auntie who worked tirelessly to keep a clean kitchen. With love and example, she taught me to appreciate beauty and to strive for excellence in everything including cooking.

I regret that this cookbook was not finished in time to show my father, although he would not have expressed his feelings with many words. Instead he would have gathered armloads and passed them out to all his friends because that's just the way he was.

The Swing

How do you like to go up in a swing,
Up in the air so blue?
Oh, I do think it the pleasantest thing
Ever a child can do!
Up in the air and over the wall,
Till I can see so wide,
River and trees and cattle and all
Over the countryside...
Till I look down on the garden green,
Down on the roof so brown...
Up in the air I go flying again,
Up in the air and down!

Robert Louis Stevenson

This poem captured my heart when I first heard it in grade school. It still touches the child inside that remembers the swing and the farm as it used to be.

Our farmyard was a child's dream playground ... expansive, unique and intriguing. It was an ideal setting to grow, learn and have imaginative fun. Always abuzz with a multitude of interesting activities and animals to observe, I was never bored. It was a perfect fit because it was home and I belonged to this little piece of ground.

Not every child is able to gather fresh eggs, to be responsible for a small flock of geese, to watch cows being milked by hand or puzzle at the magic of a separator that divides the milk into thick cream and skim milk! "Oh, that every child could grow up on a farm", was my sentiment because, 'it is the pleasantest thing ever a child can do'.

Small by usual standards, our Hutterite-style community was comprised of several homes of extended family, a huge barn and machine shop, poultry barns and lots of grain storage buildings. There were four or five of us children that usually roamed the grounds, exploring the buildings and the far-reaching belt of trees that surrounded our yard. We went from place to place and interspersed in the wanderings were detours to the big farm kitchen.

The kitchen was more than a stopover. It was a destination. I love to go back, as far back as I possibly can; close my eyes and remember and feel and smell. Ethnic food, common food, celebration food … delicious, good or ordinary; always interesting and always entertaining. Three times a day the big bell pealed out the gong that announced the meal was ready.

I had misgivings that I would ever be able to follow in the footsteps of the cooks I was observing. Preparing six plump roosters for roasting, rolling out pastry crust for 5 pies, shaping one hundred perogies … it all looked so tedious and difficult. This way of food was woven into my family life and for the time being I loved it. I would not stress about the future.

A short distance from the kitchen was the one-room elementary school I attended. When the noon bell resounded through the air, it was a welcome call; the call to dinner, the best meal of the day. It was a sound I could not ignore. I recall skipping along the sidewalk in happy anticipation of taking my place at the long wooden table.

The setting was plain and simple but the food was wonderful. My favorite feast was roasted chicken with bread stuffing, potatoes and milk gravy, peas and carrots followed by a dessert of pie or cake. A close second was the roast beef dinner minus the beets that would inevitably discolor the mashed potatoes on my plate.

Each noon we feasted on a substantial, if not lavish, main dish consisting of poultry, fish or various cuts of beef. Casseroles were non-existent, as most people preferred the separation of meat and vegetables. It wasn't until I visited Mennonite homes that I was introduced to the one-dish casserole meal.

With exception of salad ingredients and fruit, we rarely bought any produce. During the summer the freezer was stocked with vegetables from the huge garden we harvested. The refrigerated storage room had shelves that were laden with neat rows of home – canned jars of vegetables and fruit along with jam, relish and pickles. A cellar built into a hill housed the root vegetables. Fresh farm milk and cream, eggs and leftovers chilled in a walk-in refrigerator.

I am many years removed from the big kitchen but I am part of that world of food. There is something fascinating about taking the same cookie recipe that was used so long ago in the big kitchen, following it and making the same cookie in my own oven today.

I can't help but think of the people behind the food I love and how much they have contributed to the heart and soul of this cookbook. My recipes may have taken on a new look, but the striving for excellence and care in food preparation I witnessed as a child still shows through.

Over the years my life and travels have taken me to many different homes and traditions where I shared the pleasure of good company and food cooked by other hands. I think of several friends who influenced my style of cooking as I took careful note of their efficient methods and menus. The times I was blessed with invitations to sit up to their laden tables are too many to count. I was bold enough to ask for recipes that I just had to have.

Compiling this cookbook is the culmination of many hours spent in my kitchen making and testing the recipes I chose to include. It is the result of a marathon adventure in patience and perseverance along with generous encouragement from family and friends. They happily ate any dish I cooked for their enjoyment and honest evaluation. I prepared the food for the photos to illustrate a sampling of the recipes as well as celebrate the awesome beauty of Alberta in several pictures.

But a cookbook is just a starting place for cooks. It is important to give recipes your own style. Most people don't come up with recipes out of thin air; they evolve from food they've tasted or read about. You can do the same. Use the margins by each recipe to be adventuresome and make changes to suit your taste. If you are like me, once you find a recipe that works, you will use it over and over again.

My hope is that you will have fun with this cookbook ~ at home in your kitchen.

Table of Contents

Appetizers
Snacks
and Beverages

Appetizers, Snacks & Beverages

My girls loved to have friends over for evening get-togethers. It could be as simple as inviting a friend or two for a beverage and a dessert. Other times it was a special celebration with a crowd of young people. I loved helping them plan the menu and preparing the food.

Serving an appetizer or snack buffet instead of a sit-down lunch was a fun option. We usually planned a hot meat appetizer, a vegetable tray with dip, cheese, crackers and fruit along with a choice of desserts.

If you serve good food that appeals to you and your family, your friends are sure to enjoy it, too.

Fresh Fruit Dip

A fresh fruit tray makes a superb appetizer.
Here is an inviting dip to complement your choice of fruits.

1 pkg. (8 oz.) cream cheese, softened
1 cup marshmallow crème
2/3 cup sweetened condensed milk
8 oz. frozen whipped topping, thawed

In a mixing bowl, combine all ingredients; beat until well blended.

1/8 tsp. tropical punch
   or lime drink crystals
2 tbsp. pineapple juice (optional)

Add drink crystals for color and pineapple juice for flavor; stir to mix. Refrigerate until serving. Turn out into a pretty glass bowl or natural container such as a cantaloupe or musk melon half. Serve with an assortment of fresh fruit.

Beverly Gingerich
Newfield, NY

3

Amish Peanut Butter Spread

It is tempting to eat this spread by the spoonful.
My grandson Tysan relishes the taste on slices of homemade bread.

1 cup brown sugar
1/2 cup water
2 tbsp. butter
1/4 cup corn syrup

Combine sugar, water and butter in saucepan. Bring to a boil and simmer for 2 to 3 minutes. Stir in syrup.

1 1/2 cups peanut butter
1 cup marshmallow crème
1/2 tsp. vanilla

Add peanut butter, marshmallow crème and vanilla. Beat together until blended. Spread will set as it cools. Keep refrigerated.

YIELD   ABOUT 4 CUPS

Beverly Gingerich
Newfield, NY

Cheese Ball

Attractive and perfect for snacking, this cheese ball is a fine blend of texture
and taste. For optimum flavor, bring it to room temperature before serving.
Tiny individual-sized cheese balls in mini muffin papers
look very attractive on a buffet table.

1 pkg. (8 oz.) cream cheese, softened
1 cup shredded cheddar cheese
1 cup cheese spread
1 tbsp. parsley flakes
1 tsp. Worcestershire sauce
1/2 tsp. garlic powder
1/2 tsp. onion salt
1/2 tsp. seasoned salt

In a small mixing bowl or food processor, combine cheeses, mixing well. Add remaining ingredients and mix until thoroughly blended. Line a small bowl with plastic wrap; spoon cheese mixture into bowl. Cover and refrigerate for 8 hours or until firm.

Chopped pecans

Unmold cheese ball and roll in chopped nuts if desired. Place on serving plate; serve with assorted crackers.

VARIATION
Add 1 pkg. (3 oz.) finely diced chipped beef to cheese ball.

YIELD   ABOUT 3 CUPS SPREAD

Karen Yoder
Goshen, IN

Cheesy Garlic Slices

Flavored toppings on a crisp slice of bread
yields a satisfying snack or appetizer.

1 loaf French bread (about 20 inches),
   halved lengthwise

1 1/2 cups mayonnaise (no substitute)
1 cup shredded cheddar cheese
1/3 cup thinly sliced green onions,
   including tops
2 to 3 garlic cloves, minced
1/3 cup minced fresh parsley
   OR 2 tsp. dried parsley flakes
Paprika

In a small bowl, combine mayonnaise, cheese, onions and garlic. Stir until well blended; spread on bread halves. Sprinkle with parsley and paprika.

Wrap each half in foil. Refrigerate for 1 to 2 hours or freeze. Unwrap and place on a baking sheet. Bake at 400° for 8 to 10 minutes or until puffed but not brown. (If frozen, bake 20 to 25 minutes.) Cut into slices.

OPTION:
Heat on grill at a cook-out.

YIELD   12 TO 15 SERVINGS

Tasty Cracker Snack

Crackers dressed up with a tasty topping
make a perfect snack for entertaining.

Snacking crackers, 2 1/2 inches round

1 1/2 cups mayonnaise (no substitute)
2 cups shredded mozzarella cheese
2 cups shredded cheddar cheese
6 green onions, thinly sliced
1/2 tsp. garlic salt

In a mixing bowl, combine mayonnaise, cheeses, onion and garlic salt. Stir together until well blended. Spread on crackers.

Place on baking sheet.
Bake at 250° for 20 minutes.

YIELD   APPROX. 60 CRACKERS

Joann Weber
Raymond, Alberta

5

Whole Wheat Thins

I was dubious the first time I tried a recipe for crackers.
Then I discovered it was easy and now I enjoy experimenting with various seasonings.
In just over thirty minutes I have a batch of homemade crackers made to taste.

1 cup whole wheat flour
½ cup all-purpose flour
1 tbsp. brown sugar
½ tsp. baking powder
1 tbsp. vegetable seasoning*
½ tsp. salt
6 tbsp. butter or margarine

In a mixing bowl or food processor, combine dry ingredients until blended. Add butter and mix until mixture is crumbly.

⅓ cup warm water

Add water and stir or process until dough forms a ball. If necessary, add more water 1 teaspoon at a time.

Roll dough directly on ungreased 10 x 15 - inch rimmed baking sheet. Using a pastry wheel, mark off desired cracker size. (A plastic serrated knife also works well using a rocking motion.) To prevent bubbles, prick the dough all over with the tines of a fork.

The seasoning can be a personal choice. I like to use an all natural seasoning such as Spike or a favorite dry salad dressing and dip mix. Increase or decrease amount as desired.

Bake in preheated 400° oven for 15 to 18 minutes or until golden. Transfer baking sheet to rack. When cool and crisp, separate along lines.

Pictured on page 69.

YIELD 50 CRACKERS ABOUT 1½ INCHES

Party Fondue

A warm creamy dip with great flavor is just right
for an evening snack around a cozy fire.

1 pkg. (8 oz.) cream cheese
½ cup sour cream
2 tbsp. milk
1 pkg. (3 oz.) dried beef, diced
2 green onions, thinly sliced
1 tbsp. diced pimento
1 tsp. Worcestershire sauce
¼ cup chopped pecans (optional)

Soften cream cheese in microwave. Use a double boiler if microwave is not available. Add remaining ingredients; stir until mixed. Continue to heat and stir until warm and smooth.

Serve warm with raw vegetables, chips, crackers or snacking bread.

YIELD 6 SERVINGS

Graham Crackers

It feels like an accomplishment to turn out crackers that
look and taste like the ones you buy. Better yet,
these golden grahams are surprisingly easy to make.

3/4 cup all-purpose flour
1/2 cup Graham or whole wheat flour
3 tbsp. brown sugar, packed
1/2 tsp. salt
1/2 tsp. baking powder
1/4 tsp. baking soda
6 tbsp. butter or hard margarine

*In a medium mixing bowl or food
processor, combine dry ingredients
until blended. Mix in butter until
mixture is crumbly.*

3 tbsp. warm water
2 tbsp. honey
1/2 tsp. vanilla

*Stir water, honey and vanilla together
until mixed. Pour into flour mixture
and stir or process until dough forms
a ball. If necessary, add more water
1 teaspoon at a time. Roll dough
directly on ungreased 10 x 15 - inch
rimmed baking sheet. Dust rolling pin
with flour as needed.*

*Mark off lines lengthwise and
crosswise without cutting through
dough. (A plastic serrated-edged
knife works well using a rocking
motion.) Prick with fork all over in
even rows.
Bake in preheated 400° oven for 10 to
12 minutes until browned. Transfer
baking sheet to rack. When cool and
crisp, separate along lines.*

YIELD   32 TWO-INCH CRACKERS

Trail Mix

There are many options for a great natural snacking mix.
This is a combination we enjoy.

2 cups peanuts
1/2 cup almonds
1/2 cup dried cranberries
1/2 cup yogurt raisins
1/4 cup sunflower seeds

*Combine and enjoy snacking on the
trail or when travelling. Other optional
ingredients may include mixed nuts,
chopped dried fruit, or coconut.*

*Toss in 1/2 cup chocolate morsels to
make about 4 cups mix.*

Pictured on Page 91

Veggie Tortilla Roll-Ups

Dainty rolls packed with wholesome fresh veggies
are a quick cure for that snack craving.

4 ten-inch flour tortillas,
   white or whole wheat

1 pkg. (8 oz.) cream cheese, softened
4 tsp. dry Ranch-style salad dressing mix

Combine cream cheese and salad
dressing mix until well blended.

1/2 cup finely chopped broccoli florets
1/2 cup finely chopped cauliflower
1/2 cup shredded carrots
1/4 cup finely chopped green onions
1/2 cup finely chopped sweet red pepper
1/4 cup chopped stuffed olives (optional)
2 oz. dried beef, chopped (optional)

Add vegetables to cream cheese
mixture; stir to mix well. Divide filling
and spread evenly on 4 tortillas. Roll
up tightly and wrap in plastic wrap.
Refrigerate for at least 2 hours but no
longer than 24 hours. Just before
serving, cut into 1-inch slices using a
serrated knife. Serve with Onion dip,
Guacamole or salsa.

YIELD   ABOUT 40 APPETIZERS

Onion Dip

1 envelope dry onion soup mix
2 cups sour cream

Mix onion soup and sour cream.
Cover and refrigerate.

VARIATION   Add imitation crabmeat
             and garlic salt to onion
             dip for extra zip.

Guacamole Dip

1 ripe avocado, mashed
1 tomato, diced
1/4 cup chopped onion
1 small garlic clove, minced
1 tbsp. lemon juice
1 tbsp. finely chopped fresh cilantro
1/2 tsp. salt

Mix all ingredients together and spoon
into small bowl. To keep avocado
mixture from discoloring, cover with a
thin coating of mayonnaise, sealing
right to the edges. Cover and
refrigerate for 1 hour. Stir in
mayonnaise before serving.

Vegetable Dip

A nice all-round dip that is
equally good with vegetables or chips.

1 cup mayonnaise
  OR salad dressing
1 cup sour cream
2 tsp. dry parsley flakes
1 tsp. seasoned salt
1 tsp. dry dill weed
1/2 tsp. onion powder

On a buffet table, serve dip
in a natural container. Slice
top off of round bread loaf.
Remove bread on inside
and spoon dip into bread
bowl. When the dip is gone
the 'bowl' can be eaten too.

*In a mixing bowl, combine all
ingredients; mix well. Cover and
refrigerate for 1 hour or longer for
flavors to blend.*

*Serve with assorted fresh vegetables
such as broccoli and cauliflower
florets, carrot sticks, celery sticks,
cherry tomatoes or slices of colored
peppers.*

YIELD   2 CUPS

Swiss Cheese Tartlets

Here is an interesting finger food that will have folks asking for more.

16 to 20 ready-to-bake unsweetened
  tart shells (available in frozen section
  of grocery store)

1 medium onion, finely diced
1 tbsp. butter or margarine

*In a small skillet, sauté onion in butter
until onion is tender.*

2 eggs
1/2 cup mayonnaise
1/2 cup milk
2 tsp. all-purpose flour
1 cup shredded Swiss
  OR Gruyere cheese
1/2 tsp. salt
1/4 tsp. pepper
1 can (4 3/4 oz.) crabmeat

*Beat eggs until frothy; add
mayonnaise, milk and flour, beating
until mixed. Stir in onion, cheese, salt
and pepper. Remove membranes
from crab and mix in. Spoon mixture
into 16 tart shells. Set on a rimmed
baking sheet.*

*Bake on lowest rack in preheated
350° oven for 20 to 25 minutes or
until set.*

YIELD   16 TO 20 TARTLETS

Vegetable Pizza

Heaped high with colorful vegetables, this appetizer is a choice selection for a gathering or party. This recipe includes an excellent made-from-scratch crust as well as a time saving option using refrigerated rolls.

1 pkg. dry yeast (1 tbsp.) 1/4 cup warm water 1/2 tsp. sugar	Dissolve yeast in water and sugar.
1/4 cup butter or margarine 1/3 cup hot water 2 tbsp. sugar 1 tsp. salt	In a mixing bowl, combine butter, water, sugar and salt; stir together until butter is melted. Cool to lukewarm.
1 egg, beaten 1 3/4 to 2 cups all-purpose flour	Add egg, yeast mixture and 1 cup flour. Beat until smooth. Mix in enough remaining flour to make a soft dough; gather into a ball.
	With oiled fingers, pat dough over bottom and up sides of greased 10 x 15 - inch baking pan. Bake in preheated 325° oven for 10 to 15 minutes until golden brown. Place on rack for 20 minutes or until completely cooled.
	Complete pizza with spread and vegetables, page 11.

Chris Mullett
Millersburg, IN

ALTERNATE CRUST

2 tubes (8 oz.) refrigerated crescent dinner rolls	Unroll both tubes of dough; separate into 4 long rectangles. Place in ungreased 10 x 15 - inch baking pan. Press over bottom and up sides to form a crust.
	Bake in preheated 375° oven for 13 to 17 minutes or until golden brown. Place on rack for 20 minutes or until completely cooled.

Vegetable Pizza (continued)

Vegetable pizza can be completed with the toppings
several hours ahead of serving and refrigerated.

1 pkg. (8 oz.) cream cheese, softened
1/2 cup mayonnaise or salad dressing
1 to 2 tbsp. Ranch-style powdered
   salad dressing mix

broccoli   cucumbers
cauliflower   tomatoes   carrots
red, green or yellow peppers

1 to 1 1/2 cups grated
   Farmer or Colby cheese

*Combine cream cheese, mayonnaise
and powdered mix; stir until smooth
and blended. Spread over cooled
crust.*

*Prepare your favorite assortment of
fresh vegetables, 3 to 4 cups. Cut into
small bite-size pieces or slices. Layer
vegetables on top of dressing.*

*Top with grated cheese. Serve
immediately or cover and refrigerate.*

YIELD   15 SERVINGS

Pizza Cups

Pizza in a crusty bread shell is easy to prepare
and provides a warm snack or appetizer.

1 lb. ground beef
1 small onion, chopped

1 cup pizza sauce
1 tsp. Italian seasoning
1/2 tsp. salt

2 tubes (10 oz.) refrigerated biscuits
3/4 cup shredded mozzarella cheese

*In a large skillet or saucepan, cook
and stir ground beef and onion until
meat is brown and onion is tender.
Drain off fat.*

*Stir in pizza sauce and seasonings.
Cook over low heat for 5 minutes,
stirring often.*

*Place biscuits in a greased muffin tin,
pressing to cover bottom and sides.
Spoon about 1/4 cup meat mixture
into biscuit-lined cups and sprinkle
with cheese.*

*Bake in preheated 350° oven for 15
minutes or until golden brown.*

YIELD   12 PIZZA CUPS

Chicken Quesadillas

There may be reluctance to move to the main course
when this taste-tempting appetizer is served.

1 small red onion, diced
1/2 sweet red pepper, diced
1/2 sweet yellow pepper, diced
1 garlic clove, minced
1 tbsp. olive or vegetable oil
1/2 tsp. salt

*In a nonstick skillet, stir-fry onion,
peppers and garlic in oil until tender-
crisp. Season with salt.*

12 flour tortillas (8-inch)
2 whole boneless skinless chicken
  breasts; grill and cut into chunks
2 cups shredded cheddar or Monterey
  Jack cheese

*Divide vegetable mixture and spread
evenly on each of 6 tortillas. Top with
grilled or stir-fried chicken. Sprinkle
each tortilla with 1/3 cup grated
cheese; top with another tortilla.*

Olive or vegetable oil
Salsa, sour cream or guacamole

*Lightly oil skillet and brown each
Quesadilla on both sides until golden.*

*OR ALTERNATELY
Heat oven to 450°. Place prepared
tortillas on ungreased cookie sheets.
Bake about 5 minutes or just until
cheese is melted.*

*Cut into wedges and serve with salsa,
sour cream or guacamole.*

YIELD   4 TO 6 SERVINGS

Guacamole Dip

1 large ripe avocado
1/2 cup mayonnaise
1 small tomato, chopped
1 tbsp. lemon juice
1/4 tsp. onion salt

*Cut avocado lengthwise in half;
remove pit and peel. In medium bowl,
mash avocado with fork. Stir in
mayonnaise, tomato, lemon juice and
onion salt. Cover and refrigerate 1
hour to blend flavors.*

Glazed Meatballs

Bite-size meatballs are a popular choice for a party or evening snack.
This sweet-and-sour variation is easy and can be prepared ahead.
Serve with crackers or miniature rolls, a cheese platter and fresh fruit.

1 egg
1/2 cup fine bread crumbs
1/4 cup milk
1 tbsp. fresh parsley, chopped
1/2 tsp. salt
1/2 tsp. onion salt
1/2 tsp. Worcestershire sauce
1/8 tsp. pepper

In a mixing bowl, beat egg with a fork. Add bread crumbs, milk, and seasonings; stir to blend.

1 lb. ground beef

Mix in beef. Shape into 1-inch balls; place on foil-lined rimmed baking sheet. Bake in 350° oven for 15 to 20 minutes or until no longer pink inside.

1 1/2 cups chili sauce
1 1/4 cups grape jelly

In a large saucepan, combine chili sauce and grape jelly. Bring to a boil over medium heat; add meatballs, reduce heat and simmer uncovered for 30 minutes.

YIELD   APPROX. 40 MEATBALLS

TO MAKE AHEAD   Let meatballs cool after baking; enclose in plastic bag, seal and freeze for up to 3 weeks. Add frozen to boiling sauce and simmer for 10 minutes.

MAKING MEATBALLS OF EQUAL SIZE
Lightly pat meat mixture into a 1-inch thick rectangle. Cut the rectangle into squares to form the size meatballs as directed in the recipe. Gently roll each square into a ball.

Hot Hamburger Chip Dip

Make the most of convenience and flavor
in this generous recipe for a dip that is oh-so-good.

2 lbs. ground beef
1 cup chopped onions
½ med. green pepper, chopped
½ med. red pepper, chopped

Cook and stir ground beef, onion and peppers in a large skillet or Dutch oven until meat is brown and vegetables are tender. Drain off fat.

1 can (10 oz.) tomato soup
1 can (10 oz.) cream of mushroom soup
½ lb. processed cheese
  (Velveeta is good)
2 tsp. chili powder
½ tsp. garlic powder
½ tsp. salt
¼ tsp. pepper

Add soups, cheese and seasonings to meat mixture. Stir together and heat to boiling; reduce heat and simmer for 15 to 20 minutes, or until cheese is melted. Stir occasionally to blend ingredients. Serve warm with taco or tortilla chips

SLOW COOKER ALTERNATIVE
Combine cooked beef mixture, soups, cheese and seasonings in slow cooker. Cover and cook on High for 1 hour, or until cheese is melted. Stir occasionally to blend ingredients. Serve immediately, or turn to Low for serving up to 4 hours later.

YIELD   20 TO 25 APPETIZER SERVINGS

Smokey Sausage Wraps

Simple, quick and enjoyed by young and old.

2 tubes (8 oz.) refrigerated crescent
  dinner rolls

Unroll both tubes of dough; separate into 16 triangles. Cut each triangle lengthwise into thirds.

48 cocktail-sized smoked link sausages

Place sausage on side opposite point on triangle. Roll up to the point.

Place on ungreased baking sheets. Bake at 375° for 12 to 15 minutes or until golden brown. Serve warm.

Provide cheese sauce, ketchup and mustard for dipping.

YIELD   48 SNACKS

Soft Pretzels

"On a missions trip to Grenada, my host family treated our group to delicious homemade pretzels. They are easy to make and so fun to eat," says Karen Yoder.

2 pkgs. dry yeast (2 tbsp.)
2½ cups warm water
1 tsp. sugar

Dissolve yeast in water and sugar. Let rise until foamy.

²/₃ cup brown sugar
1 tsp. vanilla
1 tsp. salt
7½ to 8 cups all-purpose flour

In a large mixing bowl, combine yeast mixture, brown sugar, vanilla and salt. Add enough flour to make a moderately stiff dough. Cover and let rise 30 minutes.

2 cups boiling water
4 tsp. baking soda

Mix together and have ready for dipping.

Coarse salt

Cut dough into several portions. Shape each portion into a roll and cut into slices. Roll each slice into a rope; twist into pretzel shape. Dip each pretzel into water and soda mixture. Place onto greased baking sheet; sprinkle with coarse salt. Bake in preheated 450° oven for 8 to 10 minutes. While hot, dip in melted butter.

Melted butter

Serve plain or with cheese dip.

VARIATION
Omit sprinkling with coarse salt. After baking, dip in melted butter; then dip in blended mixture of ¹/₂ cup sugar and 1 tablespoon cinnamon.

YIELD 18 TO 20 LARGE PRETZELS

Robin Stauffer
Palmyra, PA

1.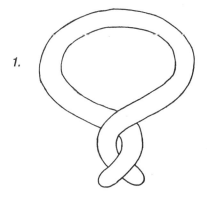

2.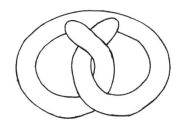

Oven Caramel Corn

It is fun to munch on these cheerful treats.
This snack is great on a road trip and keeps fresh for weeks.

8 quarts popped corn

2 cups brown sugar
1 cup butter or margarine
1/2 cup light corn syrup
1 tsp. salt

In a large saucepan, combine sugar, butter, syrup, and salt.
Bring to a boil over medium heat; boil and stir occasionally for 5 minutes.

1 tsp. vanilla
1/2 tsp. soda
2 cups salted peanuts (optional)

Remove from heat; stir in vanilla and soda until foamy. Pour over popped corn; stir until corn is coated. Stir in peanuts. Spread out in shallow baking pans.

Bake in 250° oven for 1 hour, stirring every 15 minutes.

When thoroughly cooled, store In plastic bags or containers.

YIELD   8 QUARTS

Sweet and Spicy Nuts

One handful of these uniquely seasoned nuts will have you reaching for more.

3 cups lightly salted mixed nuts
1 egg white, slightly beaten
1 tbsp. orange juice

In a medium bowl, stir nuts, beaten egg white and orange juice until nuts are coated and sticky.

2/3 cup sugar
1 tbsp. grated orange peel
1 tsp. cinnamon
1/4 tsp. ground ginger
1/4 tsp. ground allspice

In a small bowl, combine sugar, orange peel and spices; mix well. Sprinkle over nuts and stir until nuts are completely coated.

Spread in a single layer on a rimmed, ungreased 10 x 15 - inch pan. Bake uncovered at 300° for about 30 minutes or until nuts are toasted and lightly browned. Stir occasionally. Serve warm or cool completely, about 1 hour. Store in airtight container at room temperature up to 3 weeks.

Ruth Ann Stelfox
Raymond, Alberta

YIELD   4 CUPS

Butterscotch Sauce

A sauce can turn an ordinary dessert into a dazzling delight.
Add nuts and use as a topping for ice cream.

1 1/4 cups brown sugar
1/2 cup corn syrup
1/4 cup butter or margarine

Heat brown sugar, syrup and butter over low heat to boiling. Cook, stirring constantly, until soft ball stage. (See note: softball, page 298.) Remove from heat.

1/2 cup whipping cream
1 tsp. vanilla

Blend in cream and vanilla until smooth. Stir again before serving.

YIELD   APPROX. 3 CUPS

Chocolate Fudge Sauce

Enjoy an 'old-fashioned fudge' flavor in this delicious sauce.
Use it as a topping for ice cream desserts
or any recipe calling for chocolate sauce.

2/3 cup semi-sweet chocolate chips
    OR 1/4 cup baking cocoa, sifted
1/2 cup brown sugar, packed
1/2 cup whipping cream
1/4 cup butter
1/8 tsp. salt

In a heavy saucepan, stir together chips, sugar, cream, butter and salt. Cook and stir over low heat until chips are melted.

1/2 cup powdered sugar

Stir in powdered sugar. Cook over medium heat, stirring constantly until mixture boils; boil 1 minute.

1/2 tsp. rum extract
    OR 1 tsp. vanilla

Remove from heat; stir in rum. Serve warm over ice cream. Store sauce in refrigerator and reheat in microwave or saucepan over low heat.

YIELD   ABOUT 1 1/2 CUPS

Southern Ice Tea

My son-in-law, John, is the designated tea-maker in his family because his method produces a wonderful drink. Perhaps it is also because he grew up in Virginia where southern tea is a tradition. John contends that pouring the hot tea over ice is what makes it taste extra special.

5 family-size tea bags
  OR 10 regular-size tea bags
4 cups boiling water

Steep tea bags in boiling water, about 5 to 10 minutes.

4 to 5 trays ice cubes
1 1/4 cups sugar
2 to 3 tbsp. frozen lemon concentrate
Water

Place ice cubes in gallon container; add sugar. Pour hot steeped tea directly over ice cubes and sugar. Add frozen lemonade concentrate and stir to blend. Add enough water to make 1 gallon. Serve over ice.

YIELD   1 GALLON

Mint Sun Tea

As the sun's rays heat the water, the tea gently steeps.
Even after hours in the sun, it does not taste bitter.
I enjoy the refreshing flavor of mint, but you can use any other kind you prefer.

2 mint tea bags
1 lemon tea bag
6 cups cold water

In a glass container with tight fitting lid, add water and tea bags.

Close lid and set outside in a sunny place until tea is steeped into a lovely bronze color.

2 to 3 tbsp. sugar
Lemon

Sweeten if desired; stir to dissolve. Chill in refrigerator until cold or serve over ice. Garnish with lemon slices.

Pictured on Page 211.

YIELD   6 CUPS

Floating Ring of Ice

A punch bowl looks particularly nice with a floating ring of ice.

Water to fill a ring mold
Fruit such as strawberries, raspberries,
  kiwi, lemon slices
Leaves such as mint or strawberry tops
Flower petals such as pansy

Fill a ring mold about 1/3 full of water. Arrange the fruit, leaves and/or flower petals in the water so that the best parts face toward the bottom. Freeze. Fill with more water. Freeze.

Unmold ring and carefully add to punch bowl after the punch is assembled making sure the lovely bottom is now floating up top.

Quick Lemonade

Karen's girls love helping with this quick drink.
For fun they like to add a drop of food coloring... pink, green or even blue.

1 can (12 oz.) frozen lemonade
  concentrate
3/4 to 1 cup sugar
3 to 4 trays ice cubes
Water

Place concentrate, sugar and ice cubes in large container. Add enough water to make one scant gallon.

Mix together and serve.

Karen Yoder
Goshen, IN

Raspberry Quencher

A refreshing drink for summer or anytime.

1 can (12 oz.) frozen raspberry concentrate
1 can (12 oz.) frozen cranberry concentrate
6 cups water
1 can (48 oz.) pineapple juice

Carbonated pink grapefruit drink

Mix concentrate with water; stir to dissolve. Add pineapple juice; chill.

To serve, add ice and pink grapefruit drink. Garnish with whole raspberries or lemon wedges.

YIELD   ABOUT 15 CUPS

Pictured on Page 91.

Old-Fashioned Orange Lemonade with a Twist

When I was a child, I couldn't wait for some grownup to make this wonderful drink. Memories of summer include a walk-in refrigerated unit and jars of a delightful beverage mix. Tiny bits of pulp floated in the tangy syrup.

8 oranges
6 lemons
grated rind of 3 oranges
grated rind of 2 lemons
10 cups sugar
10 cups boiling water

Grate rind of 3 oranges and 2 lemons. Squeeze juice from oranges and lemons. In large pot; combine juices, grated rind and sugar. Pour boiling water over all.

2 oz. citric acid
1 oz. tartaric acid
1 oz. Epsom salts

Stir in citric acid, tartaric acid and Epsom salts. Continue stirring until sugar is dissolved. Cover and let stand overnight. Strain and put into plastic containers or glass jars. Refrigerate or freeze and use as needed.

To serve: combine 1 part orange-lemonade syrup to 4 parts water. If desired, add a carbonated drink such as ginger ale or 7-up to individual servings.

Option: Add a teaspoon of grenadine syrup to each glass of drink. It will settle to the bottom adding a striking touch of color. Stir and enjoy the flavor.

YIELD   17 CUPS SYRUP

NOTE
Citric and Tartaric acid and Epsom salts are available in the spice section of most supermarkets. Otherwise, they are available in drug stores.

Slush in the Summer

Slush is cool and refreshing anytime but perfect on a hot summer evening.
Make ahead to serve at family reunions, patio barbecues or picnics in the park.

6 cups water
2½ cups sugar
1 can (12 oz.) frozen orange juice
  concentrate
1 can (48 oz.) pineapple juice
4 bananas, mashed

Lemon/lime carbonated drink
  or ginger ale

Mix water and sugar in large saucepan. Bring to a boil and boil for 5 minutes. Add orange and pineapple juice. Mash bananas and add; mix well.

Chill in freezer until slushy, stirring occasionally. To serve, fill glasses 2/3 full and add a carbonated lemon/lime drink or ginger ale.

To freeze for later, ladle into freezer containers, cover and freeze. When serving, thaw to slush consistency in refrigerator. Pour into punch bowl or glasses and add carbonated drink.

YIELD   15 TO 20 SERVINGS

Sparkling Grape Refresher

This drink is wonderful served with appetizers and is enjoyed by young and old.

1½ cups water
½ cup sugar
1 can (12 oz.) grape juice concentrate
1 can (6 oz.) orange juice concentrate
¼ cup lemon juice
1 large (2 liter) bottle ginger ale

Boil water and sugar together until the sugar is dissolved. Cool. Add grape, orange and lemon juices. Chill well. Just before serving, add ginger ale.

YIELD   ABOUT 12 CUPS

TO MAKE AHEAD
Freeze before adding ginger ale.

Janelle Eberly
Orrville, OH

Karen's Strawberry Smoothie

This frosty cold slush is equally delicious using fresh or frozen fruit.

3 cups strawberries
1/2 cup blueberries
1/4 cup sugar
  (adjust sugar according to sweetness
  of berries)
Tray ice cubes
1 cup water, approx.

Place all ingredients into blender. Blend together until smooth. Serve immediately.

YIELD   6 TO 8 SERVINGS

Fruit Smoothie

2 cups fresh or frozen peaches
2 cups fresh or frozen strawberries
1 can (14 oz.) pineapple chunks,
  undrained
1/4 cup sugar
Tray ice cubes

Partially thaw fruit if frozen. Blend fruit, sugar and ice cubes together until smooth. Serve immediately.

YIELD   6 TO 8 SERVINGS

Mock Eggnog

Joyce says her mom, Mildred, contributes this delicious frothy beverage to their Christmas gathering each year.

2 pkgs. instant vanilla pudding
  (4 serving size)
1/3 cup sugar
1/2 tsp. nutmeg

12 cups cold milk
2 tsp. vanilla extract
1 tsp. rum or butter rum flavoring

1/2 gallon vanilla ice cream
7-up or ginger ale

Combine pudding mix, sugar and nutmeg in small bowl; stir to blend.

In a large container, stir together milk and flavorings. Add pudding mixture and whisk until smooth. Refrigerate until serving.

To serve, pour milk mixture into punch bowl. Add ice cream in scoops. Add 7-up or ginger ale to taste.

YIELD   12 SERVINGS

Joyce Ruckert
Harrisburg, OR

Yeast Breads

Yeast Breads

NOTE
All of the yeast breads were tested in Alberta using flour milled from Canadian hard red wheat. In areas where the climate is more humid, additional flour may be needed to achieve a smooth elastic dough.

Honey Wheat Bread

Baking wholesome tasty bread is a gratifying achievement.
My granddaughter Alyson loves this bread toasted and spread with jelly.

2 pkgs. dry yeast (2 tbsp.)
1 cup warm water
1 tsp. sugar

In a small bowl, dissolve yeast and sugar in warm water.

1/4 cup vegetable oil
3 tbsp. honey
2 tbsp. molasses
1 egg
1 tbsp. salt

Combine oil, honey, molasses, egg and salt. Beat with electric mixer until smooth.

1 cup warm water
1 cup warm milk
3 cups whole wheat four
4 1/2 to 5 cups all-purpose flour

In large mixing bowl, combine yeast, oil mixture, water, milk and whole wheat flour. Beat until smooth. Mix in enough remaining flour to make dough easy to handle.

Turn dough onto lightly floured surface and knead for 5 to 8 minutes. Place into a lightly oiled bowl; turning once to oil surface. Cover; let rise in warm place until doubled, about 1 hour. Punch down and let rise again, until almost doubled, about 45 minutes.

Divide dough into 3 equal parts; let rest 10 minutes. Roll each portion into rectangle, approx. 15 x 9 inches. Roll up tightly, beginning at short side; seal ends and fold under. Place seam side down in greased 9 x 5 - inch loaf pan. Brush loaves lightly with oil. Let rise until doubled, about 1 hour.

VARIATION
HONEY WHEAT BREAD WITH FLAX
Soak 1/4 cup flax seed in 1/4 cup boiling water; cool. Add to batter when mixing in flour.

Place loaves on low rack so that tops of pans are in center of oven. Bake in preheated 350° oven for 25 to 30 minutes or until deep golden brown and loaves sound hollow when tapped. Remove from pans and brush with butter if desired. Cool on wire rack.

Pictured on Page 35.

YIELD   3 LOAVES

Season after season, I was swept along in the rhythm of life on our wheat farm. It was a secure, predictable pattern. The cycle began in early spring when hard red wheat kernels were planted into the rich soil. The old seed died, giving life to tender new shoots. Fertile fields turned a promising, vibrant green.

Summers heat and showers of rain nurtured the exhilarating progression of growing grain to ripened stalk.

As a child, I loved the excitement of the harvest ... catching rides with the wheat trucks, watching the golden heads of grain sway in the wind and methodically fall prey to the combine header. I marvelled at the wonder of the combine that separated the straw and chaff from the prized wheat berries.

Sometimes I got to ride in the truck that hauled the wheat to Ellison Milling where it was milled into premium flours renowned around the globe. Sacks of white, whole wheat and pastry flour were purchased from the mill and brought back to farm completing a continuous yearly cycle.

I'll never forget the tantalizing aroma of fresh, white bread that was baked at least once a week in the old kitchen. I grew up thinking that whole-wheat bread was for those with peculiar diets! On special occasions we bought small loaves of sliced bread for sandwiches, much to my childish delight.

Fluent joys of childhood are a memory but the satisfaction of baking breads with Ellison's flour is still an important part of my life. For me, the simple task of working with yeast dough is a labour of love. I enjoy the thrill of seeing how the dough is transformed in the oven as wonderful smells permeate my kitchen. I can hardly wait for guests to share in tasting the results.

I hope some of my recipes inspire you to bake breads for yourself, your family and friends.

Be gentle when you touch bread
let it not lie uncared for, unwanted
there is such beauty in bread,
beauty of sun and soil
beauty of patient toil,
rain and wind have caressed it
Christ often blest it
be gentle when you touch bread.

– a Celtic prayer

Plain White Bread

I cannot resist the occasional slice of plain white home baked bread.
It reminds me of my heritage as a child;
magnificent bread in slices an inch thick spread with butter and honey.

2 pkgs. dry yeast (2 tbsp.)
1/2 cup warm water
1 tsp. sugar

In a small bowl, dissolve yeast and sugar in warm water.

1 cup warm milk
1 cup warm water
3 tbsp. sugar
3 tbsp. Canola or vegetable oil
1 tbsp. salt

In a large mixing bowl, combine yeast, milk, water, sugar, oil and salt.

6 to 7 cups all-purpose or bread flour

Add 3 cups flour and beat with electric mixer until smooth. Mix in enough remaining flour to make dough easy to handle.

Turn dough onto lightly floured surface and knead for 5 to 8 minutes. Place into a lightly oiled bowl, turning once to oil surface. Cover; let rise in warm place until doubled, about 1 hour. Punch down and let rise again until almost doubled, about 45 minutes.

Divide dough into 2 equal parts; let rest 10 minutes. Roll each portion into rectangle, approx. 15 x 9 inches. Roll up tightly, beginning at short side; seal ends and fold under. Place seam side down in 2 greased 9 x 5 - inch loaf pans. Brush loaves lightly with oil. Let rise until doubled, about 1 hour.

Bake in preheated 350° oven for 30 to 35 minutes or until deep golden brown and loaves sound hollow when tapped. Remove from pans, brush with butter if desired. Cool on wire rack.

YIELD   2 LOAVES

Pictured on Page 35.

Perfect French Bread

What can compare to the aroma and taste
of a perfect loaf of homemade French bread?

2 pkgs. dry yeast (2 tbsp.)
1/2 cup warm water
1 tsp. sugar

In a small bowl, dissolve yeast and sugar in warm water.

1 cup warm milk
1 cup warm water
1 egg, beaten
2 tbsp. sugar
1 tbsp. salt
1 tbsp. butter or margarine, softened
6 to 6 1/2 cups all-purpose flour

In a large mixing bowl, combine milk, water, egg, sugar, salt and butter. Add yeast and 4 cups flour; beat until smooth. Mix in enough remaining flour to make dough easy to handle.

Turn dough onto lightly floured board; knead until smooth and elastic; about 5 to 8 minutes. Place into a lightly oiled bowl; turning once to oil surface. Cover and let rise in warm place until doubled, about 1 hour. Punch dough down and let rise again until almost doubled, about 30 minutes.

Divide dough in half and let rest 5 minutes. Roll each half into rectangle, 14 x 9 inches. Roll up tightly, beginning at long side; seal edges and fold under. Place seam side down on greased baking sheet. Cut three shallow diagonal slashes in top of each loaf with sharp knife. Let rise until light, about 1 hour.

Bake in preheated 350° oven for 20 to 25 minutes or until deep golden brown and loaves sound hollow when tapped. Remove from sheet and cool on wire rack.

YIELD   2 LOAVES

Pictured on Page 35.

Baguettes

One recipe French bread dough,
   divided into 3 or 4 portions

Form each portion into a long narrow roll, the length your oven will hold. Slash before baking as for French loaves. Continue as above except reduce baking time to 15 minutes or until golden brown.

YIELD   3 OR 4 LONG LOAVES

Wholesome Harvest Bread

The unique blend of grains and seeds in this gourmet bread is equally delicious as a plain slice or toasted. Savoring can be sheer enjoyment without guilt.

2 cups water
1/2 cup cornmeal
1/2 cup honey
1/3 cup butter or margarine
1 tbsp. salt

In a medium saucepan, bring water to a boil. Add cornmeal, honey, butter and salt; stir to blend. Cool to lukewarm.

2 pkgs. dry yeast (2 tbsp.)
1/2 cup warm water
1 tsp. sugar

In a small bowl, dissolve yeast and sugar in warm water.

1 cup sunflower seeds
3 tbsp. poppy seeds
1 cup rye flour
1 cup whole wheat flour
3 1/2 to 4 cups all-purpose flour

In a large mixing bowl, combine cornmeal and yeast mixtures. Add seeds, rye and whole wheat flour; beat until smooth. Mix in enough remaining flour to make dough easy to handle.

Turn dough onto lightly floured surface; knead until smooth and elastic, 5 to 8 minutes. Place into a lightly oiled bowl; turning once to oil surface. Cover and let rise in warm place until doubled, about 1 hour.

Punch dough down; divide in thirds. Roll each third into rectangle. Roll up, beginning at short side; pinch edges to seal. Place seam down in greased 9 x 5 - inch loaf pan. Brush loaves lightly with oil. Let rise until doubled, about 1 hour.

Bake in preheated 375° oven for about 30 minutes or until loaves sound hollow when tapped.

This recipe lends itself to individual tastes so experiment. Substitute sesame seeds for poppy seeds or use both. Stir in 1/2 cup oat bran when adding whole wheat flour. Substitute 2 cups whole wheat flour for 1 cup rye flour and 1 cup whole wheat flour.

YIELD   3 LOAVES

Reba Rhodes
Bridgewater, VA

Herb 'n' Cheese Twist

Cheese and herbs are rolled into the dough then shaped into a ring.
Step-by-step instructions make it easy to assemble this attractive and savory 'Twist'.

---

1 pkg. dry yeast (1 tbsp.)
1/2 cup warm water
1 tsp. sugar

In a small bowl, dissolve yeast and sugar in warm water.

3/4 cup warm milk
2 tbsp. butter or margarine, softened
1 egg, beaten
1 tsp. salt

In a large mixing bowl, combine yeast, milk, butter, egg and salt.

2 to 2 1/2 cups all-purpose flour
1 cup shredded cheddar or mozzarella
  cheese, divided

Add 1 1/2 cups flour and 1/2 cup cheese; beat until smooth. Mix in enough remaining flour to form soft dough. Turn dough onto a lightly floured surface; knead until smooth and elastic. Place into a lightly oiled bowl; turning once to oil surface. Cover; let rise in warm place until doubled, about 1 hour. While dough is rising, prepare filling.

HERB AND ONION FILLING

2 tbsp. canola or olive oil
1 cup chopped onion
1 garlic clove, finely chopped

In a nonstick 10-inch skillet, heat oil over medium heat. Stir in onions and garlic. Cook uncovered 10 minutes, stirring every 3 to 4 minutes.

1 tbsp. snipped fresh parsley
  or 1 tsp. parsley flakes
1/4 tsp. dried tarragon, crushed

Stir parsley and tarragon into onion mixture.

TO ASSEMBLE
On a lightly floured surface, roll dough into a 9 x 20-inch rectangle. Spread dough with the herb and onion filling; sprinkle with remaining 1/2 cup cheese. Roll up dough starting with the long side; pinch edge to seal. With a sharp knife, cut roll in half lengthwise, making two 20-inch portions. Place rolls side-by-side, with cut edges up.

Herb 'n' Cheese Twist (continued)

Moisten one end of each portion; press together to seal. Twist the two pieces of dough together several times by lifting one portion of dough over the other. Moisten and seal the remaining ends. Shape into a ring; seal ends together; place ring on greased baking sheet. Cover and let rise until nearly doubled, about 45 minutes. Bake in preheated 350° oven about 25 minutes or until golden brown.

1 egg, beaten

Brush with beaten egg and bake 5 minutes more. Let cool slightly on wire rack; serve warm.

TO FREEZE
Cool completely; wrap, label and freeze for up to 2 months. To reheat: thaw frozen ring. Sprinkle lightly with water; wrap in foil. Place on baking sheet at 325° for 10 minutes or until heated through.

YIELD   1 RING

Pictured on Page 35.

Grami's Dinner Rolls

All of my growing-up years, Saturday was synonymous with fresh buns
for the noon meal. It didn't matter to me what else was served
as long as there were warm buns and strawberry jam on the table.

That was repeated at supper and thrice on Sunday.
I could not imagine a weekend without those incredibly light homemade rolls.

So it is no wonder this is my signature recipe. I love making rolls.
I love eating them and I love giving them to family and friends. Best of all, I love the
shine in the eyes of my grandchildren when I share one fresh from the oven.

2 pkgs. dry yeast (2 tbsp.)
1 cup warm water
1 tsp. sugar

In a small bowl, dissolve yeast and sugar in warm water.

1/2 cup butter or margarine, softened
1/3 cup sugar
1 egg
1 tbsp. salt

In small mixing bowl, combine butter, sugar, egg and salt. Beat together until well blended.

1 1/2 cups lukewarm milk
6 to 6 1/2 cups all-purpose flour

In large mixing bowl, combine yeast, butter mixture and milk. Add 4 cups flour and beat until smooth. Mix in enough remaining flour to form soft dough.

Turn dough onto lightly floured surface; knead until smooth and elastic. Place into a lightly oiled bowl; turning once to oil surface. Cover; let rise in warm place until doubled, about 1 hour.

TO SHAPE ROLLS OR BUNS
This method has been passed down through my family for generations.

It is easy to learn, has great results and is very quick using both hands. With practice it becomes a natural form.

Lightly grease the palm of your hand with shortening. Place cupped fingers, palm side down, over the piece of dough. Move your hand in a circular motion, putting a little pressure on the dough. Continue the movement until dough forms a smooth ball.

Punch dough down; cover and let rise again until doubled, about 40 minutes. Turn dough onto lightly floured surface and divide into 36 equal pieces. Shape each piece into smooth ball. Place about 2 inches apart on greased baking sheet. Cover and let rise until almost doubled, about 45 minutes. Bake in preheated 350° oven for 13 to 15 minutes or until lightly browned.

YIELD   3 DOZEN ROLLS

Grami's Dinner Rolls (continued)

Sandwich Buns: *make Grami's Dinner Roll dough. After second rising: shape rolls; place 3 inches apart on greased baking sheet. Flatten firmly with the palm of your hand 10 minutes after forming. Let rise and bake as on page 32.*

Pictured on page 35 and 211.

Hot Dog Buns: *make Grami's Dinner Roll dough. After second rising: roll dough into oblong, 7 x 14 inches, about 1/2 inch thick. Cut into strips 7 x 2 inches; pinch long sides together to form long roll. Place seam-side down about 2 inches apart on greased baking sheets. Cover and let rise until almost double, about 35 minutes. Bake as on page 32.*

Light Wheat Dinner Rolls

Substitute 2 cups whole wheat flour in the first addition of all-purpose flour.

Cheesy Onion Rolls

Occasionally when I am making a batch of dinner rolls, I like to use part of the dough for a cheesy roll that goes well with a garden salad or bowl of soup. You will need 1/3 of Grami's Dinner Roll dough.

2 medium onions, chopped
  (about 2 1/2 cups)
2 cloves garlic, minced
3 tbsp. olive or vegetable oil

In a non-stick 10-inch skillet, heat oil over medium heat. Stir in onions and garlic to coat with oil. Cook uncovered 10 minutes, stirring every 3 to 4 minutes. Reduce heat to medium-low and cook 20 to 25 minutes longer, stirring every 5 minutes, until onions are light golden brown

3 tbsp. butter or margarine, softened
1 cup grated cheddar cheese

Roll 1/3 of Grami's Dinner Roll dough into 12 x 15 - inch rectangle. Spread with softened butter. Sprinkle onions and cheese evenly over top.

Roll up tightly beginning with wide end. Seal well by pinching edges of roll together. Cut into 12 slices. Place on greased or parchment-lined baking sheet. Flatten rolls with the palm of your hand. Cover and let rise until doubled, 30 to 35 minutes. Bake in preheated 350° oven for 15 to 18 minutes or until lightly browned.

YIELD   12 ROLLS

Pictured on Page 35.

Variations for Grami's Dinner Rolls

Follow directions for dinner rolls until ready to shape. Divide dough into four parts. Use 1/4 of dough in your choice of the variations. Cover and let rise in warm place about 45 minutes or until dough has doubled. Bake at 350° for 13 to 15 minutes or until golden brown.

Crescent Rolls:

Roll dough into a 12-inch circle, about 1/4 inch thick. Spread with soft butter; cut into 16 wedges. Beginning at the wide end, roll up each wedge. Place rolls with points underneath, 2 inches apart on greased baking sheets.

Cloverleaf Rolls:

Grease bottoms and sides of muffin cups with shortening or spray with cooking oil. Divide one-fourth portion into 12 equal pieces. Cut each piece into thirds; shape into balls. Place 3 balls in each muffin cup.

Pictured on Page 35.

Minature Rolls:

Form pieces of dough into 1-inch balls. Place close together in 2 lightly greased round 9-inch layer pans.

Pictured on Page 35.

Square Parkerhouse Rolls:

Roll dough into oblong, 13 x 9 inches, about 1/4 inch thick. Cut into twelve 3-inch squares; brush with melted butter. With dull edge of knife, press a crease just off center of each square. Brush lightly with melted butter. Fold over so top half overlaps slightly; press edges together at crease. Place 1 inch apart on greased baking sheet.
NOTE Can also be cut with round biscuit cutter, however, cutting dough into squares eliminates the need to re-roll scraps.

Make-Ahead Potato Roll Dough

This dough is prepared the night before and can be
used for any of the variations in Grami's Dinner Rolls.

1 pkg. dry yeast (1 tbsp.)
1 1/2 cups warm water
1 tsp. sugar

*In a small bowl, dissolve yeast and
sugar in warm water.*

1 cup lukewarm mashed potatoes,
   unseasoned*
2/3 cup sugar
2/3 cup butter or margarine, softened
2 eggs
1 1/2 tsp. salt

*In a large mixing bowl, combine
yeast, potatoes, sugar, butter, eggs
and salt.*

7 to 7 1/2 cups all-purpose flour

*Add 3 cups flour; beat until smooth.
Mix in enough remaining flour to form
a soft dough.*

*Turn dough onto lightly floured
surface; knead until smooth and
elastic. Place dough into a lightly
oiled bowl, turning once to oil
surface. Cover dough tightly with
plastic wrap and refrigerate at least
8 hours.*

* in place of mashed potatoes use:
2/3 cup instant mashed potato flakes
stirred into 3/4 cup hot water.

*About 3 hours before baking, shape
dough into rolls. Cover and let rise
until doubled, 2 1/2 to 3 hours. Bake in
preheated 350° oven for 12 to 15
minutes or until lightly brown.*

YIELD   ABOUT 4 DOZEN MEDIUM ROLLS

Zwieback

Zwieback is a German word that refers to a double bun or literally translated, 'two-baked'. A small piece of dough is shaped into a ball and topped with a smaller ball. It is a novel way to shape a roll and children love them. I'd like to speculate that one day a German mother had some left over dough after filling all her pans. Being thrifty and creative, she turned the little problem into 'zwieback'.

1 pkg. dry yeast (1 tbsp.)
1 cup warm water
1 tsp. sugar

In a small bowl, dissolve yeast and sugar in warm water.

3/4 cup butter
1/2 cup sugar
2 eggs
2 1/2 tsp. salt

In a small mixing bowl, combine butter, sugar, eggs and salt. Beat together until well blended.

2 cups warm milk
8 to 8 1/2 cups all-purpose flour

In a large mixing bowl, combine yeast, butter mixture and milk. Add 4 cups flour and beat until smooth. Mix in enough remaining flour to form soft dough.

Turn dough onto lightly floured surface; knead until smooth and elastic. Place into a lightly oiled bowl, turning once to oil surface. Cover and let rise in warm place until doubled, about 1 hour.

Punch dough down; cover and let rise again until doubled, about 45 minutes. Turn dough onto a clean surface.

Cut 2/3 of dough into even sized pieces. When formed, ball should be about 1 1/2 inches in diameter. Place 2 inches apart on greased baking pans.

TO SHAPE ROLLS:
See method, page 32.

Cut remaining 1/3 of dough into slightly smaller pieces and form into balls. Press the smaller ball on top of the larger ball, pressing down with the thumb to prevent the top from sliding off during baking. Let rise until doubled, about 1 hour.

Bake in preheated 375° oven for 15 to 20 minutes or until lightly browned.

YIELD   ABOUT 3 DOZEN ZWIEBACK

Special Occasion Pan Rolls

For special occasions such as weddings or funerals,
Hutterite cooks make huge batches of dainty pan rolls.
The dough is richer and sweeter than the one used for ordinary rolls.

Make 'zwieback' dough, page 38. When dough is ready to be formed, cut into uniform pieces. When formed, ball should be about 1½ inches in diameter. Shape rolls using method on page 32. Place close together in greased baking pans. Let rise until doubled, about 1 hour.

Bake in preheated 375° oven for 15 to 20 minutes or until lightly browned.

Pictured on page 127.

YIELD   ABOUT 4½ DOZEN SMALL ROLLS

Geroestet Zwieback
or Roasted Buns

To celebrate the birth of a child, a Hutterite family is gifted
with a traditional batch of roasted buns. These dry roasted treats are
very tasty and great for snacking. When relatives and friends drop in to see the
new baby, they can expect a sampling with a cup of coffee. I was delighted
on the occasions a relative would send a gift of dried slices of 'zwieback'.
And yes, they are perfect for dunking!

Make 'Zwieback' dough, page 38. When dough is ready to be formed, divide dough into 8 uniform pieces, about 4 to 5 inches in diameter. Shape each piece into a smooth ball. Place into four greased 9 x 5 - inch loaf pans, two to a pan. Or place on greased baking sheets. Let rise until doubled, about 1 hour. Bake in preheated 375° oven for 30 to 35 minutes or until lightly browned. Cool completely.

Cut loaves into slices, about ¾ inch thick. Place in single layers on baking sheets; bake in 150° oven till roasted dry, about 6 hours. Increase oven temperature to 250°; toast until golden brown, about 15 minutes. Watch carefully.

When cool, store in airtight containers or freeze to maintain freshness.

**YIELD   8 SMALL LOAVES, CUT
INTO 9 SLICES EACH**

Flaky Croissants

Rolling, buttering and folding this special dough may seem daunting but it is not difficult. After overnight refrigeration, it is quite easy to roll and shape dough into croissants. Baked to golden perfection, they are delicious and so flaky.

1 pkg. dry yeast (1 tbsp.)
¼ cup warm water
1 tsp. sugar

In a small bowl, dissolve yeast and sugar in warm water.

1 cup warm water
1 tbsp. shortening
½ tsp. salt
2½ to 3 cups all-purpose flour

In a large mixing bowl, combine yeast mixture, water, shortening, salt and 1½ cups flour. Beat until smooth, about 2 minutes. Stir in enough remaining flour to form a soft dough.

Turn dough onto lightly floured surface; knead until smooth and elastic. Place dough into a lightly oiled bowl, turning once to oil surface. Cover and let rise in a warm place until doubled, about 45 minutes. Punch down dough. Cover and refrigerate 2 hours.

1 cup cold butter, cubed

Turn dough onto a lightly floured surface; roll into a 10 x 15 - inch rectangle. In a small bowl, beat butter until softened but still cold. Spread ¼ of butter over dough. Fold dough into thirds, starting with the short side. Turn dough a quarter turn. Repeat rolling, buttering and folding three times. Wrap in plastic wrap and place in plastic bag; refrigerate overnight.

Next day

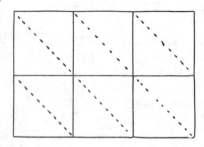

On a floured surface, roll dough into a 10 x 15 - inch rectangle. With a sharp knife, cut into half length-wise, and into thirds crosswise. Cut each square diagonally in half, forming two triangles. Roll up triangles from the wide end; place point side down 2 inches apart on greased baking sheets. Curve ends to form a crescent. Cover and refrigerate for 20 minutes.

1 egg, beaten

Brush with egg. Bake in preheated 425° oven for 15 to 18 minutes or until golden brown. Remove from pan to a wire rack.

YIELD   *12 CROISSANTS*

Oatmeal Dinner Rolls

These rolls are quick because rising time is reduced.
For a ladies tea make rolls very small and serve with chicken salad.

2 cups water
1 cup quick-cooking oats
2/3 cup brown sugar, lightly packed
1/4 cup butter or margarine
1 1/2 tsp. salt

In medium saucepan, bring water to a boil. Stir in oats; reduce heat and simmer uncovered for 1 minute. Stir in brown sugar, butter and salt. Cool to lukewarm.

2 pkgs. active yeast (2 tbsp.)
1/2 cup warm water
1 tsp. sugar

In a small bowl, dissolve yeast and sugar in warm water.

1 egg, beaten
4 1/2 to 5 cups all-purpose flour

In large mixing bowl, combine oatmeal and yeast mixtures. Add egg and 3 cups of flour; beat well. Add enough remaining flour to form a soft dough.

Turn onto a floured surface; knead until smooth and elastic. Place into a lightly oiled bowl; turning once to oil surface. Cover and let rise in a warm place until doubled, about 1 hour.

Shape into 24 rolls; place on greased baking sheets. Cover and let rise until doubled, about 45 minutes. Bake in preheated 350° oven for 15 to 20 minutes or until golden brown. Cool on wire racks.

YIELD   2 DOZEN ROLLS

Karen Yoder
Goshen, IN

41

Southern Raised Biscuits

Because these biscuits are raised, they are exceptionally delicate and flaky.
Wonderful with breakfast or brunch, they also team well with a hearty stew or soup.

1 pkg. dry yeast (1 tbsp.)
1/4 cup warm water
1 tsp. sugar
1 cup buttermilk at room temperature

In a small bowl, dissolve yeast and sugar in warm water. Stir in buttermilk.

2 1/2 cups all-purpose flour
2 1/2 tbsp. sugar
1 1/2 tsp. baking powder
1/2 tsp. soda
1 tsp. salt
1/4 cup butter or margarine
1/4 cup vegetable shortening

In large mixing bowl, blend dry ingredients. Cut in butter and shortening until mixture looks like fine crumbs. A food processor is perfect for this step.

Add buttermilk mixture to dry ingredients, stirring with a fork just until combined. Turn dough onto lightly floured surface and knead gently until smooth, about 6 times. Pat or roll dough to 1/2-inch thickness. Cut with biscuit cutter and place on lightly greased baking sheet. Cover and let rise 1 hour. Bake in preheated 400° oven for 10 to 12 minutes or until golden brown.

YIELD   12 TO 15 BISCUITS

Sweet Breads
and Brunches

Sweet Breads and Brunches

Raisin Danish Twist

*Use large luscious raisins to make a wonderfully
old-fashioned loaf that is good simply sliced and buttered.*

1 pkg. dry yeast (1tbsp.)
1/2 cup warm water
1 tsp. sugar

In a small bowl, dissolve yeast and sugar in warm water.

1/4 cup warm milk
1/4 cup sugar
2 tbsp. butter or margarine, softened
1 egg, beaten
1 tsp. salt
2 1/4 to 2 1/2 cups all-purpose flour
1 cup golden raisins

In a large mixing bowl, combine yeast mixture, milk, sugar, butter, egg and salt. Add 1 1/2 cups flour and beat until smooth. Add raisins and enough remaining flour to form soft dough. Turn dough onto a lightly floured surface; knead until smooth and elastic. Place dough into a lightly oiled bowl; turning once to oil surface. Cover; let rise in warm place until doubled, about 1 hour.

Punch dough down; turn out onto lightly floured surface. Form dough into a roll about 28 inches long. Twist the roll by turning ends in opposite directions. Carefully lift the roll onto greased baking sheet and shape into a large 'pretzel' by forming the roll into a crescent, then drawing ends into the arch and tucking them under to keep dough from untwisting.

1 egg, well-beaten
Powdered sugar

Brush twist with beaten egg and dust generously with powdered sugar. Cover and let rise in a warm place until doubled, about 1 hour. Bake in preheated 350° oven for 20 to 25 minutes or until golden brown.

*YIELD   1 TWIST CUT INTO APPROX.
16 SLICES*

Cinnamon Bread

Make Raisin Danish Twist dough. When dough is ready to be formed, punch dough down. Roll into a 6 x 20 - inch rectangle. Brush lightly with melted butter; sprinkle with a blend of 1/4 cup sugar and 1 teaspoon cinnamon. Roll up tightly beginning at wide end. Seal well by pinching edges of roll together. Twist roll; continue with shaping, rising and baking as above.

Cinnamon Rolls

Cinnamon and sugar rolled up in sweet yeast dough
is an old-time favorite for breakfast or brunch.

2 pkgs. dry yeast (2 tbsp.)
1/2 cup lukewarm water
1 tsp. sugar

In a small bowl, dissolve yeast and sugar in warm water.

1/2 cup butter or margarine, softened
1/2 cup sugar
2 eggs
2 tsp. salt
1 1/2 cups lukewarm milk
6 1/4 to 6 1/2 cups all-purpose flour

In large mixing bowl, beat together butter, sugar, eggs and salt. Add yeast mixture and milk. Add 3 cups flour and beat until smooth. Mix in enough remaining flour to make dough easy to handle.

Turn dough onto lightly floured surface; knead until smooth. Place into a lightly oiled bowl; turning once to oil surface. Cover and let rise in warm place until doubled, about 1 hour.

Note: if kitchen is cool, place dough on a rack over a bowl of hot water; cover with plastic wrap and a tea towel.

Punch dough down and let rise again until almost doubled, about 30 minutes.

1/2 cup soft butter or margarine
1/2 cup brown sugar
1/2 cup white sugar
Cinnamon

Divide dough in half; roll each half into 10 x 15 - inch rectangle. Spread each rectangle with 1/4 cup softened butter and sprinkle with 1/2 cup brown and white sugar, mixed. Sprinkle generously with cinnamon.

Roll up tightly, beginning at wide end. Seal well by pinching edges of roll together. Cut into 1-inch slices. Place on greased baking sheets. Cover and let rise until doubled, 35 to 40 minutes. Bake in preheated 350° oven for 15 to 17 minutes or until lightly browned. Frost while warm with Quick White Icing or Cream Cheese Frosting, page 215.

QUICK WHITE ICING
Measure 2 cups powdered sugar into bowl; moisten with milk to spreading consistency, about 2 tablespoons.

YIELD   2 DOZEN LARGE ROLLS

Cinnamon Nut Coffee Cake

*Winter's chill nudges us inside to enjoy a warm beverage
and great confection like this delicious coffee cake.*

1/2 cup chopped pecans
1/2 cup brown sugar, packed
1/2 tsp. cinnamon

In a small bowl, stir together nuts, sugar and cinnamon; set aside.

1/2 cup butter or margarine, softened
1/4 cup sugar
1/4 cup brown sugar
1 tsp. vanilla
2 eggs

In a mixing bowl, beat together butter and sugars until creamy; add vanilla. Add eggs, one at a time, beating well after each addition.

1 1/2 cups all-purpose flour
1 tsp. baking powder
1/2 tsp. baking soda
1/4 tsp. salt
3/4 cup sour cream

In a small bowl, blend dry ingredients. Add to creamed mixture alternately with sour cream, beating after each addition just to keep batter smooth. Spread half of batter into a greased and floured 9-inch round cake pan. Sprinkle 2/3 nut mixture over batter. Repeat with remaining batter and nut mixture.

Bake in preheated 350° oven for 45 to 50 minutes, or until a wooden pick inserted in center comes out clean. Cool for 10 minutes; remove from pan and cool completely.

1/2 cup powdered sugar
1/4 tsp. cinnamon
2 tsp. milk

Stir together powdered sugar, cinnamon and milk, adding more milk if necessary. Drizzle over cooled cake if desired.

YIELD   8 TO 10 SERVINGS

Cinnamon Blueberry Coffee Cake

*Make as above except:
Sprinkle 2/3 cup blueberries over the first layer
of cinnamon-nut mixture.*

Doughnuts

I have one memory of a long ago New Year's dinner when my diminutive aunt made the traditional 'kuchen' or doughnuts. A long wooden flour-dusted board was lined with rows of neat rounds rising to the perfect moment for the next step. Once in a while I like to recapture that legacy in my own kitchen. The results are marvelous. If anyone has the ambition to make them at home, they are beyond compare.

1 pkg. dry yeast (1 tbsp.)
1/2 cup warm water
1 tsp. sugar

In a small bowl, dissolve yeast and sugar in warm water.

1 1/2 cups milk
1 cup mashed potatoes, unseasoned*
1/2 cup butter or margarine
1/2 cup sugar
1 tsp. salt
1 tsp. nutmeg

In a saucepan, scald milk; add mashed potatoes, butter, sugar, salt and nutmeg. Cool to lukewarm.

2 eggs, beaten
5 to 6 cups all-purpose flour

In a large mixing bowl, combine yeast, milk mixture and eggs. Add 2 cups flour and beat until smooth. Mix in enough remaining flour to make a soft dough.

* in place of mashed potatoes use:
2/3 cup instant mashed potato flakes stirred into 3/4 cup hot water.

Turn dough onto lightly floured surface; knead until smooth. Place into a lightly oiled bowl; turning once to oil surface. Cover and let rise in warm place until doubled, about 1 hour. Punch down; let rise again until almost doubled, about 30 minutes.

Roll out dough 1/2 inch thick. Cut with floured 3-inch doughnut cutter. Let rise on lightly floured board until very light, 30 to 45 minutes. Leave uncovered so a crust will form on dough.

Prepare oil (3 to 4 inches deep) for deep fat frying in a heavy kettle. Heat to 375°; drop as many doughnuts as can be turned easily, into hot oil. Turn doughnuts as they rise to surface. Fry 2 to 3 minutes or just until golden brown. Lift from oil with a long fork; drain on absorbent paper.

YIELD   4 DOZEN DOUGHNUTS

Doughnuts (continued)

SUGARED DOUGHNUTS:

Place in bag with granulated sugar and shake.

GLAZED DOUGHNUTS:
3 cups powdered sugar
1/4 to 1/3 cup hot water
1 tsp. vanilla

In a mixing bowl, stir powdered sugar, 1/4 cup hot water and vanilla together until smooth. Add enough remaining water to make a thin glaze. Dip warm doughnuts into warm glaze. (Keep glaze warm by setting bowl into a pan of hot water.)

ALTERNATE ICING GLAZE:
1/4 cup butter or margarine
1 cup sugar
1/2 cup milk
1 cup powdered sugar
1/2 tsp. vanilla
1/4 tsp. salt

In a saucepan, combine butter, sugar and milk. Cook and stir over medium heat until mixture boils; boil 1 minute. Remove from heat and cool. Add powdered sugar, vanilla and salt; mix well. Dip doughnuts in glaze while doughnuts are still warm.

Berry Danish

Golden pastry is filled with a delicious
berry and cream cheese blend in this sweet delight.
Plan to prepare dough a day ahead.

1 pkg. dry yeast (1 tbsp.) 1/4 cup warm water 1 tsp. sugar	In a small bowl, dissolve yeast and sugar in warm water.
1/2 cup sour cream	In medium saucepan, heat sour cream on low just until bubbly.
1/4 cup butter or margarine 1/4 cup sugar 1/2 tsp. salt	Add butter, sugar and salt to sour cream and stir until dissolved. Cool to lukewarm.
1 egg, beaten	Add egg to sour cream mixture.
2 cups all-purpose flour	In a mixing bowl, combine yeast and sour cream mixtures. Add flour and mix thoroughly. Cover and refrigerate overnight.

CREAM CHEESE FILLING

1 pkg. (3 oz.) cream cheese, softened 3 tbsp. sugar	Beat cream cheese and sugar together until well blended.
1/2 tsp. lemon juice 1/2 tsp. vanilla	Add lemon juice and vanilla, beating until mixed. Set aside.

BLUEBERRY OR SASKATOON FILLING

3 tbsp. sugar 2 tsp. cornstarch or Clearjel 1/4 cup water 1/4 tsp. lemon juice 1 cup fresh or frozen blueberries or saskatoon berries	In a saucepan, blend together sugar and cornstarch. Add water, lemon juice and berries. Cook until thickened, stirring constantly. Cool.

Berry Danish (Continued)

TO ASSEMBLE

Divide dough into 2 equal portions. On a lightly floured surface, roll each pastry to 12 x 8 - inch rectangle. Spread 1/2 cream cheese mixture down center of each pastry. Spoon 1/2 berry filling over cream cheese.

Cut pastry on each side into 1-inch wide strips. Fold each side alternately over the top to produce a braided effect. Seal ends well to prevent leaking. Place on greased baking sheet. Cover and let rise until doubled. Bake in preheated 350° oven for 12 to 15 minutes. Do not overbake.

If desired, drizzle with a glaze while still warm.

GLAZE
1 cup powdered sugar
2 tbsp. milk
1/2 tsp. vanilla

Mix together until smooth.

VARIATION
Omit berry filling; spread each pastry with 1/4 cup of your favorite jam or jelly. Spread cream cheese filling down center and continue as above.

YIELD   2 LOAVES CUT INTO 8 SLICES EACH

BRAIDING A FILLED BREAD OR PASTRY

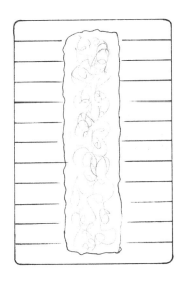
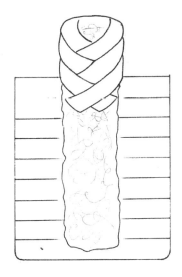

Cranberry Orange Muffins

The tartness of cranberries contrast well with the orange flavor
in this wonderful moist version of a popular muffin.

2 cups all-purpose flour
1 cup sugar
2 tsp. baking powder
1 tsp. baking soda
1/2 tsp. salt

In a large mixing bowl, blend flour, sugar, baking powder, soda and salt.

2 eggs
1/2 cup orange juice
grated peel of 1 orange
1/3 cup butter or margarine, melted
2/3 cup plain yogurt

In a small bowl, beat eggs; add orange juice, peel, butter and yogurt. Stir into dry ingredients just until moistened.

1 cup fresh or frozen cranberries
1 cup chopped walnuts or pecans

Fold in cranberries and nuts.

Spoon into 12 large greased or paper-lined muffin cups. Bake at 350° for 20 to 25 minutes or until golden brown.

YIELD   12 LARGE MUFFINS

Joann Weber
Raymond, Alberta

Those who bring

sunshine

into the lives of others,
cannot keep it from
themselves.

- James M. Barrie

I was having a recovery day when they arrived at my door.
An ordinary box decorated with sunflower decals and lined with shredded paper...
cheery notes tied to mini quiche and jumbo cranberry orange muffins ...
I was refreshed and blessed.

Orange Crescent Rolls

Pretty as well as scrumptious, these delicate pastries highlight
a tangy taste of citrus and a scattering of toasted coconut.

1 pkg. dry yeast (1 tbsp.)
1/4 cup warm water
1 tsp. sugar

In a small bowl, dissolve yeast and sugar in warm water.

1/2 cup sour cream
6 tbsp. butter or margarine, melted
1/4 cup sugar
2 eggs, beaten
1 tsp. salt
3 1/2 cups all-purpose flour

In large mixing bowl, combine yeast, sour cream, butter, sugar, eggs and salt. Gradually add 2 cups flour and beat until smooth. Mix in remaining flour until dough is easy to handle. Place into a lightly oiled bowl; turning once to oil surface. Cover and let rise in warm place until doubled, about 1 to 1 1/2 hours.

3/4 cup sugar
2 tbsp. grated orange rind
2 tbsp. butter or margarine, melted

Divide dough in half; roll each half into 12-inch circle. Combine sugar and orange rind. Brush dough with 1 tablespoon melted butter; sprinkle with half the orange/sugar mixture. Cut into 12 wedges. Roll up each wedge, beginning at rounded edge. Repeat with second half of dough. Place rolls, point side down, on two greased baking sheets. Cover and let rise until doubled, about 1 hour. Bake in preheated 350° oven for 20 minutes, or until golden brown.

GLAZE
3/4 cup sugar
1/2 cup sour cream
1/4 cup butter or margarine
2 tbsp. frozen orange juice concentrate

Combine ingredients; bring to boil and boil 3 minutes, stirring constantly. Pour warm glaze over rolls as soon as removed from oven.

3/4 cup flaked coconut (optional)

Sprinkle rolls with coconut; broil 3 to 5 minutes or until coconut is lightly browned.

YIELD   24 ROLLS

Cinnamon Twists

Slender and puffy, these twists are similar to cinnamon rolls.
They pair well with coffee or tea at a breakfast or brunch.

1 cup sour cream
3 tbsp. shortening
3 tbsp. sugar
1 tsp. salt
1/8 tsp. baking soda
1 egg, beaten

Bring sour cream to a boil; stir in shortening, sugar, salt and soda. Cool to lukewarm. Stir in beaten egg. Transfer to large mixing bowl.

1 pkg. dry yeast (1 tbsp.)
1/2 cup warm water
1 tbsp. sugar

In small bowl, dissolve yeast and sugar in warm water.

3 to 3 1/2 cups all-purpose flour

Combine yeast and sour cream mixtures. Gradually add 2 cups flour, beating until smooth. Mix in enough remaining flour to make a soft dough that is easy to handle. Turn dough onto lightly floured surface; knead until smooth and elastic. Round up dough and place into a lightly oiled bowl, turning once to oil surface. Cover; let rise in warm place until doubled, about 1 hour.

3 tbsp. butter or margarine, melted
1/2 cup brown sugar
1 tsp. cinnamon

Roll dough into a 18 x 10 - inch rectangle. Spread with melted butter. Sprinkle brown sugar and cinnamon over half the dough lengthwise. Fold the plain half dough over sugared half pressing together lightly.

Cut into 1 1/2-inch strips. Holding strips at both ends, twist in opposite directions. Place on greased baking sheets. Let rise until doubled, about 35 minutes. Bake in preheated 350° oven for 12 to 15 minutes. While warm drizzle twists with Thin Icing or Cream Cheese Frosting, page 215.

THIN ICING
Blend 2 cups powdered sugar with 2 tablespoons milk. If icing is too stiff, stir in a few more drops of milk.

YIELD   ABOUT 24 TWISTS

Raspberry Streusel Muffins

These muffins are a bit time consuming to
make but are well worth the extra effort. Serve them at a
company-special brunch or family breakfast. Leftovers freeze well.

1/4 cup slivered almonds, toasted
1/4 cup brown sugar
1/4 cup all-purpose flour
2 tbsp. butter or margarine, melted

In a small mixing bowl, combine almonds, sugar, flour and butter until mixture resembles moist crumbs. Set streusel topping aside.

1 1/2 cups all-purpose flour
1/2 cup sugar
2 tsp. baking powder

In large bowl, blend flour, sugar and baking powder.

1/2 cup milk
1/2 cup butter, melted
1 egg, beaten

In a small bowl, whip milk, butter and egg together with a fork or whisk. Stir milk mixture into flour mixture just until moistened. Spoon about 1 tablespoon batter into each of 12 greased or paper-lined muffin cups.

1 cup fresh or frozen whole
   unsweetened raspberries, divided

Divide half of the raspberries among cups. Top with remaining batter, then remaining raspberries. Sprinkle streusel topping over muffins.

Bake at 350° for 20 to 25 minutes or until golden brown. IMMEDIATELY remove from pan.

YIELD   12 MEDIUM MUFFINS

Blueberry Streusel Muffins

Substitute fresh or frozen blueberries for raspberries. If you wish to stir blueberries into batter instead of the above layer method: toss blueberries with 1/4 cup of the measured flour before blending into the batter. This keeps the muffin batter and blueberry colors separate instead of turning to shades of purple.

Refrigerator Bran Muffins

An excellent choice for breakfast is a nutritious bran muffin and
fresh fruit. Have a batch of this convenient batter on hand
and bake as needed or bake ahead and freeze for up to three months.
Reheat muffins in the microwave.

1 cup natural wheat bran 1 cup boiling water	*Pour boiling water over wheat bran. Let stand until cool.*
2 eggs 1/2 cup vegetable oil 1 1/4 cups sugar 2 cups buttermilk	*Beat eggs until frothy. Add oil and sugar; beat until creamy. Add buttermilk and bran mixture stirring until well blended.*
2 1/2 cups all-purpose flour 4 1/2 tsp. baking soda 1 1/2 tsp. salt	*Combine flour, soda and salt; stir into bran mixture.*
2 cups bran flakes	*Measure bran flakes, crush slightly; add and mix all together. Store in tightly covered container in refrigerator 24 hours or several days before baking.*

TO BAKE:

1/4 cup brown sugar
1/4 cup chopped pecans

*Grease or line 24 large muffin cups.
Stir batter thoroughly and spoon into
cups filling 2/3 full. Top with a
sprinkling of brown sugar and finely
chopped pecans, if desired.*

Bake at 350° for 25 to 30 minutes.

VARIATION
*Use half whole wheat flour. Add 1 cup
raisins or 1 cup blueberries to batter
just before baking.*

YIELD   24 LARGE MUFFINS

Waffles

Crisp on the outside and soft on the inside, homemade waffles taste marvelous.

2 eggs
2 cups buttermilk
2 cups all-purpose flour
2 tsp. baking powder
1 tsp. baking soda
1/2 tsp. salt
1/4 cup plus 2 tbsp. vegetable oil

Heat waffle iron. In a mixing bowl, beat eggs. Add remaining ingredients, beating until smooth.

Pour batter from cup or pitcher onto center of hot waffle iron. Bake about 5 minutes or until steaming stops. Remove waffle carefully with fork.

YIELD   ABOUT EIGHT 7-INCH WAFFLES

VARIATIONS
BLUEBERRY WAFFLES
Sprinkle 2 tablespoons blueberries over batter for each waffle as soon as it has been poured onto iron.

STRAWBERRY WAFFLES
Slice 1 quart strawberries. In chilled bowl, beat 1 cup whipping cream and 2 tablespoons powdered sugar until stiff. Top baked waffles with strawberries and whipped cream.

Buttermilk Pancakes

My grandchildren like these tender puffy pancakes swimming in syrup.
I prefer them with homemade strawberry jam.

1 egg
1 cup buttermilk
2 tbsp. vegetable oil
1 cup all-purpose flour
1 tbsp. sugar
1 tsp. baking powder
1/2 tsp. baking soda
1/2 tsp. salt

In medium mixing bowl, beat egg; add remaining ingredients. Beat until smooth.

Lightly grease heated griddle or skillet. To test griddle, sprinkle with a few drops of water. If bubbles skitter around, heat is just right. Pour batter from tip of large spoon or from pitcher onto hot griddle.

Turn pancakes as soon as they are puffed and full of bubbles but before bubbles break. Bake other side until golden brown.

YIELD   TEN 4-INCH PANCAKES

Cheese Scones

Karen likes to serve these scones with soup or in place of rolls for Sunday lunch.
If time is of essence, assemble dry and wet ingredients ahead of time in separate bowls
and refrigerate. They can be put together quickly for a fresh addition to a meal.

2 cups all-purpose flour
2 tbsp. sugar
1 tbsp. baking powder
1 tsp. salt
1/4 tsp. baking soda
1 1/2 cups shredded cheddar cheese

In a large mixing bowl, combine flour, sugar, baking powder, salt and soda. Stir in cheese.

1 egg
1/2 cup sour cream
1/4 cup vegetable oil
3 tbsp. milk

In a small bowl, beat egg lightly with a fork. Add sour cream, oil and milk; stir to blend. Add to dry ingredients and stir just until moistened.

Turn onto a floured surface and knead gently 10 to 12 times. Divide dough in half. Transfer to a greased baking sheet; pat into 8-inch circles. With a sharp knife, score each into 8 wedges; do not separate. Bake at 375° for 15 to 20 minutes or until lightly brown. Cool slightly; cut along wedge scores and serve.

YIELD   16 WEDGES

Karen Yoder
Goshen, IN

Golden Corn Bread

A colorful and perfect addition to a soup meal.

1 1/3 cups buttermilk
1/3 cup butter or margarine, melted
2 eggs

In a mixing bowl, beat buttermilk, butter and eggs together thoroughly with a fork or wire whisk.

1 1/4 cups cornmeal
3/4 cup all-purpose flour
1/3 cup sugar
2 tsp. baking powder
1 tsp. salt
1/2 tsp. baking soda

Stir dry ingredients together until well blended. Stir into buttermilk mixture all at once just until flour is moistened. Batter will be lumpy.

Pour batter into greased 9-inch square baking pan. Bake in preheated 400° oven for 15 to 20 minutes or until golden brown and wooden pick inserted in center comes out dry. Delicious served warm.

Pictured on page 69.

YIELD   9 SERVINGS

Buttermilk Biscuits

Warm from the oven, tender soft biscuits make any meal special.

2 cups all-purpose flour
1 tbsp. sugar
1 tbsp. baking powder
1 tsp. salt
$1/2$ tsp. baking soda

In a mixing bowl, combine flour, sugar, baking powder, salt and soda.

4 tbsp. butter or margarine

Cut in butter thoroughly, until mixture is crumbly.

$1 1/2$ cups cold buttermilk

Add to dry ingredients; stir just until blended. Dough will be moist.

$1/4$ cup flour

Spread $1/4$ cup flour into small shallow bowl or pie pan. Drop $1/4$ cup biscuit dough onto flour and roll to coat. Shape piece into a rough ball, shaking off excess flour. Place in greased 9-inch round baking pan. Continue with remaining dough.

2 tbsp. melted butter

Brush tops with melted butter. Bake at 425° for 15 minutes or until golden brown. Cool for 2 minutes; remove from pan to serve.

VARIATIONS

YIELD   9 BISCUITS

HERBED BISCUIT ROUNDS
Mix as above: stir $1/4$ cup chopped fresh parsley and $1/4$ cup chopped fresh chives into buttermilk. Brush tops with melted butter; sprinkle with onion salt and Parmesan cheese.

Erma Yoder
Millersburg, IN

CHEESE BISCUITS
Add 1 cup grated cheddar cheese and 1 teaspoon Italian seasoning to dry ingredients.

Biscuits and Sausage Gravy

This Southern style breakfast is a tradition in Mennonite restaurants.
Serve with your favorite juice and lots of fresh fruit.

*Prepare Southern Raised Biscuits,
page 42
OR Buttermilk Biscuits, page 59
OR Refrigerated Buttermilk Biscuits;
prepare as directed on package.*

1 lb. bulk pork sausage
2 tbsp. chopped onions

*Crumble sausage into a large skillet or
saucepan; add onions. Cook and stir
over medium-high heat until meat is
brown and onion is tender. Remove
sausage from skillet; drain and set
aside.*

1/4 cup butter or margarine
6 tbsp. all-purpose flour
3/4 tsp. salt
1/2 tsp. poultry seasoning
1/4 tsp. garlic powder
1/8 tsp. ground nutmeg
1/8 tsp. Worcestershire sauce
Dash hot pepper sauce
4 cups milk

*In a large saucepan, melt butter over
medium heat. With a wire whisk, stir in
flour and seasonings. Gradually stir in
milk; cook until mixture thickens,
stirring constantly. Stir in cooked
sausage.*

*Serve sausage gravy over warm split
biscuits.*

YIELD   4 TO 6 SERVINGS

Breakfast Casserole

Prepare the night before and serve for breakfast or brunch.

10 slices bread, brown or white

Cut bread into cubes and turn into a greased 9 x 13 - inch baking pan.

1 cup shredded cheddar cheese
1 lb. cooked ham, chopped
4 green onions, chopped

Layer cheese, ham and onions over bread cubes.

6 eggs
2 cups milk
1 tsp. salt
1 tsp. parsley flakes
1/2 tsp. Worcestershire sauce
1/2 tsp. dry mustard
1/4 tsp. pepper

Beat together eggs, milk and seasonings; pour over bread layers.

1 cup shredded cheddar cheese

Top with shredded cheese. Cover and refrigerate overnight. Bake at 350° for 45 to 50 minutes.

YIELD   10 TO 12 SERVINGS

Baked Oatmeal

Baked oatmeal is nothing like porridge, but rather resembles an oatmeal muffin.
It is delicious served warm with fresh sliced peaches or strawberries.

3/4 cup brown sugar
1/2 cup butter or margarine, melted
2 eggs
3/4 cup milk
2 tsp. baking powder
1 tsp. vanilla
1 tsp. salt

In a mixing bowl, combine sugar, butter and eggs; beat together thoroughly. Add milk, baking powder, vanilla and salt; mix well.

3 cups quick-cooking oats

Stir in oats until well blended.

Pour into a greased 9 x 9 - inch baking dish or 1 1/2-quart casserole. Bake at 350° for about 30 to 35 minutes or until golden and firm to the touch. Serve warm with milk.

YIELD   6 TO 8 SERVINGS

Breakfast Quiche

This simplified quiche eliminates the need to roll out dough. Very tasty!

½ cup all-purpose flour
½ tsp. baking powder
1 tbsp. shortening

Blend dry ingredients; cut in shortening until mixture is crumbly.

3 eggs
½ cup milk
2 tsp. cornstarch
⅓ cup finely chopped onion
　OR 2 tsp. dry onion flakes
⅓ cup mayonnaise
1 tsp. parsley flakes
½ tsp. salt
¼ tsp. pepper
1 cup shredded cheddar cheese
6 slices bacon, cooked and crumbled

In a mixing bowl, beat eggs slightly; whisk together with milk, cornstarch, onion, mayonnaise and seasonings. Stir in cheese, bacon and flour mixture.

1 tbsp. butter or margarine, melted
½ cup mozzarella or Swiss cheese,
　shredded

Melt butter in 9-inch pie pan. Pour mixture into pan; sprinkle with mozzarella cheese. Bake at 350° for 30 to 35 minutes or until lightly browned.

Recipe can easily be doubled and baked in 9 x 13 - inch baking pan.

VARIATION
Omit bacon; substitute ⅔ cup chopped cooked ham.

YIELD   4 SERVINGS

Karen Yoder
Goshen, IN

Cashew Crunch Granola

This recipe came to me a long way around.
Our friend Luke, from Ontario, taught school in Alberta. He married Amy from Michigan. Together with their children they served in Thailand. While home in the US on furlough, they came to my daughter's home in Indiana while I was visiting. Amy brought a gift of homemade granola. I had to have the recipe because it was some of the best I had ever tasted. Amy shared it all the way from Thailand.

10 cups quick-cooking oats
2 cups cashew pieces
2/3 cup crushed cinnamon
   graham cereal
1 cup flaked coconut

In a large mixing bowl, combine oats, nuts, graham cereal and coconut.

3/4 cup sugar
3/4 cup brown sugar
1/2 cup butter or margarine
1/4 cup vegetable oil
1/4 cup water
2 tbsp. vanilla
3/4 tsp. salt

In a medium saucepan, combine sugars, butter, oil, water, vanilla and salt. Cook and stir until boiling and sugar is dissolved. Pour over oat mixture and stir to coat evenly. Spread 1/2 inch thick on two rimmed baking sheets; pat lightly to even. Bake at 350° for 20 to 25 minutes, or until golden.

Do not stir while baking. Let cool 10 to 15 minutes before breaking apart.

Adjust this recipe to make it uniquely your own. Use your favorite nuts and add raisins or other dried fruit.

YIELD   ABOUT 16 CUPS GRANOLA

Amy Kuepfer
Lagrange, IN

63

Grape Nut Cereal

Whole wheat flour is incorporated into a dough and baked.
The cooled cake is grated into coarse crumbs and toasted. This three-step process
may sound involving, but it is easy and the resulting cereal is a popular favorite.

4½ cups whole wheat flour
1¾ cup brown sugar
1 tsp. baking soda
1 tsp. salt

In a large mixing bowl, combine flour, brown sugar, soda and salt.

2¼ cups buttermilk
¼ cup vegetable oil
1 tsp. maple flavoring
½ tsp. vanilla

Add buttermilk, oil and flavorings to dry mixture. Beat until smooth.

Spread dough into 2 greased 10 x 15 - inch rimmed baking sheets. Bake at 350° for 20 to 25 minutes or until golden brown.

Crumble cake with hands while warm or cut into small squares. When cool, grate into coarse crumbs using a grater or food processor. Spread crumbs in shallow layer on rimmed baking sheets and heat in 325° oven for 15 to 20 minutes or until crisp and dry. Store in airtight container.

YIELD   APPROX. 8 CUPS CEREAL

Soups and
Sandwiches

Soups and Sandwiches

Harvest Corn Chowder

This garden medley soup is a meal in itself.
Serve with French bread and enjoy the fruits of harvest.

2 cups water
2 cups cubed potatoes
2 cups fresh or frozen corn
1/2 cup chopped carrots
1/2 cup diced celery
1/4 cup chopped onion
1 bay leaf
1/2 tsp. salt

In saucepan combine water, vegetables and seasonings. Cook together until vegetables are tender, about 20 minutes. Do not drain. Discard bay leaf.

1/4 cup butter
1/4 cup flour
1 1/2 tsp. salt
1/4 tsp. thyme
1/4 tsp. pepper
2 cups milk
1 cup grated cheddar cheese
1 cup cubed cooked ham

Melt butter in saucepan over low heat. Whisk in flour, salt, thyme and pepper. Cook over low heat, stirring until mixture is smooth and bubbly. Remove from heat and stir in milk. Heat to boiling, stirring constantly. Add cheese and continue cooking over low heat, stirring until cheese is melted. Add ham and stir into cooked vegetables; heat through.

VARIATION
Omit carrots; substitute chopped red pepper. Omit ham; substitute fried bacon.

YIELD   6 SERVINGS

Creamy Broccoli Soup

There are vegetables aplenty in this thick, nourishing soup. Serve steaming hot on a cold winter day. Complete the meal with slices of whole wheat bread.

2 cups water
1 cup chopped celery
1 cup chopped carrots
1/2 cup chopped onions
2 cups fresh broccoli florets, cut into
    small pieces

In saucepan combine water, celery, carrots and onion. Simmer until tender, about 15 minutes. Add broccoli florets and cook 5 more minutes. Do not drain.

1/4 cup butter
1/3 cup flour
2 tsp. salt
1/4 tsp. white pepper
4 cups milk
1 tbsp. chicken bouillon granules
1/8 tsp. hot pepper sauce

In large saucepan or Dutch oven, melt butter over low heat. Blend in flour, salt and pepper; stir in milk. Heat to boiling, stirring constantly. (Stirring with a whisk will dissolve any lumps that may be left.) Boil and stir 1 minute. Add chicken bouillon granules and pepper sauce.

1 cup grated Colby or mild cheddar
    cheese
2 cups fully cooked ham, optional

Add cheese and stir until melted. Combine all ingredients; heat through.

YIELD   6 TO 8 SERVINGS

> **NOTE**
> *Instead of discarding broccoli stems and stalk; peel and chop them. Use in place of celery or in addition to celery.*

Pictured on page 69.

Chicken Broth

Homemade chicken broth is a winter comfort and a mainstay in my kitchen.
I use it as the base for a variety of soups as well as in casseroles or gravy.

To prepare broth:

8 cups water
1 stewing chicken (3 to 4 pounds),
   quartered
OR
3 whole chicken breasts, split

2 carrots, cut into chunks
1 celery stalk including leaves,
   cut in pieces
1 small onion
1 small bay leaf
1 tbsp. salt
3 peppercorns

In a large soup kettle or Dutch oven, bring water to a boil. Add chicken, vegetables and seasonings. Bring back to a boil, reduce heat; cover and simmer 1½ to 2 hours or until chicken is tender.

Remove chicken from broth to cool. When cool, remove meat from bones. Use in your favorite recipe or freeze for later use.

Strain broth, chill and skim off fat. Use in another recipe or freeze for later.

YIELD   ABOUT 8 CUPS BROTH

NOTE
To cool a large quantity of broth quickly, place the pot in an ice-water bath in the sink. Moving the broth straight from the stovetop into the fridge lengthens the cooling time and increases the temperature in the refrigerator creating food safety problems. After the broth has been refrigerated overnight, skim and remove the fat that has risen to the top; discard.

Chicken Soup with Dumplings
(Nockerl or Nock-a-la)

'Nockerl' is the Bavarian or southern German word for dumpling that goes into soup.
Adding the suffix 'a la' makes a word mean a 'smaller' version of the word.
So if we are saying the word for dumpling, we need only add 'a la'
and the meaning changes to small dumpling.
Now Nock-a-la, the name for a soup that I am very fond of, makes perfect sense.

¹/₄ cup butter or margarine, softened
2 eggs
³/₄ cup flour
¹/₄ tsp. salt

In small mixing bowl, cream butter; add eggs and beat together. Add flour and salt; continue beating until mixed. If necessary add more flour as batter should be quite stiff so dumplings hold their shape. Cover bowl and let stand for 15 to 30 minutes.

5 cups chicken broth

In large saucepan, heat broth to boiling. Scoop out rounded balls of batter with a teaspoon and drop into simmering broth. When all the dumplings are in the broth, cover and simmer 15 to 18 minutes – without peeking – until the dumplings are puffed and light. Ladle the broth and dumplings into soup bowls. Sprinkle with chives if desired and serve.

YIELD   3 TO 4 SERVINGS

NOTE
An effective way to mix the batter is in a food processor because you can quickly knead it to the proper stiffness and resilience. The batter should form a ball that rides up on the central spindle. Transfer the batter to a small bowl, cover with plastic wrap and set aside for 15 to 30 minutes or refrigerate for 2 hours or longer.

Chicken Soup with 'Gerstl' or Pasta

Reibgerstl is the name I found in an Austrian cookbook which literally translated means 'grated gerstl'. We had it often in our tradition and I grew up loving these ragged bits of homemade pasta cooked in chicken broth. It is an easy-to-digest soup that my girls loved most any day but especially when they needed comfort food.

1 egg 1 egg yolk 1 cup flour 1/4 tsp. salt	Beat egg and egg yolk together with a fork. Add flour and salt all at once and knead well. Pat into a disc and leave to dry then grate on a coarse grater. Or pulse in food processor until desired size pieces are obtained. Dry in the oven on a baking sheet. When completely dry, the 'gerstl' can be stored in an airtight container or frozen until needed.
4 cups chicken broth	Gradually sprinkle 'gerstl' into hot chicken broth and simmer for a few minutes or until soft.

YIELD 2 TO 3 SERVINGS

Chicken Soup with Buckwheat

Here is an unusual way of incorporating a healthy grain into your diet. My sister-in-law, Mary Lynn, had never tasted it before she met my brother. She sampled and savored and now it is one of her favorite soups.

1 egg 1/3 to 1/2 cup cracked buckwheat	Beat egg with a fork. Add buckwheat and mix together.
4 cups chicken broth	Pour and stir buckwheat mixture into simmering broth. Cook for 10 to 12 minutes.

YIELD 2 TO 3 SERVINGS

Chicken Soup with Bow Ties

This is a wonderful basic chicken soup
especially if your pasta is homemade.

4 cups chicken broth
1 cup chopped carrots
1 cup diced celery
1/2 cup chopped onion
2 tbsp. chicken bouillon granules

*In a large saucepan or Dutch oven,
bring chicken broth to a boil. Add
carrots, celery, onion and bouillon.
Cover and simmer about 8 to 10
minutes or until vegetables are tender.*

1 cup cooked chicken meat, diced
1 tbsp. snipped fresh parsley
  or 1 tsp. parsley flakes
1/4 tsp. dried lemon thyme (optional)
1 cup dry bowtie pasta, cooked
  according to pkg. directions
salt and pepper to taste

*Add meat, parsley, lemon thyme and
cooked bowtie pasta to broth. Season
with salt and pepper to taste.
Heat through and serve.*

VARIATION
*Use packaged or homemade noodles
in place of bow pasta*

YIELD   6 TO 8 SERVINGS

Egg Noodles

Although time consuming, the matchless flavor of
homemade noodles is worth the time and effort.

2 eggs
2 egg yolks
3 tbsp. cold water
1 tsp. salt
1 1/2 to 2 cups all-purpose flour

*Beat eggs, yolks and water together
thoroughly. Stir in salt and 1 1/2 cups
flour. Knead until flour is blended and
dough is stiff, yet workable, adding
more flour as necessary. Cover dough
with bowl and let 'rest' 30 minutes.*

*On a floured surface, roll out pieces of
dough until very thin. Lay each on a
separate cloth to dry.*

*When they are dry enough not to stick,
fold one edge over two inches and
continue to fold loosely to form a flat
tube. Place on cutting board and cut
into 1/4-inch strips or wider if you
prefer. Unroll and spread noodles on a
clean cloth and allow to dry
completely before storing in an airtight
container. May also be frozen.*

YIELD   ABOUT 6 CUPS

Chicken Tortellini Soup

Tortellini can be purchased but they are so fun to make and shape.
It's worth a try!

6 cups chicken broth
1 cup thinly sliced carrots
1/2 cup diced celery
1/2 cup chopped onion
1 tsp. parsley flakes
1/2 tsp. salt
1/8 tsp. pepper

In a Dutch oven or large saucepan, combine chicken broth, vegetables and seasonings. Bring to a boil. Reduce heat; cover and simmer for 20 minutes.

24 tortellini,
   frozen or prepare recipe below

Add tortellini to broth; bring to a boil. Cover and simmer for an additional 15 minutes or until tortellini tests done.

YIELD   3 TO 4 SERVINGS

Tortellini

1/2 cup finely chopped cooked chicken
1 tbsp. grated Parmesan cheese
1/2 to 1 tsp. water

In a small mixing bowl, add enough water to chicken and cheese to hold together. Set aside.

1 cup all-purpose flour
2 eggs
1/4 tsp. salt

In a mixing bowl, combine flour, eggs and salt. Mix together to form a stiff dough; divide in half.

On a lightly floured surface, roll dough until very thin. Cut into 2-inch circles. Place 1/4 teaspoon filling on each circle; moisten edges with water. Fold in half and press edges to seal. Pull ends together to form a circular shape; seal with a touch of water.

VARIATION
Beef Tortellini Soup; replace chicken broth with beef broth and chopped chicken with chopped beef.

Pictured on page 69.

NOTE: *these can be made ahead and frozen.*

YIELD   24 TORTELLINI

To make a Tortellini

1.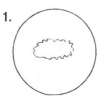

2.

3.

Basic Turkey Broth

This broth is made from the leftover Thanksgiving or Christmas turkey.
It can be made into delicious soup or used in any recipe that calls for chicken broth.

1 leftover turkey carcass
8 to 10 cups water
1 chicken bouillon cube
1 celery rib with leaves
1 small onion, halved
3 whole peppercorns
1 garlic clove
1 tsp. seasoned salt
1/4 tsp. thyme

Place all broth ingredients in a large soup kettle; cover and bring to a boil. Reduce heat; simmer for 2 hours. Strain broth; discard bones and vegetables. Cool; skim off fat.
* see note on cooling broth, page 71.

YIELD   6 TO 8 SERVINGS

Turkey Vegetable Soup

8 cups turkey broth
4 cups diced carrots, celery and/or
    other vegetables
2 chicken bouillon cubes
    OR 2 tbsp. chicken bouillon granules
1/2 cup chopped onion
1 tsp. salt
1/2 tsp. pepper

In a large saucepan or Dutch oven, combine broth, vegetables and seasonings. Cover and simmer for 15 to 20 minutes or until vegetables are tender.

4 cups diced cooked turkey
1 tbsp. fresh snipped parsley
    OR 1 tsp. parsley flakes

Add turkey and parsley; heat through.

YIELD   8 TO 10 SERVINGS

NOTE
Add cooked noodles to soup, if desired.

Basic Beef Stock

Rich dark broth stands alone as the base for wonderful soups
but is also used in gravy and meat sauces.

3 lbs. cut-up soup bones and beef shank

Place bones and beef shank in large shallow roasting pan. Roast in 375° degree oven, turning occasionally until meat is browned, about 1 hour.

12 cups water
1 small onion
1 celery stalk including leaves,
   cut in pieces
2 large carrots, cut in pieces
3 sprigs fresh parsley
   or 1 tsp. parsley flakes
1 garlic clove
1 bay leaf
2 tsp. salt
1/4 tsp. pepper
   OR 4 peppercorns

Bring water to a boil in large soup kettle. Add meat and bones along with all remaining ingredients. Bring to a boil over high heat; reduce heat and skim off foam. Bring back to a boil and skim again. Reduce heat, cover and simmer until meat is very tender, about 3 hours.

Lift out meat, cool and dice for use in beef soup or sandwiches. Strain stock, discarding bones and vegetables. Cool stock and chill; lift off and discard fat. Use in beef soup or freeze for later use.

YIELD   ABOUT 10 CUPS BEEF STOCK

Chunky Beef Barley Soup

With the barley, vegetables and beef,
this soup represents a healthy, balanced meal.

2 tbsp. canola or vegetable oil
2 garlic cloves, minced
1 medium onion, chopped
1/2 cup celery, sliced

1 1/2 lbs. stewing beef, cut in 1/4" to 1/2"
  cubes, fat removed
1 tbsp. vegetable oil

5 1/2 cups beef broth or consommé
1 cup carrots, sliced
2 whole tomatoes, chopped (optional)
1/2 cup pearl barley
1 1/2 tsp. salt
1 to 2 tsp. chili powder
1/2 tsp. cumin
1/2 tsp. ground pepper

Pictured on page 69.

In Dutch oven or large saucepan, heat oil; add garlic, onion and celery. Cook over medium heat for 5 minutes until onion is soft. Remove from pan and reserve.

Dredge beef cubes in flour; shake or sieve out excess flour. Heat oil in pan; brown beef all over in batches adding more oil if necessary. Return beef cubes and onion mixture to pan.

Add beef stock, carrots, tomatoes, barley, and seasonings. Simmer over low heat for 2 hours.

Soup can be allowed to cool and then reheated to boiling point before serving. If too thick, add more beef stock, tomato juice or red cooking wine.

YIELD   5 TO 6 SERVINGS

Kathy's Chili Soup

This soup increases in flavor the longer it simmers
so it is a great make-ahead dish. An excellent choice for a work crew.

1 lb. ground beef
1 large onion, chopped
1 can (28 oz.) canned tomatoes
1 can (15 1/2 oz). chili beans
1 can (10 oz.) condensed tomato soup
1 can (4 oz.) mushroom pieces
1/2 cup brown sugar
1/2 cup ketchup
1 1/2 tsp. chili powder
1 1/2 tsp. salt

Brown beef and onion in skillet. Drain. In large saucepan or Dutch oven, combine all ingredients. Heat to boiling; reduce heat and simmer 1 to 2 hours stirring occasionally.

YIELD   6 TO 8 SERVINGS

CROCK POT ALTERNATIVE:
Brown beef and onion in skillet. Drain. Combine all ingredients in slow cooker; mix well. Cover. Cook on Low for 3 to 4 hours.

Kathy Yoder
Goshen, IN

Bread Soup Bowls

Cut tops off mini bread loaves and remove dough to leave a hollow container.
Soup served in a 'bread bowl' tastes extra special.

1 pkg. dry yeast (1 tbsp.)
1/3 cup warm water
1 tbsp. sugar

1/2 cup warm milk
2 tbsp. butter or margarine, melted
1 tsp. salt
1/2 cup whole wheat flour
1 3/4 to 2 cups all-purpose flour

In a small bowl, dissolve yeast in sugar and water.

In a mixing bowl, combine yeast, milk, butter, salt and whole wheat flour. Beat until smooth; mix in enough remaining flour to make dough easy to handle. Turn dough onto lightly floured surface and knead until smooth. Place into lightly oiled bowl; turning once to oil surface. Cover and let rise in warm place until double, about 1 hour.

Divide dough into 6 pieces; shape each piece into smooth ball. Place 2 inches apart on greased baking sheet. Flatten slightly with the palm of your hand 10 minutes after forming. Cover and let rise until almost doubled, about 45 minutes.

Bake in preheated 350° oven for 15 to 18 minutes or until golden brown. For a crisp exterior, place a bowl of water in oven while bread is baking.

YIELD   6 BREAD BOWLS

Hamburger Soup with Pasta

A soup meal is a wonderful relaxing way to entertain close friends.
This fragrant filling variety is great on a cold winter day.

1 lb. lean ground beef
1 medium onion, chopped

Brown beef and onion in a skillet; drain.

4 cups beef broth
1 can (28 oz.) diced tomatoes
1 can (10 oz.) condensed tomato soup
1 cup water
1 cup sliced carrots
1/2 cup chopped celery
1/2 cup small pasta shells
 OR 1/2 cup pearl barely
1 bay leaf
1 tsp. salt
1/2 tsp. dried parsley
1/4 tsp. thyme
1/4 tsp. basil
1/4 tsp. pepper

In a Dutch oven or large pot, combine all ingredients. Cover and simmer for 2 hours or until vegetables are tender. Discard bay leaf. Extra liquid may be added to obtain desired consistency.

YIELD   10 SERVINGS

SLOW COOKER ALTERNATIVE
Combine all ingredients in slow cooker. Cover and cook on High 3 hours, or Low 6 to 8 hours.

Swedish Flatbread

Thin crisp flatbread is an ideal accompaniment to serve with soups and salads.

1 1/3 cups all-purpose flour
1 tbsp. sugar
1/2 tsp. baking soda
1/2 tsp. salt
1/4 cup butter or margarine

In a mixing bowl or food processor, combine dry ingredients; add butter. Mix with hands or pulse until mixture is crumbly.

1/3 cup buttermilk

Add buttermilk; stir or process until dough forms a ball. Roll dough directly on ungreased 10 x 15 - inch rimmed baking sheet. Mark off desired cracker size with pastry wheel or plastic serrated knife using a rocking motion. Prick dough all over with tines of a fork.

Bake in preheated 400° oven for 15 to 18 minutes or until lightly browned. Transfer baking sheet to rack. When cool and crisp, separate along lines.

Pictured on page 69.

YIELD   35 CRACKERS

Barbecued Beef On A Bun

Alberta ranchers pride themselves on raising superior beef.
This barbecued version is exceptional.

3 to 4 lb. beef roast
1 medium onion, chopped

Place beef and onion in a Dutch oven; add water to almost cover meat. Bring to a boil; reduce heat. Cover and simmer for 2¹/₂ to 3 hours or until meat is tender. Remove meat; slice or shred and return to Dutch oven.

Strain and reserve cooking liquid. Chill cooking liquid; skim and discard fat.

1¹/₂ cups ketchup
¹/₄ cup brown sugar, packed
¹/₄ cup vinegar
2 tbsp. molasses
1 tbsp. prepared mustard
2 tsp. salt
2 tsp. Worcestershire sauce
1 tsp. chili powder
¹/₂ tsp. paprika
¹/₂ tsp. garlic salt
¹/₄ tsp. liquid smoke
few drops hot pepper sauce
2 cups strained liquid

Combine ketchup, brown sugar, vinegar, molasses and seasonings in saucepan. Add 2 cups strained liquid. Pour over meat. Cover and simmer for 1 hour, stirring occasionally. If mixture becomes too thick, add additional reserved cooking liquid. Serve on hamburger buns.

YIELD   10 TO 12 SERVINGS

MAKE-AHEAD OVEN ALTERNATIVE

Roast meat at 300° for 3 hours, until medium done. Slice or shred the meat. Combine sauce seasonings and simmer for 10 minutes to blend flavors. Pour over and between layers of meat. Cover with foil and place in 275° oven for 1 to 2 hours or until ready to serve. OR pile into a slow cooker and keep on Low until ready to serve.

Wheat Focaccia Sandwich

A flavorful Italian flat bread filled with an assortment of
meat and vegetables makes a great lunch or supper sandwich.

1 pkg. dry yeast (1 tbsp.)
1 cup warm water
1 tsp. sugar

*In small bowl, dissolve yeast and
sugar in warm water.*

1 tbsp. vegetable oil
1/2 cup whole wheat flour
1 tsp. salt
2 cups all-purpose flour

*In a large mixing bowl, combine
yeast, and oil. Add whole wheat flour;
salt and 1 cup all-purpose flour; beat
until smooth. Add enough remaining
flour to form soft dough that is easy
to handle.*

*Turn onto a floured surface; knead
until smooth and elastic. Place dough
into a lightly oiled bowl, turning once
to oil surface. Cover and let rise in a
warm place until doubled, about 35
minutes.*

*Press dough into a 12-inch circle on a
well-greased baking pan. Cover and
let rise in a warm place until doubled,
about 30 minutes.*

1 tbsp. vegetable oil
1 tbsp. grated Parmesan cheese
1/4 tsp. basil leaves
1/4 tsp. garlic powder
1/8 tsp. salt
1 tbsp. sesame seeds

*Brush oil gently over dough. Blend
Parmesan cheese and seasonings;
sprinkle over bread. Sprinkle seeds
over bread.*

*Bake in preheated 350° oven for 25 to
30 minutes or until golden brown.
Remove to a wire rack to cool.*

TO ASSEMBLE SANDWICH
1/4 cup mayonnaise
1 tbsp. butter, softened
1 tsp. prepared mustard (optional)

Split the focaccia bread in half horizontally. Whisk together mayonnaise, butter and mustard; spread over cut sides of bread.

Lettuce leaves
4 oz. thinly sliced fully cooked ham
4 oz. thinly sliced cooked turkey
1 small green pepper, thinly sliced
2 slices red onion, separated into rings
6 slices Swiss, cheddar, provolone
  OR Havarti cheese.
2 medium tomatoes, thinly sliced

On bottom half, layer with remaining filling ingredients. Replace top half. Chill until serving. Cut into wedges.

YIELD   12 SERVINGS

Chicken Salad Sandwich

Chicken salad packs lots of nutrition and crunch.
It is a versatile sandwich filling that can be served in many different ways.
Spread filling on bread or open-faced buns or roll up in a wrap.
For special luncheons, tuck into croissants or pile into miniature cream puffs.

1 cup finely chopped cooked chicken
1/3 cup mayonnaise
1/4 cup finely chopped celery
2 tbsp. finely choppen green onion
2 tbsp. finely chopped dill pickle
  (optional)
1/4 tsp. salt
1/8 tsp. pepper

Combine all ingredients; stir well. Cover and chill.

4 sandwich rolls
Butter or margarine

Split rolls; spread with butter. Divide chicken filling and spread on rolls.

YIELD   4 SANDWICHES

Ham and Cheese Sandwich

This handy sandwich has a melted cheese and meat filling that is equally good cold or hot. A great standby to keep in the freezer.

1 pkg. dry yeast (1 tbsp.)
1/2 cup warm water
1 tsp. sugar

In a small bowl, dissolve yeast and sugar in warm water.

1/3 cup hot water
1/4 cup instant potato flakes
1/4 cup butter or margarine, softened
1/4 cup sugar
1 egg
1 tsp. salt

Stir potato flakes into hot water; cool to lukewarm. In large mixing bowl, combine potato mixture, butter, sugar, egg and salt. Beat together until well blended.

3/4 cup warm milk
3 1/2 to 4 cups all-purpose flour

Add yeast mixture, milk and 1 1/2 cups flour; beat until smooth. Mix in enough remaining flour to form a soft dough. Turn dough onto lightly floured surface; knead until smooth and elastic. Place into a lightly oiled bowl; turning once to oil surface. Cover; let rise in warm place until doubled, about 1 hour.

Punch dough down; cover and let rest 10 minutes. On lightly floured surface, roll a portion of dough into rectangle. Cut into rectangles, approx. 4 x 5 inches.

16 slices cooked ham
16 slices American or mozzarella cheese

Layer a slice of ham and cheese on each piece of dough. Fold in half length-wise; seal edges by pressing with a fork. Place on greased baking sheet. Let rise until nearly doubled, about 40 minutes.

Bake in preheated 350° oven for 15 to 17 minutes or until golden.

YIELD   16 SANDWICHES

Salads

Salads

Vegetable Salads

Fruit Salads

Gelatin Salads

Cran Spinach Salad

Vibrant green spinach is not only flavorful, it is a nutritional powerhouse.
Toss in a few other healthy ingredients and enjoy an energy boosting meal.

1 pkg. (6 oz.) fresh baby spinach
3 cups salad greens,
   torn into bite-size pieces
1 cup cucumber slices, quartered
1/2 cup shredded mozzarella cheese
1/2 cup dried cranberries
1/3 cup pecans, sugared

Pictured on page 211.

In a large salad bowl, combine spinach and salad greens. Arrange spinach and greens on serving platter or divide onto individual salad plates. Top with cucumbers and shredded cheese; sprinkle with cranberries. Drizzle with desired amount of Poppy Seed dressing. Garnish with sugared pecans.

YIELD   6 SERVINGS

VARIATION
POMEGRANATE PEAR SPINACH SALAD
Omit dried cranberries; substitute 1/2 cup pomegranate seeds and 1 pear, cut into thin slices. Garnish with sugared almonds.

Poppy Seed Dressing

1/4 cup sugar
1/4 cup balsamic vinegar
1/4 cup mayonnaise
1/4 tsp. salt
1/4 tsp. ground mustard
1/8 tsp. pepper
6 tbsp. canola or vegetable oil
1 tsp. poppy seed

In a blender, combine sugar, vinegar, mayonnaise, salt, mustard and pepper. Cover and process until blended. While processing, gradually add oil in a steady stream. Blend until thick and creamy; pour into container. Stir in poppy seeds. Store tightly covered in refrigerator.

YIELD   ABOUT 1 CUP

Sugared Pecans

1 cup pecans
1/4 cup sugar
2 tbsp. water
1/4 tsp. vanilla

Walnuts or almonds may be substituted for pecans. Use same measurement and method to sugar 3/4 cup sunflower seeds.

In a medium non-stick skillet, cook all ingredients over medium heat, stirring constantly until water disappears and nuts are coated and dry. Pour onto baking sheet; cool.

Layered Lettuce Salad

If I need an attractive salad that can be
prepared ahead of time, this is a favorite choice.

6 cups bite-size pieces mixed salad greens
4 medium green onions, sliced
1 cup chopped cauliflower
1 cup diced celery
1 cup shredded carrots
1 pkg. (10 oz.) frozen peas, thawed

*Place salad greens in a large glass
bowl or glass 9 x 13 - inch baking dish.
Layer onions, cauliflower, celery,
carrots, and peas on salad greens.*

1 1/2 cups mayonnaise or salad dressing
1/4 cup Parmesan cheese (optional)
2 tbsp. sugar
pinch salt

*Prepare dressing by whisking together
mayonnaise, Parmesan cheese, sugar
and salt. Spread over salad, covering
top completely and sealing to edge of
bowl or dish.*

2 cups shredded cheddar cheese
12 slices bacon,
  crisply cooked and crumbled
Tomatoes (optional)

*Sprinkle with shredded cheese and
bacon. Cover and refrigerate 4 to 6
hours or overnight. When ready to
serve, garnish with tomato if desired.*

YIELD   6 TO 8 SERVINGS

Salad Topping Medley

Have this topping on hand to sprinkle over a mix of lettuces in the amount
you desire. Toss with a favorite dressing and enjoy a fast nutritious lunch.

3 tbsp. mayonnaise
1 tsp. sugar
1/2 cup sunflower seeds
1 pkg. raman noodles
1/2 cup slivered almonds

*Stir together mayonnaise and sugar;
toss with seeds, noodles and
almonds to coat.*

*Place in rimmed baking pan and bake
in 250° oven, stirring every 15
minutes until toasted, about 1 hour.*

YIELD   ABOUT 2 1/2 CUPS

Italian Vegetable Salad

This salad has it all… great color, flavor and nutrition.

5 cups broccoli, in bite-size pieces
5 cups cauliflower, in bite-size pieces
4 plum tomatoes, chopped
1 medium cucumber, quartered and sliced
1 medium red onion, coarsely chopped
1 cup carrots, thinly sliced
2 cans (2¼ oz.) black olives (optional)

In a large mixing bowl, combine the first seven ingredients.

1 cup Italian dressing
1 cup Creamy Italian dressing

Stir dressings together. Pour over vegetable mixture; toss to coat. Cover and refrigerate for 4 hours.

2 cups shredded mozzarella cheese

Just before serving, add cheese to salad. Toss and serve.

YIELD   12 SERVINGS

NOTE
Ingredient amounts can easily be halved to serve six.

Sherri Martin
Parry Sound, Ontario

Celery Seed Salad Dressing

Homemade dressing tastes better, contains fewer preservatives and costs less than a commercial kind. I keep this one on hand because it is marvelous on a tossed salad.

½ cup sugar
⅓ cup white vinegar
¼ cup mayonnaise
1 tsp. celery seed
1 tsp. salt
½ tsp. onion powder
¼ tsp. ground mustard
⅛ tsp. pepper
1 cup canola or vegetable oil

In a blender, combine all ingredients except oil. Cover and process until blended. While processing, gradually add oil in a steady stream. Blend until thick and creamy. Store tightly covered in refrigerator.

YIELD   ABOUT 2 CUPS

Toss salad with dressing adding a little at a time
to ensure you don't over sauce.

Fresh Broccoli Salad

This tasty blend of flavors and textures team together perfectly
as a salad that would complement any dinner.

2 bunches fresh broccoli
10 slices bacon
1 to 2 small carrots
1 small red onion
1/2 cup dried cranberries

Wash and trim broccoli; cut into small florets. Cut bacon into 1/2-inch pieces; fry until crisp; drain on paper towel. Cut carrots into julienne strips (approx. 1/2 cup 1-inch match-like strips). Slice onion into very thin slices or chop if preferred.

In mixing bowl, combine broccoli, bacon, carrots, onion and dried cranberries. Cover and refrigerate. Just before serving toss with desired amount of dressing. Turn out into serving dish.

3 tbsp. chopped peanuts
OR 1/2 cup slivered almonds, toasted

Sprinkle with nuts if desired.

YIELD   6 TO 8 SERVINGS

Dressing

1 cup salad dressing or mayonnaise
1/4 cup sugar
1 tbsp. vinegar

In a small mixing bowl, whisk salad dressing, sugar and vinegar together until well blended. Cover and refrigerate.

VARIATIONS
Omit dried cranberries, substitute 1/2 cup golden raisins.

Omit nuts, substitute 3 tablespoons toasted sunflower seeds.

Add 1 can (11 oz.) mandarin oranges, drained.

What a fabulous place for a picnic! Spectacular
mountain scenery at Cameron Lake located in
Waterton Lakes National Park, Alberta. Beyond the
southern shore of Cameron Lake is Glacier National
Park in Montana. Waterton Lakes and Glacier National
Parks were designated in 1932 as the world's first
International Peace Park, commemorating the long
friendship between Canada and the United States.

1. Amish Church Cookies, page 262

2. Picnic Potato Salad, page 96

3. Raspberry Quencher, page 19

4. Savory Strombolli, page 139

5. Sesame Snap Wafers, page 282

6. Fresh Vegetable Marinade, page 97

7. Trail Mix, page 7

8. Dill Pickles, page 172

Two Cheese Tossed Salad

This is ideal for those times when you're looking for something you can prepare in advance. Make dressing a day ahead and refrigerate. Prepare vegetables in advance and put the final product together at the last minute.

Dressing

1/2 cup vegetable oil	*Combine all ingredients, mixing well.*
1/4 cup sugar	*Cover and refrigerate.*
1/4 cup vinegar	
1 tsp. poppy seeds	
1/2 tsp. prepared mustard	
1/2 tsp. minced onion flakes	
1/4 tsp. salt	

5 cups torn fresh spinach	*In a large mixing bowl, combine*
5 cups torn iceberg lettuce	*greens, onion, mushrooms, cheeses*
1/2 cup chopped red onion	*and bacon. Just before serving, toss*
1/2 lb. sliced fresh mushrooms	*salad with desired amount of*
1 carton (8 oz.) cottage cheese	*dressing. Serve immediately.*
1 cup shredded mozzarella cheese	
3 to 4 bacon slices, cooked and crumbled	

VARIATION
Omit cottage cheese and substitute
1 cup Feta cheese, cubed

YIELD   6 TO 8 SERVINGS

Joanne Weber
Raymond, Alberta

Vegetable Parmesan Toss

Here is a crunchy refreshing salad with a tasty dressing that adds a burst of flavor to every bite. It is a perfect choice for a church dinner or potluck meal.

Dressing

2 cups salad dressing or mayonnaise
1/2 cup Parmesan cheese
1/4 cup sugar
1/2 tsp. basil leaves
1/2 tsp. salt

In a mixing bowl, whisk together dressing ingredients until sugar is dissolved. Cover and refrigerate.

5 cups iceberg lettuce,
  torn into bite-size pieces
4 cups broccoli, in bite-size pieces
4 cups cauliflower, in bite-size pieces
1 medium red onion, chopped
1 can (8 oz.) water chestnuts,
  drained and sliced
1 lb. bacon, crisply cooked and
  crumbled
2 cups croutons

In a large mixing bowl, combine vegetables, bacon and croutons. When ready to serve, pour dressing over vegetable mixture; toss to coat. You may not wish to use all the dressing; refrigerate leftovers in covered container.

YIELD   *12 to 15 SERVINGS*

Lorna Bender
Goshen, IN

Salad Croutons

12 slices bread

Cut bread into small cubes, about 1/2 inch.

1/3 cup melted butter or margarine

In a large mixing bowl, drizzle melted butter over bread cubes; toss to coat. Place bread cubes on 2 rimmed baking sheets.

2 tbsp. Ranch-style powdered
  salad dressing mix
1/2 tsp. garlic salt
1/2 tsp. onion salt

Mix seasonings and sprinkle evenly over bread cubes. Bake in 250° oven for 20 minutes or until crisp.

Increase oven temperature to 350° and continue baking until lightly browned about 12 to 15 minutes.

Store in airtight container or freeze to maintain freshness.

YIELD   *ABOUT 8 CUPS*

Festive Tossed Salad

As summer arrives, it's the perfect time to enjoy fresh greens
with dried cranberries and walnuts in this interesting salad.

I cup coarsely chopped walnuts
3 tbsp. butter

In a skillet, cook and stir walnuts in butter until toasted, about 5 minutes. Remove from heat.

1/4 cup sugar
1/2 to 1 tsp. black pepper
  (less if you prefer)
1/4 tsp. salt

Stir sugar, pepper and salt into walnuts.

12 cups torn mixed salad greens
3/4 cup dried cranberries
4 oz. crumbled feta or blue cheese
1 small red onion, thinly sliced

In a large mixing bowl, toss greens, cranberries, cheese, onions and walnuts. Just before serving, toss with desired amount of dressing. Serve immediately.

YIELD   12 SERVINGS

Salad Dressing

2/3 cup sugar
1/2 cup cider or red wine vinegar
1 garlic clove
1 tsp. parsley flakes
1/2 tsp. oregano
1/8 tsp. salt
1/8 tsp. pepper
1/2 cup vegetable oil

In a blender, combine all ingredients except oil. Cover and process until blended. While processing, gradually add oil in a steady stream. Blend until thick. Store tightly covered in refrigerator.

Lorene Petersheim
Catlett, VA

Marinated Bean Salad

This salad has lots of zip and travels well to a summer picnic or potluck meal.

1 can (16 oz.) red kidney beans
1 can (16 oz.) green wax beans
1 can (16 oz.) yellow wax beans
1 medium green pepper, chopped
1 medium red onion, thinly sliced
1 can chick peas (optional)

Drain beans.
In a large mixing bowl, toss beans with green pepper, onion and chick peas.

2/3 cup vinegar
1/2 cup sugar
1/3 cup canola or vegetable oil
1 tsp. salt
1/8 tsp. pepper

Mix together vinegar, sugar, oil, salt and pepper vigorously with a whisk or shake well in tightly covered jar. Pour over vegetables, tossing well. Cover and chill several hours or overnight; toss again before serving.

YIELD   10 TO 12 SERVINGS

Picnic Potato Salad

Can it really be a picnic without potato salad? I don't think so.
Some people feel that potato salad tastes better the next day.
I like it so well that I can't wait that long and think it tastes great
in the immediate and hope there is enough left over for later.

6 cups cooked potatoes, shredded or cubed
3 green onions, chopped
1/2 cup celery, finely chopped
3 to 4 hard-boiled eggs, diced

In a large mixing bowl, combine potatoes, onions, celery and eggs.

NOTE
Toss with dressing while potatoes are warm to help them absorb the flavors.

Dressing

1 cup salad dressing
1/3 cup sugar
1 1/2 tbsp. vinegar
1 tbsp. prepared mustard
3/4 tsp salt
1/8 tsp. pepper

Mix all ingredients together until smooth. Pour over potatoes; toss to coat. Cover and refrigerate until cold and ready to serve.

Paprika
Radishes

Sprinkle with paprika before serving. Garnish with radishes, if desired.

YIELD   8 TO 10 SERVINGS

Pictured on page 91.

96

Fresh Vegetable Marinade

This is a beautiful and tangy way to use fresh garden vegetables. Make it well ahead to allow the flavors to blend. Vary amounts and kinds according to your taste.

3 cups broccoli florets
1 small cauliflower
3 cups carrot slices
2 cups cherry tomatoes
2 cups celery slices
1 small red pepper,
   cut in strips or rings

Wash, prepare and cut vegetables into bite-size pieces. Put into container that has a tight-fitting cover.

1 cup Italian dressing
1 tsp. sugar (optional)

Stir Italian dressing and sugar together. Pour dressing over all and toss to distribute dressing.

Cover and chill for several hours or overnight. Drain and serve.

Pictured on page 91.

YIELD   ABOUT 12 CUPS

Cucumber Salad

Crisp and cool, this original is a great little side salad using fresh cucumbers from the garden. I often take it with a meal to the field during the wheat harvest. The crew loves it.

4 cups peeled sliced cucumbers
1/4 medium red onion, thinly sliced.
2 tsp. coarse pickling salt
2/3 cup vinegar
1/3 cup sugar
1/2 tsp. celery seed
10 ice cubes

In a medium bowl, combine all ingredients and mix well. Cover and refrigerate for at least 1 hour before serving.

YIELD   4 TO 6 SERVINGS

One taste of fresh garden fare reminds me why I don my gloves and grab my trowel. The season wouldn't be the same without the refreshment of home-grown tomatoes and cucumbers from the vine.

Oriental Cabbage Salad

The dressing and noodles give this crunchy salad an Oriental twist.

3 to 4 cups finely shredded cabbage
1 cup shredded carrots
1/2 cup thinly sliced celery
1 small red onion, thinly sliced
1/2 cup Oriental style noodles, toasted
   OR chow mein noodles
2 tbsp. sunflower seeds, toasted

In a large salad bowl, toss cabbage, carrots, celery and onion. Break noodles into bite-size pieces and stir in. Add desired amount of dressing and toss. Garnish with sunflower seeds.

Dressing

4 tbsp. sugar
3 tbsp. white vinegar
1 tbsp. chicken bouillon granules
1/8 tsp. pepper

In small saucepan, combine sugar, vinegar, chicken seasoning and pepper. Bring to a boil, reduce heat and simmer for 2 minutes. Remove from heat and cool.

3 tbsp. vegetable or olive oil

Add oil and stir until well blended or put in a glass jar and shake well.

YIELD   6 TO 8 SERVINGS

NOTE
Use Nappa cabbage for a change of texture

Fruited Chicken Salad

I spent a month with Ginny at her picturesque hilltop home in Michigan
while I awaited the arrival of my first grandson, Ethan.
Later when my daughter Beverly and I visited, Ginny served this delectable salad.
It was a special lunch in good company.

3 cups diced cooked or canned chicken
1 cup thinly sliced celery
1 can (11 oz.) mandarin orange sections,
  drained
1 can (9 oz.) pineapple tidbits, drained
1/2 cup slivered almonds, toasted

In small mixing bowl, combine all ingredients.

2 tbsp. canola or vegetable oil
2 tbsp. orange juice
2 tbsp. white vinegar
1/2 tsp. salt
Dash marjoram

Blend oil, orange juice, vinegar and seasonings. Pour over chicken mixture. Cover and chill 1 hour. Drain and discard marinade.

1/2 cup mayonnaise

Add mayonnaise to salad; toss gently to blend. Serve with lettuce leaf.

Pictured on page 211.

YIELD   8 TO 10 SERVINGS

Ginny Ryan
Dexter, MI

Watergate Pistachio Salad

I don't know the origin of this odd name for a great holiday treat.
It is embarrassingly easy to make for something that tastes so good.

2 pkgs. instant pistachio pudding
  (4 serving size)
1 can (20 oz.) crushed pineapple,
  undrained

In a medium mixing bowl, whisk together pudding and undrained pineapple. Chill in refrigerator for 30 minutes.

1 container (8 oz.) frozen whipped
  topping, thawed
1/2 cup miniature marshmallows
1/4 cup sliced almonds, toasted

Fold in whipped topping, marshmallows and nuts. Cover and refrigerate until ready to serve. Turn out into a serving dish; garnish with additional almonds if desired.

YIELD   8 TO 10 SERVINGS

Frosted Hawaiian Fruit Salad

This is an appealing and colorful combination of fruit;
however, you may choose your own favorites or vary
with selections of fruit that are in season. The topping is a firm favorite!

1 can (20 oz.) pineapple tidbits
  (drain and reserve liquid)
1 can (11 oz.) mandarin orange
  segments, drained
2 medium bananas
1 pint strawberries, sliced
1 cup seedless green grapes, halved
2 kiwi, peeled and sliced

1/2 cup flaked coconut, toasted
1/2 cup slivered almonds, toasted

*Peel bananas; slice into bowl. Cover
completely with other fruit. Cover
bowl and chill. Just before serving
toss fruit and spoon into individual
serving bowls. Top with a mound of
topping.*

*Garnish with coconut and almond
slivers if desired.*

YIELD   7 OR 8 SERVINGS

Fruit Salad Topping

1/2 cup sugar
2 tbsp. plus 2 tsp. all-purpose flour
1 cup pineapple juice
1 egg, beaten

*In medium saucepan, combine sugar
and flour. Add pineapple juice and
beaten egg; stir to mix. Cook over
medium heat until thickened, stirring
constantly with a whisk. Chill in a
bowl of ice water or refrigerator. (This
mixture stiffens after chilling; whip
before adding whipped cream.)*

1/2 cup whipping cream
1/8 tsp. almond extract
Drop of green food coloring (optional)

*Whip cream and almond flavoring
until thick. Add to cooked mixture;
beat until light and creamy.*

YIELD   ABOUT 2 CUPS

Frozen Fruit Slush

Peaches are synonymous with summer. I love to eat them fresh when they arrive locally, picked mere hours earlier in the Okanagan valley of British Columbia. Some I preserve and some I freeze to use in smoothies.
The rest of these juicy treasures go into this slush to savor during the winter months.
Serve at a brunch or as a light dessert with cookies.

3 cups water
1½ cups sugar

In medium saucepan, heat water to boiling; add sugar and stir to dissolve.

1 can (6 oz.) frozen orange juice
   concentrate
1 can (20 oz.) crushed pineapple

Add orange juice concentrate and crushed pineapple; stir to mix.

4 cups sliced fresh peaches
4 bananas, diced
1 can (11oz.) mandarin oranges, drained

Add peaches, bananas and oranges and mix all together. Freeze in containers or freezer bags. When serving, thaw to slush consistency. If desired, add fresh fruit such as blueberries or strawberries in season.

YIELD   ABOUT 10 TO 12 SERVINGS

Overnight Fruit Salad

A lovely creamy fruit salad that can be prepared well ahead of time.

2 eggs
½ cup pineapple juice
¼ cup sugar
2 tbsp. lemon juice
1 tbsp. butter
⅛ tsp. salt

Beat all ingredients together. Cook in saucepan over low heat, stirring constantly, just to boiling. Remove from heat; cool.

½ cup cup whipping cream, whipped
1 can (20 oz.) pineapple tidbits
   (drain and reserve liquid)
1 can (11 oz.) mandarin orange
   segments, drained
2 cups seedless red or green grapes,
   halved
1 cup miniature marshmallows

Fold whipped cream into cooled dressing. Fold fruit and marshmallows with dressing. Cover and refrigerate overnight.

YIELD   8 TO 10 SERVINGS

Tropical Cream Cheese Salad

My girls and I keep coming back to our favorite salad that is so good it can take the place of a dessert. Since it was always on the menu when I had dinner guests, it became my most requested recipe. It's creamy, a bit crunchy and simply luscious.

1 pkg. orange gelatin
  (4 serving size)

In a medium saucepan, mix gelatin as directed on package. (Use reserved pineapple juice, below, as part of the liquid.) Reserve 1 cup gelatin mixture; set aside.

1 pkg. (3 oz.) cream cheese, softened
16 regular marshmallows

To the gelatin in saucepan, add cream cheese and marshmallows. Cook and stir over medium heat until marshmallows are melted and mixture is smooth. Remove from heat and chill until mixture is thickened but not set.

NOTE Whip the thickened gelatin with an electric mixer before adding the pineapple and whipped cream to make it very smooth and creamy.

1 can (14 oz.) crushed pineapple, drained
  (reserve juice)
1 cup whipping cream, whipped
  (or 2 cups frozen whipped topping,
  thawed)
1/2 cup slivered or shaved almonds,
  toasted

Fold crushed pineapple, whipped cream and almonds into thickened gelatin. Turn into glass serving bowl; chill for several hours until very cold and set. When set, pour 1 cup reserved gelatin mixture over top. (If reserved gelatin mixture is too thick to pour, melt slightly; do not heat.) Chill until topping is set.

YIELD   10 TO 12 SERVINGS

Orange Tapioca Salad

Carol brought a meal which included this salad to my daughter's home
after the birth of one of my granddaughters. We sat around the table exclaiming
at the creamy texture and delicate flavor. It is a light treat with a
heavy meal or can serve as the dessert course at a summer luncheon.

1 pkg. orange gelatin
1 pkg. instant vanilla pudding mix
1 pkg. tapioca pudding mix
  (4 serving size each)
2 cups water

2 cans (11 oz.) mandarin oranges,
  drained
1 carton (8 oz.) frozen whipped topping,
  thawed

VARIATION
**ORANGE PINEAPPLE
TAPIOCA SALAD**
*Fold 1 can (8 oz.) crushed pineapple,
drained, into pudding mixture along with
oranges. Use drained pineapple juice as
part of the water in the first step.*

NOTE
*My daughter Beverly uses
gelatin powder from a bulk
food store. She combines
peach and orange gelatin
for a truly delightful flavor.*

*In medium saucepan, combine gelatin
and pudding mixes. Add water and
stir until blended. Cook over medium
heat until mixture boils, stirring
constantly; boil for 1 minute. Remove
from heat and chill completely.*

*Whisk cooled pudding vigorously until
smooth. Fold oranges and whipped
topping into pudding mixture. Spoon
into a serving bowl. Cover and
refrigerate for 2 hours or longer.*

YIELD   8 TO 10 SERVINGS

Carol Schrock
Shipshewana, IN

Stained Glass Torte

My mother made this long-time favorite often when I was a child.
It is a large recipe that keeps well in the refrigerator.

1 pkg. strawberry gelatin
1 pkg. lime gelatin
1 pkg. orange gelatin
   (4 serving size each)
boiling water

Dissolve each package of gelatin separately in $1^1/_2$ cups boiling water. Pour into 9 x 9 - inch baking pans and chill until firm; several hours or overnight.

$1^1/_2$ cups pineapple juice
   (use juice from pineapple tidbits plus
   other fruit juice such as peach or pear)
$1/_4$ cup sugar
8 marshmallows
1 pkg. lemon gelatin
   (4 serving size)

In a medium saucepan, combine pineapple juice and sugar; bring to a boil. Add marshmallows and lemon gelatin; cook and stir until dissolved. Chill until mixture begins to set.

2 cups whipping cream
1 tsp. vanilla
1 can (19 oz.) pineapple tidbits, drained

In small mixing bowl whip cream and vanilla until stiff. Cut strawberry, lime and orange gelatin into small cubes; reserve $1/_2$ cup of each color.
In a large mixing bowl gently fold together, lemon gelatin mixture, whipped cream, gelatin cubes and pineapple tidbits. Spoon into two serving bowls; spoon reserved cubes on top. Cover and chill until ready to serve.

YIELD   15 TO 20 SERVINGS

Rainbow Row Gelatin Salad

This is a cute treat to make for a child's party. Not only is it colorful,
it also tastes delicious. I chose the colors of the rainbow for this recipe
but you can vary the flavors to reflect your own creativity.
Select the number of layers you wish to make and choose flavors that
match your color theme. Arrange on a mirror for a kaleidoscope effect.

1 pkg. cherry gelatin
   (4 serving size)
boiling water

*In a small bowl, dissolve cherry
gelatin in 1 cup boiling water.
Divide in half.*

2 cups sour cream, divided

*To one half add 1/3 cup sour cream;
blend together. Pour into a 9 x 9 - inch
baking pan. Chill in refrigerator 15 to
20 minutes or until firm.*

Cold water

*To the second half of gelatin, add 3
tablespoons cold water; stir to blend.
(see note below)
Pour on top of first layer. Return to
refrigerator and chill 15 to 20 minutes
or until firm.*

1 pkg. orange gelatin
1 pkg. lemon gelatin
1 pkg. lime gelatin
1 pkg. berry blue gelatin
1 pkg. grape gelatin
   (4 serving size each)

*Repeat steps with each gelatin flavor
in order given. Chill until completely
set, several hours or overnight. Cut
into squares and arrange on serving
platter or mirror.*

YIELD   ***SIXTEEN 2 1/4-INCH SQUARES***

NOTE
*This sounds like a time-
consuming recipe but you
can do other things while
layers are chilling and
setting. It also takes less time
if you chill each individual
mixture in bowl of ice water
until cold but not set.*

Creamy Layered Gelatin Salad

This recipe is nostalgic since it comes from long-time friends in Virginia.
They got it from friends in Indiana and it was known as Virginia/Indiana salad.

1 large pkg. orange gelatin
   (6 serving size)
2 cups hot water
2 cups cold water
1 can (14 oz.) crushed pineapple,
   drained (reserve juice)

Mix gelatin in water as directed on pkg. Add crushed pineapple and stir to mix. Pour into a 9 x 13-inch glass dish or large glass bowl. Chill until set.

1/2 cup sugar
2 tbsp. cornstarch
1 cup pineapple juice
   (add water to reserved juice to make
   1 cup)
3 eggs, beaten

In a small saucepan, combine sugar and cornstarch. Add juice and beaten eggs; cook and stir until thickened. Cool and spread over orange gelatin. Chill until set.

4 oz. cream cheese, softened
1 cup powdered sugar
1 tsp. vanilla
1 1/2 cups whipping cream, whipped
1/4 cup flaked coconut,
   toasted (optional)

Combine cream cheese, powdered sugar and vanilla, mixing until well blended. Add whipped cream and beat until smooth. Spread over second layer. Garnish with a sprinkling of toasted coconut if desired.

YIELD   12 TO 15 SERVINGS

Marlene Miller
Judy Witmer
Dayton, VA

Festive Cranberry Mold

Erma's holiday spread isn't complete without this salad.
It is tart, sweet and festive all at the same time.
Plan to prepare topping a day ahead.

Topping

1 pkg. (3 oz.) cream cheese, softened
1 cup whipping cream
16 large marshmallows, quartered

In a small mixing bowl, beat cream cheese with mixer. Gradually add whipping cream at low speed. Do not whip. Stir in marshmallows; cover and refrigerate overnight.

NEXT DAY *Whip chilled marshmallow topping until thick and creamy.*

Cranberry Layer

1 pkg. (12 oz.) cranberries
1 apple, peeled and cored
1 cup sugar

Chop cranberries and apple using food processor or grinder. Stir in sugar until blended.

1 pkg. large cherry gelatin
  (6 serving size)
2 cups boiling water

In a medium bowl, dissolve gelatin in boiling water. Chill until thick like syrup. Stir in cranberry mixture.

Turn into a 9 x 13 - inch glass dish. Chill for several hours or overnight until set. Spread with topping and refrigerate.

YIELD   ***12 TO 14 SERVINGS***

Erma Yoder
Millersburg, IN

Finger Jello

This is a novel treat for children.
As mixture cools, it divides into two color tones which looks pretty and tastes great.

3 pkgs. jello, any flavor
   (4 serving size each)
3 pkgs. unglavored gelatin
3½ cups boiling water

Dissolve jello and gelatin in boiling water.

1 cup whipping cream

Stir in cream. Pour into 9 x 13 - inch baking dish. Refrigerate immediately. When firm cut into squares.

YIELD   20 SQUARES

Main Dishes

Main Dishes

Crispy Baked Chicken

For years I pan fried chicken until I discovered this healthier method.
It tastes so good... you can hardly tell the difference.

1 frying chicken (2 1/2 to 3 lb.),
   cut in pieces

1/2 to 2/3 cup butter or margarine, melted
4 cups crisp rice cereal, crushed
1 tsp. salt
1/4 tsp. pepper

Seasoning salt

Remove skin from chicken pieces; wash and dry thoroughly.

Combine cereal crumbs, salt and pepper. Dip chicken in melted butter, roll in crumbs until well coated. Place in shallow glass baking dish or rimmed baking sheet; do not crowd.

*Sprinkle with seasoning salt. Bake at 350° uncovered for 1 hour.
OR place in grill on medium heat with hood closed for 1 hour.*

YIELD 6 SERVINGS

NOTE
In order for the white meat to stay juicy and fork-tender it does not need to be baked as long as the dark meat. Bake dark pieces for 15 minutes before adding the white pieces.

Spicy Crisp Baked Chicken

Add additional flavor to baked chicken with this medley of spices.

1 tsp. parsley flakes
1/2 tsp. sage
1/2 tsp. onion salt
1/2 tsp. garlic salt
1/2 tsp. celery salt

Combine seasonings and add to the crisp rice cereal crumbs. Continue with recipe as above.

Golden Chicken Tenders

Tender chicken strips are coated with wonderfully seasoned bread crumbs before baking in this easy to prepare dish. It is great for company but also perfect any day. The accolades abound whenever I make it for the seeding and harvest crews.

½ cup shredded cheddar cheese
¼ cup grated Parmesan cheese
1 cup bread crumbs
1 tsp. basil leaves
½ tsp. thyme
½ tsp. salt
¼ tsp. pepper

In a shallow dish, mix cheeses, crumbs and spices until well blended.

4 skinless, boneless chicken breasts;
   cut into ¾-inch strips
½ cup butter or margarine

Melt butter in small skillet. Roll chicken in melted butter, then into crumb mixture.

Arrange chicken on a rimmed baking sheet. Bake in 350° oven for 25 to 30 minutes or until chicken is tender. Broil in oven for 2 to 3 minutes until chicken is lightly browned. Serve with a dipping sauce if desired.

YIELD   4 TO 6 SERVINGS

Janet Showalter
Dayton, VA

Teriyaki Sauce

¼ cup water
1 tbsp. brown sugar, packed
2 tbsp. soy sauce
1 tbsp. lemon juice
1 tbsp. canola or vegetable oil
1 garlic clove, finely chopped
¼ tsp. ginger
¼ tsp. ground mustard

In a small saucepan, combine all ingredients. Heat to boiling, stirring constantly; boil and stir 1 minute.

YIELD   1/2 CUP SAUCE

Stuffed Chicken Breasts

Baked in a creamy sauce, this entrée is an impressive presentation
for a special occasion. Serve with mashed potatoes and a garden salad.

1 pkg. chicken flavored stuffing mix
  OR prepare stuffing below

Prepare stuffing according to package directions; set aside.

8 chicken breast halves,
  (skinless, boneless)

Place chicken breasts between pieces of plastic wrap or waxed paper. Using flat side of meat mallet or rolling pin, gently pound chicken breasts until 1/2 inch or less in thickness.

8 slices Swiss or mozzarella cheese
Seasoned salt

Place one slice of cheese on each breast; sprinkle with seasoned salt. Divide stuffing mix and spread on each breast. Roll up and secure with a wooden pick. Place rolled breasts in a 9 x 13 - inch baking dish.*

1 can (10 oz.) cream of chicken soup
3/4 cup milk
1/2 cup sour cream

In a small mixing bowl, combine soup, milk and sour cream; mix thoroughly. Pour over chicken. Bake at 350° for 1 hour.

*As a variation, chicken can be prepared to this point, rolled in melted butter and soft bread crumbs. Place on rimmed baking sheet and bake at 350° for 40 to 45 minutes or until chicken tests done. Serve with gravy or Rich White Sauce, page 116.

YIELD   8 SERVINGS

Bread Stuffing

Use in place of stuffing mix in recipe above.

3 tbsp. butter or margarine
1/3 cup chopped onion
1/2 cup chopped celery

In small skillet, sauté onion and celery in butter until tender.

2 1/2 cups soft bread crumbs
1 tsp. parsley flakes
1/2 tsp. salt
1/4 tsp. poultry seasoning
1/8 tsp. pepper
Water or chicken broth

Combine onion mixture with bread crumbs and seasonings. Add enough water or chicken broth to moisten, approximately 1/3 cup.

Chicken Marsala

This is a splendid way to prepare chicken
that is succulent in taste and a feast for the eye.

2 tbsp. butter or margarine
2 cups sliced mushrooms
2 garlic cloves, minced
1/4 tsp. seasoned salt
1/4 tsp. onion salt
1/4 tsp. salt
1/8 tsp. pepper
1 tbsp. cooking wine

Melt butter in medium non-stick skillet. Stir in mushrooms, garlic and seasonings; sauté until mushrooms are tender-crisp. Add cooking wine and cook an additional minute. Set aside.

6 chicken breast halves,
   (skinless, boneless)
1/2 cup flour
1/2 tsp. salt
1/4 tsp. pepper

Flatten chicken breasts between sheets of plastic wrap or waxed paper to 1/2 inch thickness. In shallow dish, blend flour, salt and pepper. Coat chicken with flour mixture; shake off excess flour.

2 tbsp. canola or vegetable oil

In a large skillet, heat oil over medium-high heat. Add chicken to skillet; cook for several minutes, turning once, until brown. Turn into a greased 9 x 13-inch baking dish.

3/4 cup Marsala cooking wine
1/2 cup chicken broth
1 tsp. lemon juice

Add cooking wine and broth to empty skillet; cook over medium heat for 10 to 12 minutes or until liquid is reduced to 1/2 cup. Add lemon juice; pour over chicken.

1/2 cup grated Parmesan cheese
6 slices mozzarella cheese
1/4 cup green onion, sliced

Top chicken breasts with Parmesan and mozzarella cheese. Spoon mushrooms on top of cheese. Sprinkle onions overall. Bake at 350° for 20 minutes. Broil in oven until cheese is bubbling and lightly browned.

NOTE
In place of Marsala cooking wine, use 1/3 cup chicken broth, 3 tablespoons white grape juice and 2 teaspoons white wine vinegar.

YIELD   6 SERVINGS

Pictured on Page 127.

Chicken Divan

Chicken and broccoli team well together in this appealing main dish.
A rich creamy sauce offers a perfect topping.

2 to 3 bunches fresh broccoli

Wash and separate broccoli into florets. Cook in boiling water until tender-crisp, about 3 minutes. Plunge broccoli into cold water until cool. Drain and place in 8 x 12 - inch baking dish or 2-quart casserole.

1/4 cup butter or margarine
6 tbsp. all-purpose flour
2 cups chicken broth
1/2 cup whipping cream
1 tbsp. vinegar
  OR 3 tbsp. white cooking wine

Melt butter in medium saucepan over low heat. Blend in flour and stir until mixture is smooth. Remove from heat and stir in chicken broth and cream. Heat to boiling, stirring constantly. Boil 1 minute. Stir in vinegar. Pour half the sauce over broccoli.

6 chicken breast halves,
  (skinless, boneless)
2 tbsp. canola or vegetable oil
1/4 cup Parmesan cheese

In a large skillet, heat oil over medium-high heat. Add chicken to skillet; cook for several minutes, turning once, until brown. Layer chicken over broccoli. Add Parmesan cheese to remaining sauce and pour over chicken. Sprinkle additional cheese over all if desired.
Bake at 350° degrees for 20 to 25 minutes or until chicken tests done.

YIELD   6 SERVINGS

Chicken Cordon Bleu

I serve this delicious entrée at many holiday and other special meals.

6 chicken breast halves,
  (skinless, boneless)
3 large Swiss cheese slices, halved
3 large, thin ham slices, halved

Place chicken breast halves between sheets of waxed paper or plastic wrap. Using flat side of meat mallet or rolling pin, flatten chicken breasts until 3/8 inch thick. Cover each breast with slice of cheese and ham. Roll up tightly. (Chicken can be prepared to this point ahead of time. Cover and refrigerate; the next step is easier when they are very cold.)

1/2 cup butter or margarine
2 cups soft bread crumbs
1/4 cup Parmesan cheese

Melt margarine in a small skillet or saucepan. In another bowl, blend bread crumbs and Parmesan cheese. Dip chicken rolls in melted butter then bread crumb mixture to coat all sides. Arrange chicken in a baking pan. Bake in 350° oven for 40 to 50 minutes until lightly browned. Turn out onto a serving platter. Pour your choice of sauce over center of each roll; serve remaining sauce on the side. Garnish with sprigs of fresh parsley.

YIELD   6 SERVINGS

Rich White Sauce

1/4 cup butter or margarine
6 tbsp. flour
2 cups chicken broth
1/2 cup whipping cream
1 tbsp. vinegar
  OR 3 tbsp. white cooking wine
1/4 cup Parmesan cheese

Melt butter in medium saucepan over low heat. Blend in flour and stir until mixture is smooth. Remove from heat and whisk in chicken broth, cream and vinegar. Heat to boiling stirring constantly; boil 1 minute. Stir in Parmesan cheese and mix well.

Mushroom Sauce

1/4 butter or margarine
1 cup chopped mushrooms

In a medium saucepan, melt butter; add mushrooms and sauté.

2 cups milk
1/4 cup flour
1/2 tsp. salt
1/4 tsp. pepper

Blend milk and flour in a glass jar with lid; shake until smooth. Gradually pour into saucepan, stirring constantly. Cook until mixture is boiling and thickened. Season with salt and pepper.

Swiss Chicken Bake

Swiss cheese, soup and stuffing mix layered
over chicken breasts makes a tempting main dish that is simple to prepare.
Add mashed potatoes, a vegetable and tossed salad for an ideal company meal.

6 chicken breast halves,
  (skinless, boneless)
6 slices Swiss cheese

Flatten chicken between sheets of plastic wrap or waxed paper to uniform thickness. Arrange chicken pieces in a greased 9 x 13 - inch baking pan. Place cheese slices on top of chicken.

1 can (10 oz.) cream of chicken soup
1/2 cup sour cream
  OR chicken broth
1/4 tsp. pepper

Mix soup, sour cream and pepper together until blended; spread over cheese layer.

1 pkg. (6 oz.) chicken flavored
  stuffing mix
1/2 cup hot water
2 tbsp. butter or margarine

Stir together stuffing mix, water and butter. Spread stuffing mixture evenly over chicken soup mixture. Bake uncovered in 350° oven for 40 to 45 minutes or until chicken tests done.

YIELD   6 SERVINGS

Pockets of Chicken

These substantial hot bundles are extremely attractive and very tasty.
Serve with a vegetable and garden salad.

6 oz. cream cheese, softened
1/4 cup melted butter or margarine
4 cups cooked cubed chicken
1/4 cup milk
2 tbsp. finely chopped onion
   OR 2 tbsp. chopped fresh chives
1/2 tsp. salt
1/4 tsp. pepper

In mixing bowl, blend cream cheese and butter until smooth. Add chicken, milk, onion and seasonings; mix well.

2 tubes (8 oz.) refrigerated crescent
   dinner rolls

Unroll both tubes of dough; separate dough into 8 rectangles. Firmly press diagonal perforations to seal. On lightly floured surface, roll each portion into a 6-inch square. Divide chicken mixture evenly and spoon onto centre of each square. Pull 4 corners of dough to top centre of chicken mixture; twist firmly. Pinch edges to seal.

2 tbsp. melted butter or margarine
1 cup seasoned croutons, crushed
   (store-bought or salad croutons,
      page 94)

Brush tops with butter, sprinkle with crushed croutons. Place on parchment-lined or greased baking sheet. Bake in preheated 350° oven for 20 to 25 minutes or until golden brown. Delicious topped with Mushroom Sauce, page 116.

YIELD   8 SERVINGS

Chicken and Stuffing Casserole

This bubbling casserole is quick to prepare for a family meal, to take to a potluck
or to someone in need of comfort food. The chicken and stuffing team
well together with a vegetable or tossed salad and fruit for dessert.

1/3 cup butter or margarine
1/2 cup chopped onion
1/2 cup chopped celery

*Melt butter in frying pan. Add onion
and celery; sauté slowly until tender.*

1 pkg. (6 oz.) chicken seasoned
   bread stuffing mix
2 1/2 cups diced cooked chicken
3/4 cup water

*Stir vegetables, bread stuffing, chicken
and water together until blended. Pour
into greased 9 x 13 - inch baking dish
or 2-quart casserole.*

2 eggs, beaten
1 can (10 oz.) cream of chicken soup.
1/3 cup mayonnaise
3/4 tsp. salt
1/4 tsp. garlic powder
1 1/2 cups milk

*Combine eggs, soup, mayonnaise,
salt, garlic and milk, stirring until well
blended. Pour over chicken mixture in
dish. Bake uncovered at 350° for 30 to
35 minutes or until bubbly.*

1 cup grated cheddar cheese

*Sprinkle with cheese and bake 10
minutes longer or until cheese is
melted.*

VARIATION
Omit chicken; substitute cooked turkey.

YIELD   8 TO 10 SERVINGS

Deep Dish Chicken Pie

Creamed chicken and vegetables topped with a crisp crust
is comfort food at its best.

1/4 cup butter or margarine
5 tbsp. all-purpose flour
1 tbsp. chicken bouillon granules
1 tsp. salt
1/8 tsp. pepper
1/8 tsp. thyme
3 cups milk

Melt butter in large saucepan or frying pan over low heat. Blend in flour and seasonings, stirring until mixture is smooth. Gradually add milk stirring with a whisk until smooth. Heat to boiling, stirring constantly until thickened.

1/2 cup water
1 cup chopped carrots
1/2 cup chopped celery
1/2 cup chopped onion

In saucepan combine water, carrots, celery and onion. Simmer until tender, about 10 minutes. Do not drain.

3 cups cubed cooked chicken or turkey
1/2 cup frozen peas

Stir chicken and vegetables into sauce. Pour into greased 9 x 13 - inch baking dish.

Top Crust

2 cups all-purpose flour
3 tsp. baking powder
1/2 tsp. salt
1/2 cup butter or margarine
1 egg
1/2 cup milk

In mixing bowl stir together flour, baking powder and salt. Cut in butter until mixture resembles coarse crumbs. Whip egg with fork; stir in milk. Make a well in center of dry ingredients; add milk mixture. Stir with fork until dough clings together. Turn dough out onto lightly floured surface; roll into 9 x 13 - inch rectangle. Cut slits in dough to allow air to escape; place on top of chicken mixture. Bake at 350° degrees for 35 to 40 minutes or until golden brown.

VARIATIONS
Add 2 cups sliced mushrooms cooked in 2 tablespoons butter.

Cook 2 cups cubed potatoes with the carrots and celery.

Substitute 1 cup cooked broccoli florets in place of peas.

YIELD   6 TO 8 SERVINGS

120

Chicken Crescent Almondine

Celery, water chestnuts and mushrooms
add texture and crunch to this hearty chicken casserole.
The toasted almonds on the buttery crescent dough add a final touch.

1 can (10 oz.) cream of chicken soup
$2/3$ cup mayonnaise
$1/3$ cup sour cream
2 tbsp. minced onion flakes
　OR $1/2$ cup chopped onion
$1/2$ cup chopped celery
3 cups cooked chicken, cubed
1 can (8 oz) water chestnuts, sliced
1 can (4 oz) mushroom pieces, drained

In a large saucepan, combine soup, mayonnaise, sour cream, onion and celery. Stir in chicken, water chestnuts and mushrooms. Cook over medium heat until hot and bubbly. Pour into ungreased 8 x 12-inch baking dish or 2-quart casserole.

Topping

1 can (8 oz.) refrigerated crescent rolls

Separate crescent dough into two rectangles. Place dough over hot chicken mixture easing to fit dish.

$2/3$ cup shredded Swiss
　or cheddar cheese
$1/2$ cup slivered almonds
2 tbsp. butter or margarine, melted

Combine cheese and almonds; sprinkle over dough and drizzle with butter. Bake in 375° oven for 20 to 25 minutes or until crust is a deep golden brown.

YIELD　4 TO 6 SERVINGS

Karen Yoder
Goshen, IN

Deep-Fried Pineapple Chicken

Crispy chicken drizzled with a smooth pineapple sauce is a favorite pick
at our local Chinese restaurants. It can be made at home with great success.
Serve with rice and stir-fried vegetables.

Chicken breast halves, (skinless, boneless)
  cut into ¾-inch pieces, about 4 cups
Oil, for deep frying
Tempura batter

*Heat cooking oil (3 to 4 inches) to 375°
in heavy kettle. With tongs or fork, dip
chicken cubes into tempura batter,
allowing excess batter to drip into bowl.
Deep-fry in batches for about 5
minutes, turning until golden brown on
all sides. With slotted spoon remove
chicken pieces into colander or onto
paper towel to drain. Arrange chicken
on serving platter; pour desired amount
pineapple sauce over top. Serve
remaining sauce on side.*

YIELD   8 TO 10 SERVINGS

Pineapple Sauce

1 can (14 oz.) pineapple tidbits, undrained
½ cup brown sugar
3 tbsp. vinegar
½ tsp. salt
¼ tsp. ground ginger

*In medium saucepan, combine
pineapple in juice, brown sugar,
vinegar, salt and ginger. Bring to a
boil.*

½ cup unsweetened pineapple juice
  or water
2 tbsp. cornstarch

*Stir cornstarch into pineapple juice.
Add to pineapple mixture; heat and
stir until boiling and thickened.*

YIELD   3 CUPS SAUCE

Tempura Batter

Tempura refers to a classic method of frying batter-dipped meat and vegetables.
This includes larger pieces of chicken, whole shrimp, scallops or fish fillets
as well as bite-size pieces of cauliflower, sliced carrots and peppers.

2 cups all-purpose flour
⅓ cup cornstarch
2 tbsp. baking powder
1 tsp. baking soda
1 tsp. salt
1 egg
1¾ cups ice water

*Measure all ingredients into bowl;
beat with electric mixer until smooth.*

122

Chicken Scallopini

I make this recipe often when I have only a short time to fix a satisfying meal.
This chicken goes well with a green vegetable and Creamy Chicken Rice, page 164.

6 chicken breast halves,
  (skinless, boneless)

Flatten chicken between sheets of plastic wrap or waxed paper to uniform thickness.

1/4 cup all-purpose flour
1/4 cup whole wheat flour
2 tsp. chicken bouillon granules
1/2 tsp. seasoned salt
1/4 tsp. salt
1/8 tsp. pepper

In shallow bowl, combine flour, bouillon, and seasonings.

1 egg
2 tbsp. milk

In small bowl, beat egg and milk. Dredge chicken in flour mixture, then dip in egg mixture. Dredge in flour again.

2 to 3 tbsp. vegetable oil

Heat oil in large skillet over medium-high heat; cook chicken for 3 to 4 minutes on each side or until meat juices run clear and coating is golden brown.

ALTERNATELY, brown chicken quickly in oil. Place in casserole dish; cover and bake at 350° for 20 minutes or until chicken tests done.

VARIATIONS
This recipe can be used for chunks or strips of chicken as well. Omit egg; moisten with milk and dredge in flour mixture. Cook in skillet as above.

YIELD   6 SERVINGS

Orange-Ginger Chicken Stir-Fry

*A generous amount of wholesome vegetables and a
slightly sweet gingery sauce team up in this colorful chicken stir-fry.*

1 lb. chicken breasts, (skinless, boneless)
   cut into 1-inch pieces
1 tbsp. vegetable oil
2 tsp. soy sauce
1/4 tsp. ginger

*Combine chicken, oil, soy sauce and
ginger; marinade for 30 minutes,
stirring occasionally.*

3 tsp. cornstarch
1/2 tsp. ginger
   OR 1 tsp. fresh grated gingerroot
1 cup chicken broth
1 medium naval orange, juiced
1 tbsp. soy sauce
1 tbsp. brown sugar

*In a small bowl, combine the
cornstarch and ginger. Stir in broth,
orange juice, soy sauce and sugar
until blended; set aside.*

2 garlic cloves, minced
1 medium onion, thinly sliced
1 tbsp. vegetable oil

*In a large non-stick skillet or wok, stir-
fry onion and garlic in the oil for 2 to
3 minutes.*

1 tbsp. vegetable oil
2 cups broccoli florets
1/2 cup thinly sliced carrots
1 cup thinly sliced, red pepper
1 cup thinly sliced, yellow pepper
1 1/2 cups sliced fresh white mushrooms

*Add more oil if necessary; stir in
broccoli, carrots, peppers and
mushrooms. Stir-fry for 5 to 7 minutes
until tender crisp. (If you prefer
vegetables softer, add 2 tablespoons
water; cover and cook for about 2
minutes.) Turn out onto serving platter
or casserole serving dish; keep warm.*

*In same skillet, stir-fry chicken for 2 to
3 minutes or until chicken is done.
Stir broth mixture and add to the pan.
Bring to a boil; cook and stir for 2
minutes or until thickened.*

1/3 cup unsalted cashews
1 tbsp. sesame seeds,
   toasted (see note below)

*Remove from heat; stir in cashews.
Pour over vegetables; sprinkle with
sesame seeds. Serve with cooked
Chinese-style steam-fried noodles or
rice.*

TO TOAST SESAME SEEDS
*Place seeds in single layer in
ungreased shallow pan. Bake in
300° oven for 5 to 10 minutes,
stirring or shaking often, until
desired doneness.*

YIELD   4 TO 6 SERVINGS

Chicken Fajitas

Roll up the goodness of chicken and vegetables in this tasty Mexican treat.

2 whole chicken breasts,
   (skinless, boneless) cut into strips
1/4 cup lime juice
1 garlic clove, minced
1 tsp. chili powder
1/2 tsp. ground cumin

In a small bowl, combine lime juice, garlic, chili powder and cumin. Add chicken; stir. Marinate for 15 minutes. In a nonstick skillet or frying pan, cook chicken and marinade for 4 to 5 minutes or until chicken is done. Remove to a dish.

2 tbsp. vegetable oil
1 medium onion, cut into thin wedges
2 1/2 cups thinly sliced
   red, yellow and green peppers

In the same nonstick skillet, cook onion and peppers for 3 to 5 minutes or until crisp-tender.

1/2 cup salsa

Stir in salsa and chicken; heat through.

12 flour tortillas (8-inch)
   (store bought or make recipe below)
1 1/2 cups shredded cheddar
   or Monterey Jack cheese

Divide mixture among tortillas; top with cheese. Roll up and serve.

YIELD   6 SERVINGS

Flour Tortillas

Flour tortillas are easy to make and fresh-from-the-skillet, are tough to beat.

2 cups all-purpose flour
1 tsp. salt
1/4 tsp. onion salt
1/4 tsp. garlic salt
1/4 cup vegetable shortening
1/2 to 2/3 cup warm water

In a bowl, blend dry ingredients; cut in shortening. Stir in enough water to make stiff dough. Form into 2 logs; divide each into 6 pieces.

One at a time, place dough on lightly floured surface; roll out to about 8 inches. Heat a large skillet over medium-high heat. Place one tortilla on skillet and cook until tortilla just begins to puff up and the bottom has a few scorch marks. Flip and cook for another 20 to 30 seconds. Remove to platter and cover with clean tea towel. Repeat process with remaining dough.

YIELD   12 TORTILLAS

Sour Cream-Chicken Enchiladas

Karen says her friend Gina's kitchen boasts some of the best Mexican food.
These enchiladas are one of their favorites.

1 can (10 oz.) cream of chicken soup
1 cup sour cream
3/4 cup water
1/4 cup all-purpose flour
1 can (4 1/3 oz.) chopped green chilies
　(or use 1/2 cup jalapeño chilies)
1 1/2 tsp. salt
1/2 tsp. pepper

In a medium saucepan, combine soup, sour cream, water, flour, green chilies, salt and pepper. Cook over medium heat, stirring constantly until mixture is thickened.

1/2 cup picante sauce
3 cups cooked chicken, diced
8 tortillas (10-inch)
　(or twelve 6-inch tortillas)
3 cups shredded cheddar cheese

Spread picante sauce on the bottom of a 9 x 13 - inch baking pan. In a mixing bowl, combine chicken and half of the thickened soup mixture. Spoon 1/4 cup chicken mixture and scant 1/4 cup cheese down center of each tortilla; roll up. Place seam side down in baking pan. Spoon remaining soup mixture over filled tortillas. Cover tightly with foil.

Bake in 350° oven for 20 to 30 minutes or until hot and bubbly. Remove from oven; uncover and sprinkle with remaining cheese. Return to oven; bake uncovered about 5 minutes longer or until cheese is melted. If desired, serve with chopped tomato and shredded lettuce.

YIELD　5 TO 6 SERVINGS

Gina Schrock
Hutchinson, KS

1. Special Occasion Pan Rolls, page 39

2. Baked Apple Dumplings, page 188

3. Chicken Marsala, page 114

4. Buttery Green Beans with Almonds, page 166

Pizza Turnovers

Wrap the traditional filling in envelopes of homemade pizza crust.

1 pkg. dry yeast (1 tbsp.)
1 cup warm water
1 tsp. sugar

In a small bowl, dissolve yeast and sugar in warm water.

2 tbsp. vegetable oil
1 tsp. salt
2½ to 3 cups all-purpose flour

In mixing bowl, combine yeast, oil, salt and 1½ cups flour; beat until smooth. Mix in enough remaining flour to make a moderately stiff dough. Turn out onto lightly floured surface and knead until smooth and elastic. Cover; let rise until doubled, about 1 hour.

1 lb. ground beef
½ cup chopped onion
1 cup pizza sauce
1 tsp. Italian seasoning
½ tsp. salt

Cook and stir ground beef and onion until meat is brown and onion is tender. Drain off fat. Stir in pizza sauce and seasonings. Cook over low heat for 5 minutes, stirring often.

Divide dough into 8 pieces. Cover; let rest 10 minutes. On floured surface roll each into a 6-inch circle. Spoon equal portions of meat mixture onto half of each circle.

2 cups shredded mozzarella cheese
1 egg, slightly beaten
1 tsp. water

Sprinkle each portion with ¼ cup cheese. Moisten edge of ½ circle with mixture of egg and water. Fold in half; seal edge by pressing with fork. Prick tops; brush with remaining egg mixture. Place on greased baking sheets. Bake at 375° for 30 to 35 minutes or until golden brown.

YIELD   8 SERVINGS

I had my first taste of homemade pizza in a college dining hall. The crust was thick and chewy and all I remember of the topping is lots of tomato sauce with meat and cheese. To supplement the bagged lunches we were given for Sunday evening, the girls in the dorm would make pizza in the kitchenette. The box of mix came complete with crust mix that needed only water, a tin of sauce and tin of Parmesan cheese. I thought our efforts produced a fantastic snack. Today we are much more creative.

Classic Pizza

1 pkg. dry yeast (1tbsp.)
1/2 cup warm water
1 tsp. sugar

1 cup warm milk
3 tbsp. vegetable oil
1 tbsp. sugar
1 tsp. salt
1/4 tsp. garlic salt
3 1/2 to 4 cups all-purpose flour
Cornmeal (optional)

In a small bowl, dissolve yeast and sugar in warm water.

In mixing bowl, combine yeast mixture, milk, oil, sugar, seasonings and 2 cups flour. Beat together until well mixed. Add remaining flour and knead until smooth. Place in a greased bowl, turn to grease top. Cover and let rise in warm place until doubled, about 1 hour.

Divide dough in half; roll into two 14-inch circles. Generously oil two 14-inch pizza pans; sprinkle with cornmeal. Place dough on pans, pressing up sides to form an edge. Prick dough with a fork and let rise again for about 20 minutes. If you like a firm crust, partially bake in preheated 375° oven for 7 to 8 minutes or until crust just begins to brown. Use immediately with your favorite toppings or freeze for later use.

YIELD   TWO 14-INCH CRUSTS

Hawaiian Pizza

1/2 cup pizza sauce
1/2 lb. ham, shaved or chopped
1 cup pineapple tidbits

1 1/2 to 2 cups shredded mozzarella
   cheese

Spread one crust with pizza sauce. Layer ham evenly over sauce. Top with pineapple tidbits.

Sprinkle with shredded cheese. Bake at 400° for 25 to 30 minutes or until cheese is melted and lightly browned.

YIELD   ONE 14-INCH PIZZA

Saucy Chicken Pepper Pizza

It seems there is no limit to what can go on a pizza.
I had never tasted one with chicken until I experimented and came up with this recipe.
My family decided it was a keeper.

1 small can tomato sauce, (about 1 cup)
2 tbsp. brown sugar
1 tbsp. vinegar
1/4 tsp. chili powder
1/4 tsp. paprika
1/4 tsp. salt

In a small saucepan, combine all ingredients. Simmer over low heat for about 10 minutes, until mixture is slightly reduced. Set aside.

2 boneless chicken breast halves,
  cut into small chunks
1 garlic clove, minced
1/2 tsp. chili powder
1/4 tsp. ground cumin
1 tbsp. vegetable oil

In a small bowl, stir together chicken, garlic and seasonings. Marinate for 15 minutes.

2 cups thinly sliced,
  red, yellow and orange peppers
1 cup sliced mushrooms (optional)
1 small onion, thinly sliced
1 tbsp. vegetable oil

In a non-stick skillet, sauté peppers, mushrooms and onions in oil until tender-crisp; set aside. In the same skillet, stir-fry chicken for 3 to 4 minutes or until chicken is no longer pink.

14-inch pizza crust

Spread 1/2 cup prepared tomato sauce over pizza crust. (Freeze remaining sauce for another use.)

1/2 cup shredded cheddar cheese
1 1/2 to 2 cups shredded
  mozzarella cheese

Sprinkle with cheddar cheese. Layer vegetables and chicken on pizza. Top with mozzarella cheese. Bake at 400° for 20 to 25 minutes until crust and cheese are lightly browned.

YIELD   ONE 14-INCH PIZZA

Italian Classic Lasagna

It is easy to create this robust layered wonder which features home-cooked meat sauce and lots of cheese. This entrée can be prepared ahead, covered tightly and refrigerated overnight. Add 5 to 10 minutes to baking time.

1 1/2 lbs. ground beef
1 large onion, chopped

Cook and stir ground beef and onion in a large saucepan or Dutch oven until meat is brown and onion is tender. Drain off fat.

1 can (20 oz.) tomatoes
   put through sieve or blended
1 can (10 oz.) condensed tomato soup
2 tbsp. brown sugar
1 tbsp. vinegar
1 tbsp. parsley flakes
1 tsp. dried basil leaves
1 tsp. salt
1/2 tsp. ground oregano
1/4 tsp. garlic powder
1/8 tsp. cayenne pepper

Add tomatoes, soup, sugar, vinegar and spices to meat mixture. Heat to boiling. Reduce heat and simmer for 30 to 40 minutes, stirring occasionally.

9 lasagna noodles
1 tsp. oil
1 tsp. salt

Cook lasagna noodles in 4 quarts of water with oil and salt as directed on package; drain.

1 lb. mozzarella cheese, shredded;
   reserve 1 cup
1/4 cup grated Parmesan cheese

In ungreased 9 x 13 - inch baking dish, layer 1/4 of the sauce and 1/3 noodles and mozzarella cheese, in that order. Repeat layers ending with meat sauce. Sprinkle with Parmesan cheese and reserved 1 cup mozzarella cheese. Bake uncovered in preheated 350° oven for 1 hour or until lasagna is bubbly and top is golden brown. Remove from oven and cover with foil. Let stand 10 to 15 minutes before serving.

VARIATION
Follow recipe as above except:
Divide 3 cups creamed cottage cheese mixed with 1 beaten egg and spread evenly on each layer of noodles.

YIELD   8 TO 10 SERVINGS

Barbecued Meatballs

These saucy meatballs are tasty enough for company,
but practical enough for a regular family meal, too.

1 1/2 lbs. lean ground beef
3/4 cup evaporated milk
1 cup quick-cooking oats
1/4 to 1/2 cup finely chopped onion
1 egg, beaten
1 tsp. chili powder
1 tsp. salt
1/4 tsp. garlic powder
1/4 tsp. pepper

In a large mixing bowl, combine milk, oats, onion, egg and spices. Crumble beef over mixture and mix well. Shape into 24 meatballs. (See method for making same-size meatballs on page 13.) Place in 9 x 13 - inch baking pan in single layer. Cover with barbecue sauce. Bake at 350° for 1 hour.

Barbecue Sauce

1 cup ketchup
3/4 cup brown sugar, lightly packed
1/4 cup chopped onion
1 tsp. liquid smoke
1/4 tsp. garlic powder

In a medium saucepan, combine the sauce ingredients. Cook over medium heat until mixture boils. Reduce heat and simmer for 10 to 15 minutes.

YIELD   6 TO 8 SERVINGS

Lorene Petersheim
Catlett, VA

NOTE
If I am not using lean ground beef, I always pre-bake the meat balls. Shape meatballs and place on a foil-lined rimmed baking sheet. Bake in 350° oven for 20 minutes. Transfer to baking pan or casserole; discard drippings. Cover with barbecue sauce and continue baking for 30 to 35 minutes or until bubbly.

Simple Spaghetti

An old favorite that is quick and easy to make.
Serve with tossed salad, crusty rolls and fresh fruit.

1 lb. ground beef
1 large onion, chopped

Cook and stir ground beef and onion until meat is brown and onion is tender. Drain off fat.

2 cans (10 oz.) condensed tomato soup
1/4 cup water
2 tbsp. brown sugar
1 can (8 oz.) sliced mushrooms (optional)
2 tsp. chili powder
1 tsp. salt
1/2 tsp. Worcestershire sauce
1/2 tsp. onion powder
1/2 tsp. garlic powder
1/4 tsp. pepper

In a large saucepan, combine soup, water, brown sugar, mushrooms and seasonings. Simmer for 5 to 10 minutes to blend flavors. Add beef mixture and simmer for 15 to 20 minutes, stirring occasionally.

8 oz. spaghetti,
   broken into 4-inch pieces

In a large saucepan, cook spaghetti according to package directions; drain. Serve tomato beef sauce over spaghetti.

YIELD   6 TO 8 SERVINGS

Spaghetti and Meatballs

Substitute meatballs for ground beef in recipe above.

1 egg
1/2 cup bread crumbs
1/4 cup milk
2 tsp. grated Parmesan cheese
1 tsp. Worcestershire sauce
1/2 tsp. dried basil, crushed
1/2 tsp. garlic powder
1/4 tsp. oregano powder
1/4 tsp. onion powder
1/2 tsp. salt
1/4 tsp. pepper

1 lb. lean ground beef

In a mixing bowl, beat egg with a fork. Add bread crumbs, milk, cheese and seasonings; stir to blend.

Mix in beef. Shape into 1 1/2-inch balls; place on foil-lined rimmed baking sheet. Bake in 350° oven for 15 to 20 minutes or until no longer pink inside. Discard drippings.

Combine meat balls and tomato sauce mixture. Simmer gently for 15 to 20 minutes, stirring occasionally. Serve with spaghetti as above.

Baked Beef Burgers

This dish, also known as 'Poor Man's Steak', consists of tender,
well-seasoned meat patties smothered in mushroom sauce.
For optimum flavor, it is imperative to prepare beef a day ahead.

2 lbs. ground beef
2 eggs, slightly beaten
1 small onion, finely chopped or grated
1 cup bread crumbs
  OR quick-cooking oats
1/2 cup milk
1 tbsp. parsley flakes
1 tsp. salt

In large mixing bowl, combine all ingredients except ground beef. Crumble the beef over the mixture and mix well. Handle the mixture as little as possible to keep the final product light in texture. Refrigerate for 8 hours or overnight.

Shape ground beef mixture into 12 large, thick patties. Brown on both sides in greased frying pan. Patties will not necessarily be cooked through, just browned. Arrange in 9 x 13 - inch baking dish; pour brown gravy sauce over all. Bake at 350°, uncovered, for 1 hour.

Brown Gravy Sauce

1/4 cup butter or margarine
1/4 cup all-purpose flour
2 cups water
2 tsp. instant beef powder
  OR 2 beef bouillon cubes
1 can (10 oz.) cream of mushroom soup

In medium saucepan, melt butter and stir in flour. Add water and beef powder. Cook over medium heat, stirring until thickened. Blend in mushroom soup until smooth.

YIELD   6 TO 8 SERVINGS

Barbecued Burgers

Juicy jumbo burgers are perfect for that backyard get-together.
The bold-flavored sauce is a cut above the ordinary.

Barbecue Sauce

1 cup ketchup
1/2 cup brown sugar, scant
1/4 cup honey
1/4 cup molasses
2 tsp. prepared mustard
1 1/2 tsp. Worcestershire sauce
1/4 tsp. liquid smoke
1/4 tsp. salt
1/4 tsp. pepper

In a small saucepan, combine all ingredients; bring to a boil. Remove from heat. Reserve 1 cup barbecue sauce to serve with burgers.

Jumbo Burgers

1 1/2 lbs. lean ground beef
1 egg, beaten
1/3 cup quick-cooking oats
1/4 cup barbecue sauce
1/4 tsp. onion salt
1/4 tsp. garlic salt
1/4 tsp. salt
1/4 tsp. pepper

In mixing bowl, combine egg, oats, 1/4 cup sauce and seasonings. Crumble beef over mixture; mix well. Shape into 6 patties. Grill, covered over medium heat, for 6 to 8 minutes on each side, basting with 1/2 cup barbecue sauce during the last 5 minutes.

6 hamburger buns, split
Toppings of your choice

Serve on buns with toppings of your choice and reserved barbecue sauce.

YIELD   6 SERVINGS

Lorene Petersheim
Catlett, VA

Beef Enchiladas

Corn tortillas spread with tomato sauce, filled, rolled and covered with more sauce are the focus in this flavorful Mexican dish.

1 lb. lean ground beef
1/2 cup chopped onion

Cook and stir beef and onion over medium heat until meat is brown and onion is tender. Drain off fat.

1 cup shredded cheddar cheese
1/2 cup sour cream
1/2 tsp. salt
1/8 tsp. pepper

Stir cheese, sour cream and seasonings into beef mixture; set aside.

1 can (10 oz.) tomato soup
2/3 cup tomato juice
1 garlic clove, minced
1 tbsp. chili powder
1/2 tsp. oregano leaves
1/4 tsp. ground cumin

In a medium saucepan, combine tomato soup, juice, garlic and seasonings. Cook over medium heat until boiling, stirring occasionally. Reduce heat and simmer uncovered for 5 minutes.

8 six-inch tortillas
   (store-bought or use recipe below)

Spread 1 tablespoon tomato mixture over tortilla; spoon about 1/4 cup meat filling down center of each tortilla. Roll up and place seam side down in ungreased 8 x 12 - inch baking dish. Repeat with remaining tortillas. Spoon remaining sauce over enchiladas.

Cover and bake in 350° oven for 20 to 30 minutes or until bubbly.

3/4 cup sour cream
1 cup shredded cheddar cheese
3 green onions, sliced (optional)

Garnish with sour cream, shredded cheese and chopped onions.

YIELD   4 TO 6 SERVINGS

Corn Tortillas

3/4 cup all-purpose flour
1/3 cup cornmeal
1/4 tsp. salt
1 egg
1 1/4 cups cold water

Combine all ingredients in a mixing bowl; beat until smooth. Spoon about 3 tablespoons batter onto a medium hot ungreased, non-stick skillet to make a very thin 6-inch pancake. Turn tortilla when edges begin to look dry, but not brown. Bake on other side; remove to platter. Continue with remaining batter.

YIELD   8 TORTILLAS

Judy's Chili

This is a mild chili but could be heated up with more spices.
Delicious used as a baked potato topping.

2 lbs. ground beef
1 medium onion, chopped
1 can (10 oz.) condensed tomato soup
1 cup tomato juice
1/4 cup ketchup
2 tbsp. brown sugar
1 tbsp. chili seasoning mix
1 tsp. salt
1/4 tsp. pepper
1/4 tsp. garlic salt
Dash of cayenne pepper (optional)

Cook and stir ground beef and onion in large skillet or Dutch oven until meat is brown and onion is tender. Drain off fat. Stir in remaining ingredients and heat to boiling. Reduce heat; cover and simmer for 1 hour, stirring occasionally.

1 can (14 oz.) red kidney beans, drained
Green onion
Sour cream
Grated cheddar cheese

Stir in beans and heat through. Top individual servings with green onion, sour cream and grated cheddar cheese if desired. Serve with crusty rolls or Golden Corn Bread, page 58.

YIELD   8 TO 10 SERVINGS

VARIATION
For additional flavor, stir in 2 to 3 teaspoons finely chopped jalapeño pepper and 3 cups sliced mushrooms.

SLOW COOKER ALTERNATIVE
This chili is excellent made in a slow cooker. Cook on High 30 minutes; reduce heat to Low, cook 2 to 3 hours. Add beans 20 minutes before serving.

Savory Strombolli

My girls returned from a trip to Virginia with this grand recipe.
It was a specialty that Beverly became proficient at putting together.
I have tweaked the recipe to use a very soft dough.
However, if time is a factor, the loaf can be made with frozen dough.

1 pkg. dry yeast (1 tbsp.)
1/2 cup warm water
1 tsp. sugar

In a small bowl, dissolve yeast and sugar in warm water.

1 cup warm milk
3 tbsp. vegetable oil
1 tsp. salt
1 tbsp. sugar
3 1/2 to 4 cups all-purpose flour

In large mixing bowl, stir together yeast, milk, oil, salt, sugar and 2 1/2 cups of the flour. Beat until smooth. Mix in enough remaining flour to make dough easy to handle.

Turn dough onto lightly floured surface; knead until elastic, about 5 minutes. Place in greased bowl; turn greased side up. Cover; let rise in warm place until doubled, about 1 hour.

Filling

3 tbsp. mustard
12 slices processed cheese
12 slices salami
1 lb. ham, thinly sliced or shaved
1 lb. ground beef, browned
  with 1 med. onion and drained
5 cups shredded mozzarella cheese

Divide dough in half. On lightly floured surface, roll each half into rectangle, 12 x 15 inches; spread with 1 1/2 tablespoons mustard. Layer 1/2 of the ingredients in order given down the center 1/3 of rectangle. Cut the exposed dough on each side into 1-inch strips. (They should be about 3 inches deep) Fold each side alternately over the top to produce a braided effect.* Seal ends well to prevent leaking. Carefully lift onto a greased baking sheet.

*see page 51, braiding a filled bread

1 egg, beaten
Parsley flakes and/or oregano

Brush top with beaten egg and sprinkle with parsley flakes. Repeat with other half of dough and remaining filling ingredients.

Let rise until light, about 15 to 20 minutes. Bake at 350° for 20 to 25 minutes or until golden brown. Cool slightly before cutting into 1-inch slices.

Pictured on page 91.

Ethel Showalter
Mt. Crawford, VA

YIELD   14 TO 16 SERVINGS

Calzoní

This attractive bread has meat, cheese and seasonings tucked inside.
Slice and serve as a main dish or alongside a bowl of soup or salad.

1 loaf frozen bread dough*
3 tbsp. butter or margarine, softened
1/4 to 1/2 tsp. garlic powder
1 lb. shaved ham
1 1/2 cups grated Swiss cheese
3 green onions, chopped
6 to 8 thinly sliced salami

*instead of using frozen bread dough,
use dough recipe for Pizza Turnovers,
page 129.

Allow dough to thaw. On a lightly
floured board, roll dough out to a
rectangle, 10 x 15 - inches. Spread
dough with butter up to within 3/4 inch
of sides. Sprinkle garlic powder evenly
over butter. Spread ham evenly over
dough. Sprinkle with grated cheese
and green onions; add salami slices.

Carefully fold one-third of topped
dough over the center third. Fold
remaining third of dough over folded
layer to make a 3-layer rectangle.
Pinch all edges of dough to seal
tightly.

1 tbsp. vegetable oil
1 tsp. poppy seeds (optional)

Brush with oil; sprinkle with poppy
seeds. Slide onto lightly greased
10 x 15 - inch baking sheet. Bake at
350° for 30 to 35 minutes or until
golden brown. Let stand 5 minutes.
To serve, cut in slices.

VARIATION
CALZONI WITH BROCCOLI
*Cook 1 pkg. (16 oz.) frozen chopped
broccoli according to pkg.
directions; drain and cool.*

*OR use 1 bunch fresh broccoli,
separated into florets.
Cook in water until tender crisp;
drain and cool.*

*Spread prepared broccoli over ham
layer in recipe above.*

YIELD   6 TO 8 SERVINGS

Soft Taco Bake

Hearty and mildly seasoned, this one-dish Mexican meal is great for a quick supper.

1 1/2 lbs. ground beef
1/2 cup chopped onion

In a skillet or heavy saucepan, cook and stir ground beef and onion until meat is brown and onion is tender; drain.

1 can (10 oz.) condensed tomato soup
2 tbsp. taco seasoning mix
1/2 cup milk
8 flour tortillas (6 to 8-inch),
   cut into 1-inch pieces
1 cup shredded cheddar cheese

In a large mixing bowl, combine beef, soup, taco seasoning, milk, tortillas and cheese. Spoon into a 2-quart shallow baking dish. Bake at 350° for 30 to 40 minutes or until bubbly.

1/2 cup sour cream
3 to 4 cups shredded lettuce
2 medium tomatoes, coarsely chopped
1/2 cup shredded cheddar cheese

Top with sour cream, lettuce, tomatoes and cheese.

YIELD   6 TO 8 SERVINGS

NOTE
A simple way to spread sour cream as topping: spoon sour cream into small plastic bag; seal. Cut off one corner about 1/4 inch; squeeze sour cream in a stream back and forth over hot meat mixture.

VARIATION
Substitute 2 tbsp. fajita seasoning mix for the taco seasoning.
OR
Omit taco seasoning, add 1 cup salsa.

Beverly Gingerich
Newfield, NY

Taco~In~A~Bag

The idea for this Mexican favorite came from my sister-in-law Mary Lynn, who suggested it for a concession. This 'bag lunch' became an instant hit and I put together more than I care to count. My daughter Beverly served them at a large picnic she hosted and delighted her guests with the novel pocket idea. Everything can be prepared ahead of time and all you need to do is keep the meat sauce warm. Guests can complete their own taco to individual preference. The recipe can be easily adapted to serve a large crowd.

1 ½ lbs. ground beef
1 medium onion

Cook and stir beef and onion until meat is brown and onion is tender. Drain off fat.

1 can (10 oz.) tomato soup, undiluted
1 pkg. taco seasoning mix

In medium saucepan, combine soup and taco mix. Cook over medium heat until boiling. Add beef mixture and simmer for 10 to 15 minutes

8 to 10 pkg. Nacho cheese taco chips
 (individual serving size)
1 cup sour cream
3 cups shredded lettuce
1 ½ cups chopped tomatoes
2 cups shredded cheddar cheese

For each serving, cut package of taco chips open length-wise; squeeze bag slightly to crush chips. Spoon about ⅓ cup meat sauce into bag. Add 2 tablespoons sour cream, a handful of lettuce, 2 tablespoons tomatoes and a sprinkling of cheese.

Salsa

Serve salsa on the side, if desired.

YIELD   8 TO 10 SERVINGS

Taco Ring

This taco meat ring is very quick to assemble using refrigerated crescents.
The result is extremely attractive and very tasty.

½ lb. ground beef
2 tbsp. chopped onion

Cook and stir beef and onion over medium heat until meat is brown and onion is tender. Drain off fat.

2 tbsp. taco seasoning mix
½ cup water

Stir ground beef, taco seasoning and water together. Cook over medium heat for about 5 minutes, stirring frequently, until water has evaporated. Remove from heat.

2 cans (8 oz. each) refrigerated crescent dinner rolls

Unroll dough; separate into triangles. Arrange triangles on large greased cookie sheet with pointed ends facing the outer edge of pan and wide ends overlapping into wreath shape and leaving a 4-inch round opening in center. Lightly press overlapping sides of dough to flatten slightly.

1 cup shredded cheddar cheese

Spoon beef mixture onto widest part of dough. Sprinkle with shredded cheese. Fold points of triangles over filling and tuck under dough to form ring.

Bake at 375° for 20 to 25 minutes or until deep golden brown.

Transfer ring to large round platter.

Shredded lettuce
Chopped tomato
Green or red bell pepper
Salsa
Sour cream

Arrange shredded lettuce around taco ring on platter; top with chopped tomato. Cut thin slice from stem end of pepper to remove top of pepper. Remove seeds and membranes; rinse pepper and fill with salsa. Place pepper in center opening.

Serve sour cream on the side.

YIELD   6 TO 8 SERVINGS

Karen Yoder
Goshen, IN

143

Roast Beef in Crock Pot

Whenever I make roast for Sunday dinner, I use this easy method.
Late Saturday evening, I place the frozen roast in the slow cooker turned on High.
Early in the morning when the delicious aroma is all over the house,
I turn it on Low. After I get home from Church it is deliciously tender and all
I need to do is make the gravy and carve the meat. If you wish,
you can do all this a day ahead and refrigerate. Reheat in the slow cooker.

3 to 4 lb. roast, frozen
1 envelope dry onion soup mix
1 tsp. salt
1/4 tsp. pepper
1 cup hot water

Place roast in slow cooker. Sprinkle with seasonings. Pour water over roast. Cover and cook on high for 4 hours. Reduce heat to Low and cook 4 to 5 hours longer. (If you are away, it can stay on Low for a few more hours.) Remove roast from cooker and keep warm.

Gravy

2 cups meat broth
1/2 cup cold water
4 tbsp. all-purpose flour
Salt and pepper

Strain broth into glass or metal dish, skim excess fat. Measure broth; pour amount desired into saucepan. Shake water and flour in jar with tight fitting lid. (It is important to put water into jar first, then flour.) Using whisk, gradually stir flour mixture into broth. Heat to boiling, stirring constantly. Boil and stir 1 minute. Season with salt and pepper. Serve gravy with sliced roast beef.

YIELD   6 TO 8 SERVINGS

Oven Pot Roast

Use this easy method to prepare a roast when you need to go out.

3 lb. roast
1 envelope dry onion soup mix

Sprinkle one-half package onion soup in the center of large piece of heavy foil. Place roast on onion mix and pat some of the mix on sides. Sprinkle rest of mix on top; bring foil up around roast and seal. Place wrapped roast in heavy covered pot or Dutch oven. Bake at 300° for 3 to 4 hours. Place roast and brown juices on warm serving platter. Or make gravy with the cooking juices as above.

YIELD   6 TO 8 SERVINGS

Beef Rouladen

This interesting entrée features 'rouladen' which are very thin slices of beef. The beef is topped with a seasoned filling, rolled up and baked in a tasty sauce. Delicious served with a baked potato and garden salad.

2 tbsp. butter or margarine
1/2 cup chopped celery
1/3 cup chopped onion

In a large skillet, sauté celery and onions in butter until tender.

2 cups soft bread crumbs
1 tsp. parsley flakes
1/2 tsp. salt
1/4 tsp. poultry seasoning
1/8 tsp. pepper

In a bowl, combine celery mixture with bread crumbs and seasonings.

6 slices beef rouladen
1/2 cup all-purpose flour
2 tbsp. vegetable oil

Place about 1/3 cup stuffing mixture on each slice of beef; roll up and fasten with a wooden pick. Roll in flour. In same skillet, over medium heat, brown roll-ups on all sides in oil. Place into a casserole dish.

1 tbsp. butter or margarine
1 tbsp. flour
1 tsp. beef bouillon granules
1/4 tsp. salt
1/8 tsp. pepper
1/4 cup cooking sherry
3/4 cup water

In skillet, melt butter; stir in flour and seasonings. Gradually add sherry and water; bring to a boil. Cook and stir until thickened. Pour over beef rolls. Bake at 350° for 35 minutes or until heated through and bubbly.

YIELD   6 SERVINGS

Strips and Rice

My nine-year-old niece was being interviewed during a national riding competition.
She was asked to name her favorite food. Her answer was,
'my aunt Judy's Strips and Rice.' I offer this recipe especially for Raylee.

1 lb. sirloin steak
1 tbsp. vegetable oil

Cut steak across grain into 1/8-inch thick slices. Heat frying pan or heavy saucepan on medium high until hot. Add oil and stir-fry beef in batches until brown, adding more oil if necessary.

1 envelope dry onion soup mix
Water

Place beef in a 2-quart casserole; add onion soup mix. Add enough water to almost cover. Bake at 325° for 1 1/2 hours.

1/4 cup water
1 1/2 tbsp. all-purpose flour

Mix together water and flour; stir into beef mixture. Return to oven and continue to bake for an additional 20 minutes or until thickened. Season with salt and pepper to taste. Serve on a bed of rice with green peas or steamed broccoli.

YIELD   4 SERVINGS

Slow Cooker Beef and Gravy

With the convience of a slow cooker, I can fix a main dish and forget about it.
Chunks of beef simmer in rich broth while I concentrate on other things I enjoy
doing. Much later, tender beef and smooth gravy hits the spot. Serve over mashed
potatoes with peas and carrots on the side.

2 to 3 lbs. stewing beef or round steak,
    cubed
Vegetable oil

Heat oil in frying pan or Dutch oven. Brown beef cubes in batches and place in slow cooker.

1 envelope dry onion soup
1 bay leaf
1 tsp. steak spice
1 tsp. salt
1/4 tsp. pepper
3 to 4 cups boiling water

Add onion soup, bay leaf and spices. Pour water over top almost covering meat. Cover and cook on High 4 to 5 hours.

One hour before serving, mix together 1/4 cup flour and 1/4 cup water. Gradually stir into slow cooker. Cover and cook for remaining time. Discard bay leaf.

YIELD   6 TO 8 SERVINGS

146

Cottage Meatloaf

*Ground beef, bread crumbs and seasonings are brought together
into a moist firm loaf in this satisfying homey dish.*

2 lbs. lean ground beef
1/2 cup milk
1 1/2 cups soft bread crumbs
2 eggs, beaten with fork
1/4 cup chopped onion
1/4 cup ketchup
1 tbsp. prepared mustard
2 tsp. Worcestershire sauce
1 1/2 tsp. salt
1/2 tsp. pepper
1/8 tsp. garlic salt

*In large mixing bowl, combine all
ingredients except ground beef.
Crumble the beef over the mixture and
mix well. Handle the mixture as little as
possible to keep the final product light
in texture. Pat into 2 loaf pans or
shape into oblong loaf in a 9 x 13 - inch
baking pan.*

1/4 cup ketchup
2 tbsp. brown sugar
1 tsp. prepared mustard

*In a small mixing bowl, stir ketchup,
sugar and mustard together until
blended. Spread over meat loaf.*

*Bake uncovered at 350° for 60 to 70
minutes or until meat is no longer pink.
Let stand 5 minutes; remove to serving
platter.*

YIELD   8 TO 10 SERVINGS

Beef and Broccoli Stir-Fry

This quick and easy stir-fry showcases tender slices of beef,
while crisp-tender broccoli adds a nice crunch.

1 tbsp. vegetable oil 2 tbsp. lemon juice or sherry 2 garlic cloves, minced 1 tbsp. soy sauce 1 tsp. sugar 1/8 tsp. pepper	In a mixing bowl, combine oil, lemon juice, garlic, soy sauce, sugar and pepper.
1 lb. sirloin steak	Cut steak across grain into thin strips; stir into marinade. Let stand at room temperature for 30 minutes.
1 tbsp. vegetable oil 1 lb. fresh broccoli, cut into 1 1/2-inch florets 1 small onion, thinly sliced 1 tsp. finely chopped gingerroot 1/2 cup chicken broth	Heat wok or large non-stick skillet on medium–high until hot. Add oil, broccoli, onion and ginger; stir-fry for 2 minutes. Stir in broth; cover and cook for 3 or 4 minutes until broccoli is tender crisp. Transfer to bowl.
1 tbsp. vegetable oil	Add oil to wok or skillet. Stir-fry beef and marinade for 3 to 4 minutes until beef is tender. Add broccoli mixture to beef.
3 tbsp. water 3 tsp. cornstarch	Stir water into cornstarch in small dish; add to beef and broccoli stirring until boiling and thickened.

Serve with rice or noodles.

YIELD   4 TO 6 SERVINGS

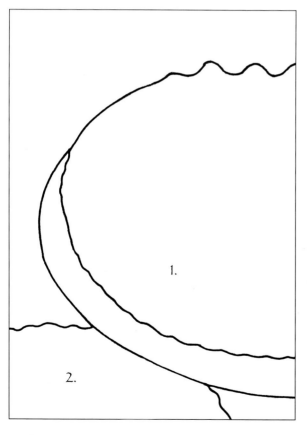

Ham and Sausage Quiche

Quiches are easy to make and simple to serve. They are perfect for a brunch, company luncheon or supper. Though their base is always milk and eggs, their main ingredients can be any variety of combinations. Use your personal favorites.

Pastry for 10-inch One-Crust Pie, page 177

Prepare pastry; line quiche dish or deep dish pie pan. Trim pastry to fit; flute edge.

1/4 lb. mild Italian sausage or ground beef
1/2 cup chopped onion

Sauté sausage and onion in frying pan until sausage is browned and onions are clear. Drain off fat; sprinkle sausage over pastry crust.

1/4 lb. minced cooked ham
1 cup shredded cheddar cheese

Sprinkle ham and cheese over sausage.

4 eggs
3/4 cup milk
1 tbsp. cornstarch
1/2 tsp. salt
1/4 tsp. oregano
1/8 tsp. black pepper

Beat eggs slightly; whisk together with remaining ingredients. Pour mixture into pastry shell.

1 cup shredded mozzarella cheese

Sprinkle cheese over top. Bake at 350° for 30 to 35 minutes or until lightly browned.

YIELD   6 SERVINGS

Ham and Broccoli Quiche

Follow recipe for Ham and Sausage Quiche; except omit sausage and oregano.

1/4 cup chopped fresh broccoli
1/4 cup chopped red pepper
1/4 cup chopped fresh mushrooms
1/4 cup chopped onions
1 garlic clove, minced
1 tbsp. vegetable oil
2 cups chopped cooked ham, divided
2 cups shredded Swiss, mozzarella or cheddar cheese or combination

Sauté broccoli, pepper, mushrooms, onions and garlic in oil until tender. Sprinkle half the ham and cheese into pastry crust. Cover with the vegetables; add remaining ham and cheese. Prepare egg mixture as above and pour over ham and cheese. Bake as above.

Ham Balls with Mustard Sauce

Try this for a change from the usual ground beef meatballs.
The tangy sauce perks up the whole dish.

1 lb. cooked ham, minced
1 lb. ground pork
1/2 lb. ground beef
2 cups soft bread crumbs
1 cup milk
2 eggs, beaten
1/2 tsp. salt
1/8 tsp. pepper

In large bowl combine ham, pork and beef; add bread crumbs, milk, eggs, salt and pepper. Shape into 1-inch balls; place on foil-lined rimmed baking sheet. Bake at 350° for 30 minutes. Discard drippings; pile into casserole dish.

Mustard Sauce

1 cup brown sugar
1/2 cup vinegar
1/2 cup water
1 tbsp. cornstarch
2 tsp. ground mustard

In medium saucepan combine sugar, vinegar, water, cornstarch and mustard. Heat to boiling, stirring constantly. Pour over balls. Cover and bake an additional 30 minutes.

This dish can be prepared ahead of time and refrigerated. Reheat in oven until bubbly.

SLOW COOKER ALTERNATIVE
Pile prepared ham balls into slow cooker. Pour sauce over all. Cook on Low for 3 to 4 hours.

YIELD   8 TO 10 SERVINGS

Sweet and Sour Spare Ribs

*After slow baking, a liberal addition of a zesty sauce is the secret
to ribs that are tender, juicy and perfectly glazed.*

5 to 6 lbs. pork spare ribs
  or pork loin back ribs

Cut ribs into serving-size pieces. Place in a large roasting pan. Cover and bake in preheated 350° oven for 1 1/2 hours, turning every 30 minutes. Drain juices and discard; pour sweet and sour sauce over ribs. Cover and continue to bake at 325° for 1 to 1 1/2 hours, stirring occasionally.

Sweet and Sour Sauce

3/4 cup brown sugar
3 tbsp. cornstarch
1 cup ketchup
2/3 cup water
1/3 cup vinegar
3 tbsp. soy sauce

In a medium saucepan, combine sugar and cornstarch. Stir in ketchup, water, vinegar and soy sauce. Bring to a boil, cook and stir until thickened and clear.

YIELD   6 TO 8 SERVINGS

Honey Garlic Ribs

*Bake 4 lbs. ribs as in the recipe above.
Prepare honey garlic sauce and use in place of the sweet and sour sauce.*

1/2 cup soy sauce
1/2 cup honey
2 tbsp. water
2 garlic cloves, minced
1 tsp. vegetable oil

Combine all ingredients in a saucepan and heat to boiling. Reduce heat and simmer for about 5 minutes. Pour over browned and drained ribs in roasting pan. Cover and continue to bake for 1 hour longer, turning to baste after 30 minutes.

YIELD   4 TO 5 SERVINGS

Herbed Halibut

A simple marinade adds a zesty flavor to any mild white fish.

4 fresh or frozen halibut steaks
2 tbsp. lemon juice

Thaw fish, if frozen. Rinse and pat dry. Arrange fish steaks in a shallow baking pan. Sprinkle with lemon juice; set aside.

1/3 cup chopped onion
1/2 tsp. dried basil, crushed
1/2 tsp. dillweed
1 garlic clove, minced
2 tsp. vegetable oil
1/4 cup snipped fresh parsley

In a small saucepan, cook onion, basil, dillweed and garlic in oil until onion is tender. Stir in parsley.

1/3 cup plain yogurt

Bake fish, uncovered, at 400° for 10 minutes. Remove from oven and spread with yogurt. Sprinkle with onion-herb mixture. Bake 5 to 10 minutes longer or until fish flakes easily with a fork.

Lemon wedges and parsley sprigs

If desired, garnish with lemon wedges and parsley sprigs.

YIELD   4 SERVINGS

Vegetables
and
Side Dishes

Vegetables & Side Dishes

To my youthful mind, weeding vegetables was a chore lessened by the outcropping of brilliant flowers that dotted the huge garden. I especially loved the showy row of sweet peas that was as much a part of the arrangement as the row of carrots. Not a summer passed without the pleasure of inhaling the fragrant scent of those glorious blooms! The tradition lives and thrives in my own small garden.

Memories of overflowing baskets of fresh vegetables are synonymous with endless hours of gathering, freezing and canning. Tiring work to be sure, but readily forgotten when the bounty was placed on the table during the long winter months.

Vegetables are beautiful and need little enrichment. I grew up with the clear flavors of plainly cooked vegetables finished with a small amount of butter and seasonings. Simple unadorned vegetables are still my preference but that does not deter my enjoyment of experimenting with palatable vegetable and side dishes that add interest and variety to mealtime.

Stuffed Baked Potatoes

Seasoned, whipped potatoes re-baked in their own shell look and taste marvelous.

6 large baking potatoes, scrubbed
1 tsp. vegetable oil

Rub potatoes with oil; pierce with a fork. Place in a shallow baking pan. Bake at 400° for about 1 hour or until tender. Allow potatoes to cool to the touch. Slice tops off potatoes; scoop out pulp, leaving a 1/4-inch shell. Set shells aside.

1/2 cup sour cream
2 tbsp. butter or margarine
1/4 cup milk
1 1/2 cups shredded cheddar
  or Colby cheese, divided
1/4 cup sliced green onions
1/2 tsp. salt
1/2 tsp. pepper

In a mixing bowl, combine pulp, sour cream, butter and milk; beat until creamy. Stir in 1 cup cheese, onions, salt and pepper. Spoon filling into shells; sprinkle with remaining cheese; return to baking pan. Bake at 350° for 20 to 25 minutes or until heated through. Serve with additional sliced green onion and bacon bits if desired.

YIELD   6 SERVINGS

NOTE
Potatoes may be prepared up to 1 day in advance. Wrap in plastic wrap and refrigerate until ready to bake.

Potatoes can also be prepared, wrapped and frozen. Allow additional time for reheating.

Golden Parmesan Potatoes

Crisp wedges of potato roasted with Parmesan
is a healthy substitute for the fried kind.

6 large potatoes, raw

Wash, peel and cut each potato into 8 wedges.

1/3 cup butter or margarine

Melt butter in a 10 x 15 - inch rimmed foil-lined baking sheet. Set aside.

1/4 cup all-purpose flour
1/4 cup grated Parmesan cheese
1/2 tsp. salt
1/8 tsp. pepper

Combine flour, cheese and seasonings in a heavy plastic bag. Moisten potatoes with water. Add a few at a time to bag and shake, coating potatoes well with cheese mixture. Place on baking sheet.

Bake at 375° for 1 hour and 15 minutes, turning every 15 minutes until they are crisp and golden brown.

YIELD   6 TO 8 SERVINGS

Butter Baked Potato Rounds

Arrange rows and rows of potato rounds in a dish and add the seasonings.
This is pleasing to the eye as well as the palate.

1/4 cup butter or margarine
1/4 cup chopped onion

Sauté onions in butter until transparent.

4 large potatoes, peeled
2 tbsp. water
1/2 tsp. parsley flakes
1/4 tsp. seasoned salt
1/4 tsp. salt

Slice potatoes crosswise into 1/4-inch thick slices. Fan out in rows in a buttered 9 x 13 - inch baking dish or casserole with slices overlapping. Add water; spread onion mixture evenly over potatoes. Sprinkle with seasonings.

Bake at 350° for 50 minutes or until potatoes are tender and slightly golden.

YIELD   4 TO 6 SERVINGS

Make-Ahead Mashed Potatoes

This dish can be served immediately after preparing or refrigerated to be baked later. It also travels well to a potluck meal in a crock pot.

5 lbs. potatoes, peeled

Cook potatoes in salted water until tender; drain.

1 pkg. (8 oz.) cream cheese, softened
1 cup sour cream
1/4 cup melted butter or margarine
1 tsp. salt
1/2 tsp. garlic salt
1/4 tsp. onion salt
1/8 tsp. pepper

In a large mixing bowl, mash the potatoes. Add all other ingredients and whip together until smooth. Transfer into serving dish; sprinkle with paprika, if desired. Keep hot if serving immediately.

To serve later, transfer into a greased 2-quart casserole or baking dish. Cover and refrigerate. About 1 hour before serving, remove from refrigerator. Sprinkle with paprika if desired. Bake, uncovered, at 350° for 45 to 55 minutes or until heated through.

SLOW COOKER ALTERNATIVE
Transfer prepared potatoes into slow cooker. Cover. Cook on Low 5 to 6 hours.

YIELD   12 TO 14 SERVINGS

Topping For Baked Potatoes

Try this tasty blend of toppings for a baked potato feast!

1 pkg. (8 oz.) cream cheese, softened
1 cup sour cream
1 to 2 tbsp. lemon juice
1/2 cup shredded cheddar cheese
1/4 cup chopped onion
2 tbsp. parsley flakes
1/2 tsp. salt

In small mixing bowl, combine cream cheese, sour cream and lemon juice. Beat together until well mixed. Stir in cheese, onions, parsley, and salt. Serve over baked potatoes.

YIELD   ABOUT 2 1/2 CUPS

Reba Rhodes
Bridgewater, VA

Cheesy Company Potatoes

This is a nice way to serve potatoes for Sunday dinner or a company meal.
Prepare and refrigerate overnight or freeze for later.

7 cups cooked shredded
  or diced potatoes
2 cups shredded Colby, Cheddar
  or Monterey Jack cheese

In a large mixing bowl, combine potatoes and cheese.

1/4 cup butter, melted
1/4 cup chopped onion

Sauté onions in butter until onions are tender.

1 can (10 oz.) cream of chicken soup
1 cup sour cream
3/4 cup milk
1 tsp. salt
1/4 tsp. pepper
Paprika

Mix onions, soup, sour cream, milk, salt and pepper together until well blended. Pour over potatoes and mix gently. Spread in 9 x 13 - inch greased baking dish or 3-quart greased casserole dish. Sprinkle with paprika.

Bake in 350° oven, uncovered for 40 to 45 minutes or until browned and bubbly.

OPTIONAL TOPPING
1/4 cup butter or margarine
2 cups crushed cornflake cereal

Melt butter and stir in crushed cereal. Sprinkle evenly over potato mixture just before baking.

YIELD   8 TO 10 SERVINGS

SLOW COOKER ALTERNATIVE
*Use 7 cups cooked diced potatoes **OR** 7 cups frozen hash brown potatoes. Prepare as above except omit cereal topping. Spoon into slow cooker. Cover. Cook on High 1 1/2 hours, and then on Low 2 1/2 hours or until heated through.*

New Potatoes and Peas

This a summertime feast.

12 small new potatoes
3 small green onions
1 tsp. salt

Wash potatoes and leave in their papery skins, or gently scrape with a knife so that only the thin shell is removed. Cut green onions to 3-inch lengths. Cook potatoes and onions in a small amount of water until almost soft.

3 cups fresh peas
1 tsp. salt

Add peas and salt; cook just until the potatoes and peas are tender. Spoon into serving dish and pour white sauce over.

YIELD   4 TO 6 SERVINGS

White Sauce

2 tbsp. butter or margarine
1½ tbsp. flour
1 tsp. chicken bouillon granules
1½ cups milk

YIELD   ABOUT 1½ CUPS

Melt butter in small saucepan; whisk in flour and chicken granules. Gradually add milk, stirring constantly over medium heat until smooth and thickened. Season with salt and pepper to taste.

Seasoned Peas and Carrots

Additional seasonings add subtle accents to these everyday vegetables.

½ cup water
2 cups sliced carrots
2 tsp. chicken bouillon granules
1 tsp. butter or margarine
1 tsp. minced onion flakes
½ tsp. salt

Bring water to a boil in medium saucepan. Add carrots, bouillon granules, butter, onion flakes and salt. Cover and cook over low heat until carrots are tender crisp.

3 cups frozen peas

Add peas to carrots and continue cooking for several minutes until peas are tender. Drain; pour peas and carrots into serving dish.

1 tbsp. butter or margarine
Salt and pepper to taste

Stir in butter, salt and pepper; serve immediately.

YIELD   6 SERVINGS

California Veggie Blend

Tender-crisp vegetables are cooked to perfection in a creamy cheese sauce.

1 bunch fresh broccoli,
  separated into florets
2 cups carrots, cut into chunks
2 cups bite-size cauliflower pieces

Steam or cook vegetables in batches in boiling water until tender crisp, about 3 minutes. Plunge into cold water. This stops the cooking process and preserves color and texture. Turn into an 8 x 12 - inch baking dish or 2-quart casserole.

1/4 cup butter or margarine
3 tbsp. all-purpose flour
1/2 tsp. salt
1/4 tsp. pepper
2 cups milk

Melt butter in a medium saucepan over low heat. Blend in flour, salt and pepper. Cook over low heat, stirring until mixture is smooth and bubbly. Remove from heat and stir in milk. Heat until boiling, stirring constantly; boil 1 minute.

1 cup shredded cheddar cheese

Add cheese and continue stirring, until cheese is melted and sauce is smooth. Pour over vegetables.

1 cup crushed butter-flavored crackers
  (Ritz are good)

Sprinkle crushed crackers over top. Bake at 350° for 30 minutes or until edges are bubbly.

YIELD   *6 TO 8 SERVINGS*

VARIATION
Substitute 5 cups frozen California Blend vegetables in place of prepared vegetables.

NOTE
This dish can be prepared the night before. Add crushed crackers just before baking.

Herb-Roasted Vegetables

Roasting vegetables that have been tossed with oil
and seasonings brings out their natural flavor.

4 cups mixed vegetables
3 to 4 tbsp. olive or vegetable oil
1/2 tsp. salt
1/2 tsp. dried rosemary
1/4 tsp. garlic salt

Wash and chunk vegetables such as
new potatoes, onions, colored
peppers and carrots. Toss vegetables
with oil and seasonings to coat.
Arrange in a single layer on rimmed
baking sheet lined with parchment
paper or foil.

Roast in preheated 425° oven for 20
to 25 minutes or until vegetables are
tender. If desired turn vegetables
halfway through baking.

YIELD   ABOUT 6 SERVINGS

Baked Corn

This is a nice change from plain corn.

4 cups canned or frozen corn
3 tbsp. flour
1/4 cup sugar
  (adjust sugar according to
  sweetness of corn)
3 eggs, beaten
3/4 cup milk
1/2 cup butter or margarine, melted
1 tsp. salt
1/4 tsp. pepper

In a mixing bowl, combine all
ingredients and stir until blended.
Turn into a greased 2-quart casserole
or baking dish. Bake at 375° for 45
minutes.

YIELD   6 TO 8 SERVINGS

Lorene Petersheim
Catlett, VA

163

Creamy Chicken Rice

This mild and creamy rice is an enduring recipe I've used for many years.
Delicious served with chicken and a green vegetable.

1 cup water 1 chicken bouillon 　OR 1 tbsp. chicken bouillon granules 1 cup long grain rice	In a medium saucepan, bring water and bouillon to a boil; stir in rice. Cover and cook over low heat until all water is absorbed, 10 to 15 minutes. OR bake in preheated 350° oven for 20 minutes.
1 can (10 oz.) cream of chicken soup 1 cup milk 1 tsp. salt 1/4 tsp. pepper	Add soup, milk, salt and pepper to rice; stir well. Turn into a greased 1½-quart casserole dish.
1 medium onion	Slice onion thinly and arrange over rice mixture. Cover and bake in preheated 350° oven until rice is thick and set but not dry, 50 to 55 minutes.

YIELD   4 TO 6 SERVINGS

Wild Rice Casserole

This melange of rice and vegetables is quick to prepare and loaded with nutrition.

1 cup brown and wild rice blend	Wash and drain rice.
1/4 cup butter or margarine 1/2 cup chopped celery 1/2 cup chopped mushrooms 1/4 cup chopped onion	Sauté vegetables in butter until tender. Stir in rice and continue cooking for 3 minutes.
2 cups beef broth or consommé	Pour rice mixture into ungreased 1½-quart casserole. Heat broth to boiling; stir into rice. Cover and bake in preheated 350° oven for 1½ hours or until all liquid is absorbed and rice is tender and fluffy.
1/4 cup slivered almonds, toasted	Sprinkle with almonds just before serving, if desired.

YIELD   4 TO 6 SERVINGS

Rice Pilaf

Pilaf is a simple preparation that calls for coating grains of rice in butter,
then cooking it slowly with onion and liquid in a covered pot.
When cooked this way, the rice remains firm, dry and separate.
Carrots give this pilaf a vibrant orange hue.

6 tbsp. butter or margarine
1/2 cup green onions, thinly sliced
1 cup shredded carrots
2 1/2 cups long grain rice

In a 3-quart saucepan, melt butter over medium heat. Stir in onions and carrots; cook about 3 minutes, stirring occasionally. Stir in rice and sauté until opaque, about 4 minutes.

4 1/2 cups water
5 chicken bouillon cubes
1 tsp. salt
1 bay leaf
1/4 tsp. thyme

Add water, bouillon and seasonings to rice; heat to boiling, stirring once or twice. Reduce heat to low; cover and simmer for 20 minutes. Remove from heat; let stand covered 5 minutes. Remove and discard bay leaf.

1/4 cup minced fresh parsley
  OR 1 tbsp. dried parsley flakes

Stir in parsley. Turn into serving dish.

YIELD   8 TO 10 SERVINGS

Erma Yoder
Millersburg, IN

Baked Confetti Rice

Very simple to prepare, this variegated side dish
is perfect to serve alongside chicken.

1 3/4 cups water
1 cup shredded carrot
1 cup chopped celery
3/4 cup long grain rice
1/4 cup chopped onion
3 tbsp. minced fresh parsley
  OR 1 tsp. dried parsley flakes
2 tbsp. butter or margarine, melted
1 tbsp. chicken bouillon granules
1 garlic clove, minced
1/2 tsp. salt

Combine all ingredients in an ungreased 2-quart baking dish. Cover and bake at 375° for 25 minutes. Stir mixture and continue baking for 20 to 25 minutes or until rice is tender.

YIELD   4 SERVINGS

Saucy Green Beans

When the much-loved green beans need something extra, try this.

½ cup chopped onion
1 tbsp. butter or margarine

In small skillet, sauté onion in butter until tender.

2 pkgs. (10 oz.) frozen green beans
   OR 1 qt. canned green beans, drained
1 can (8 oz.) sliced mushrooms, optional

Cook frozen beans according to package directions; drain. Layer beans into a 9 x 9 - inch baking dish or 1½-quart casserole. Spread mushrooms and onions evenly on top.

3 tbsp. butter or margarine
2 tbsp. flour
1 tsp. salt
¼ tsp. pepper
1 cup sour cream
1 cup shredded cheddar cheese

In small skillet, melt butter; stir in flour and seasonings. Blend in sour cream, stirring constantly until mixture thickens. Pour over bean mixture. Sprinkle with cheese. Bake at 350° for 25 to 30 minutes or until bubbly.

YIELD   4 TO 6 SERVINGS

Buttery Green Beans with Almonds

The almonds add a distinctive crunch to this simple but elegant dish.

¼ cup slivered or sliced almonds

Spread nuts on ungreased pie pan. Toast in a 350° oven for 5 to 7 minutes. Watch carefully to avoid burning. Cool in the pan on a wire rack.

4 cups fresh or frozen green beans

Steam beans in a steamer for 8 minutes or cook in a saucepan with a small amount of water until crisp-tender.

2 tbsp. butter or margarine
1 small onion, chopped
Salt

In a large skillet, melt butter. Add onion and sauté until tender. Add green beans and stir-fry for 2 to 3 minutes, until the beans are hot and well coated with butter. Season with salt to taste. Transfer to a serving dish and sprinkle with almonds. Serve immediately.

Pictured on page 127.

YIELD   4 TO 6 SERVINGS

166

Home-Baked Beans

When I was growing up, our family doctor was a close neighbor and friend.
He graciously made old-fashioned house calls whenever we needed him, and his wife
shared her recipes. This is one of them. The sauce has a wonderful flavor and
improves the longer the beans are baked, although you may have to add more cream.
Some days the beans baked all day filling the kitchen with a tantalizing aroma.

2 cups dried brown beans
4 cups water
1 tsp. salt

Wash and drain dry beans. In medium saucepan, cook beans in water and salt until tender, about 1 hour. Drain.

1 cup whipping cream
1 cup ketchup
1/4 cup brown sugar
2 tbsp. vinegar
2 tbsp. honey
2 tsp. prepared mustard
1/2 tsp. chili powder
1/2 tsp. salt

Combine beans with remaining ingredients in large casserole. Cover and bake at 325° for 2 hours or longer, stirring occasionally.

SLOW COOKER ALTERNATIVE
Combine cooked beans and remaining ingredients in slow cooker. Cover; cook on High until contents come to boil. Turn to Low and cook an additional 6 hours, stirring occasionally.

YIELD   ABOUT 6 SERVINGS

Sweet Potato Casserole

Sweet potatoes are a natural addition to the classic holiday turkey dinner.
Marshmallows form a glistening topping on this bright casserole.
Or substitute a crunchy streusel topping with equally delicious results.

3 cups mashed, cooked sweet potatoes
1/2 cup milk
1/4 cup butter, melted
2 tbsp. brown sugar
1 egg
1 tsp. vanilla
1/4 tsp. cinnamon
1/4 tsp. nutmeg
1/4 tsp. salt

In a mixing bowl, beat together all ingredients until smooth. Pour into a greased 9 x 9 - inch baking dish or 1 1/2 -quart casserole.

1/2 cup miniature marshmallows

Top with marshmallows. Bake in preheated 350° oven for 30 minutes or until marshmallows are puffed and golden brown.

YIELD   6 SERVINGS

Streusel Topping

Use this streusel topping in place of marshmallows in recipe above.

1 cup chopped pecans
1/2 cup brown sugar
1/4 cup all-purpose flour
2 tbsp. melted butter or margarine

In a small bowl, stir together until ingredients are moistened. Sprinkle over prepared sweet potatoes. Bake in preheated 350° oven for 30 minutes or until golden brown.

Cottage Cheese Perogies

This recipe is the Hutterite version of perogies,
which are pasta pockets stuffed with cottage cheese.
Unlike Mennonite wareneki, these 'krapfen' are deep fried after boiling.
Serve with sausage or beef.

1½ cups all-purpose flour
½ tsp. salt

In a mixing bowl, blend flour and salt.

1 egg, beaten
1 tbsp. vegetable oil
⅓ cup warm water

Combine egg, oil and water; add to flour and mix well. Turn onto a lightly floured surface and knead until dough is smooth, adding more flour if necessary. Cover with a bowl and let 'rest' for 15 minutes.

COTTAGE CHEESE FILLING
2 tbsp. butter or margarine
⅓ cup finely chopped onions

In a small skillet, fry onions in butter until opaque.

2½ cups dry cottage cheese
1 egg, beaten
⅓ cup soft bread crumbs
2 tbsp. cream
1 tbsp. sugar
½ tsp. salt

In a mixing bowl, combine onions with remaining ingredients. Mix together until well blended.

Divide dough in half. On a lightly floured surface, roll out dough 1/8 inch thick. Cut into 2 x 3-inch rectangles. Place a heaping teaspoon filling in the center. Fold 2-inch edges together. With floured fingers pinch edges together to seal well.

6 to 8 cups water
1 tsp. salt

In a large saucepan or Dutch oven, add water and salt; bring to boil. Drop perogies into boiling water, 8 to 10 at a time. Boil for 8 minutes. Remove from water with a slotted spoon and place on a rack to cool.

Perogies may be frozen at this stage. Place in single layer on baking sheet; freeze. When frozen, place in freezer bags. Thaw before deep-frying.

Oil for deep-frying

Heat oil in saucepan and fry perogies, a few at a time until a light golden brown. Serve hot.

YIELD   ABOUT 24 PEROGIES

169

Crock Pot Dressing or Stuffing

Stuffing can be baked in the cavity of a chicken or turkey but it needs less liquid to keep it moist. The crock pot method is perfect for transporting to a potluck meal. It may be prepared and refrigerated overnight, if desired.

3/4 cup butter or margarine
2 cups chopped onion
2 cups chopped celery
  (stalks and leaves)

In large skillet, cook and stir onion and celery in butter until vegetables are tender.

12 cups slightly dry bread cubes
2 cans (8 oz.) mushroom pieces
1/4 cup fresh chopped parsley
  (or 1 tbsp. dried parsley flakes)
1 1/2 tsp. salt
1 1/2 tsp. sage
1 tsp. poultry seasoning
1 tsp. dried thyme
1/2 tsp. pepper

Turn bread cubes into a deep bowl. Add onions, celery, mushrooms and seasonings; toss.

2 eggs, well beaten
3 1/2 to 4 cups chicken broth
  (broth can be made with water and chicken soup base mix)

Pour over bread cubes and mix well. Pack lightly into a large greased slow cooker. Cover and cook on High for 45 minutes; turn to Low for 3 to 4 hours or until meat thermometer reaches 168°.

VARIATION
Bake in greased 3-quart casserole dish at 350° for 1 hour or until puffed and lightly browned.

YIELD   12 TO 15 SERVINGS

Cranberry Sauce

This is a must when serving roast turkey.

1 cup water
1 cup sugar
1 pkg. (12 oz.) fresh or frozen cranberries
1 tsp. lemon juice

In a medium saucepan, mix sugar and water; stir to dissolve sugar. Bring to a boil; add cranberries and lemon juice, return to boil. Reduce heat; simmer gently for 10 minutes, stirring occasionally. Remove from heat. Cool completely at room temperature and refrigerate.

YIELD   2 GENEROUS CUPS

Brown Rice Stuffing

Rice stuffing is a nice alternative to bread stuffing
but it can also serve as a side dish when baked in a casserole.

1 cup brown rice

In medium saucepan, cook rice
according to package directions.

1/4 cup butter or margarine
1/2 cup finely chopped onion
1/2 cup finely chopped celery
2/3 cup sliced mushrooms
1 small green pepper, chopped (optional)

Melt butter in skillet; add onions,
celery, mushrooms and pepper. Cook
and stir until onion is tender. Combine
with cooked rice.

1 tsp. parsley flakes
1/2 tsp. salt

Stir in parsley and salt. Pack into a
3 lb. roasting chicken or bake in
casserole dish at 350° for 1 hour.

YIELD   6 SERVINGS

Yorkshire Pudding

Yorkshire pudding is to roast beef what bread stuffing is to roast turkey.
The batter puffs high during baking, then hollows in center leaving high crispy edges.

1 cup all-purpose flour
1 cup milk
3 eggs
1/2 tsp. salt

Combine flour, milk, eggs and salt in a
mixing bowl. Beat together until
smooth. Cover and refrigerate for
4 hours or overnight.

1 tbsp. cold water

Thirty minutes before roast beef is
served, add water to batter and beat
again.

Fat from roast drippings or oil

Reserve pan drippings from roast,
adding enough oil to measure 1/4 cup;
pour into 9-inch square pan. Place pan
in 350° oven until hot. Increase
temperature to 425°. Pour batter into
pan of drippings. Bake for 20 to 25
minutes or until puffy and golden
brown. Cut into squares and serve
immediately with roast beef gravy.

NOTE
To make individual servings, heat
1/2 tsp. oil in each cup of 12 cup
muffin tin. Pour batter into muffin
cups and bake as directed in
recipe.

YIELD   6 TO 9 SERVINGS

Dill Pickles

Strictly speaking, this is not a vegetable, but I tucked the recipe in here because dill pickles are a staple in my kitchen when the grandchildren visit.

Garlic cloves
Fresh dill
Cucumbers

Prepare 6 one-quart canning jars; to each jar add 1 to 2 garlic cloves and 2 sprigs fresh dill. Pack washed cucumbers into jars.

12 cups water
3 cups pickling vinegar
2/3 cup coarse pickling salt

In a large kettle or Dutch oven, heat water, vinegar and salt to boiling. Pour brine over cucumbers in jars, leaving 1-inch headspace.

Prepare metal lids and rings according to package directions. Place on jars and tighten firmly with hands. Place jars on rack in canner; add warm water to cover jars. Heat to boiling; turn off heat and allow jars to remain in water for 5 minutes. Remove jars from water; jars should seal while they cool. Remove bands after 24 hours; wipe jars clean and store. Pickles will be ready to serve in 3 to 4 weeks.

Pictured on page 91.

YIELD   6 QUARTS

When my girls were young the neighbor children would often drop in for visits, at times enjoying a snack before they left. One of their favorite treats were these crunchy, dill pickles. We were puzzled one day to find an empty pickle jar sitting in the fridge, but dismissed it as an oversight. The dawning that someone was helping themselves to the pickles happened the day the empty jar was left sitting on the table. One penitent child was in a bit of a 'pickle', but also attested to the fact that the dill pickles were irresistible!

Cucumber Relish

Add flavor to a grilled burger with this zesty relish as part of the toppings.
Try it on hot dogs, brats and sausages as well.

6 large cucumbers, peeled
6 large onions
1 green pepper
1 red pepper

Wash and prepare vegetables; remove seeds and membranes from peppers. Chop vegetables coarsely using a grinder or food processor.

1/2 cup pickling salt
2 1/2 cups water

Sprinkle with pickling salt; add cold water. Let stand for 1 hour.

2 cups sugar
1/3 cup flour
3 tbsp. dry mustard
1 1/2 cups water
1 1/2 cups vinegar
1 1/2 tsp. mustard seed
1 1/2 tsp. celery seed
1 1/2 tsp. turmeric

In medium saucepan, blend sugar, flour and dry mustard. Add water, vinegar and spices. Cook over medium heat until mixture boils, stirring constantly.

Drain cucumber mixture and place in large Dutch oven or saucepan. Add cooked sauce and bring to a boil. Reduce heat and boil gently for 30 minutes, stirring frequently.

Sterilize 6 pint jars with lids. Pour hot relish into heated jars. Place the lids on the hot jars immediately and tighten rings so they will seal without processing. OR process in boiling water bath for 10 minutes, if desired.

YIELD   6 PINTS

Notes

Pies and Pastry

Pies and Pastry

Many people find baking a pie or tart more threatening than preparing other desserts. I come from a culture where pie making was as natural as baking cookies. I think it must be in my genes because I love working with pastry.

The overall success of a pie begins with a good crust. Superb pastry is easy to achieve with the help of a food processor. I use it whenever possible to combine the dry ingredients and fat to form fine crumbs. Although you can add the liquid through the feed tube, I prefer adding the liquid with my hands to get the perfect texture. The dough should just hold together. If it gets sticky and wet stir in a little extra flour.

Handle dough gently and as little as possible for a pie crust that is delicate, flaky and unmistakably homemade.

Pastry for Single-Crust Pie

1 1/4 cups all-purpose flour
1/4 tsp. salt
1/3 cup butter or margarine
1 tbsp. shortening

In a medium mixing bowl, blend flour and salt. Cut in butter and shortening until mixture is crumbly using your hands or a food processor.

4 to 5 tbsp. ice water
1/2 tsp. vinegar

Combine water and vinegar; sprinkle half of the water over flour mixture. Toss gently with fork. Add enough water until all flour mixture is moistened and dough holds together. Turn dough onto a sheet of plastic wrap; flatten into a disc and wrap. Chill 30 minutes.

Place dough on lightly floured surface; flatten slightly with hand. Roll dough from center to edge into a 12-inch circle. Fold pastry in half; gently transfer to 9-inch pie plate with fold in center. Unfold and ease pastry to fit pie plate without stretching it.

Complete to this step for pies that will be filled before baking.

Trim pastry to 1/2 inch beyond edge of pie plate. Fold under extra pastry; flute edge as desired.

For recipes that need a pre-baked shell:

Line pastry with double thickness of foil; bake at 450° for 8 minutes. Remove foil and bake an additional 5 to 6 minutes or until pastry is golden.

YIELD   1 SINGLE CRUST

The meeting of rolling prairie and lofty mountains is the experience of visitors to Waterton Lakes National Park. The town of Waterton is bordered by a deep glacial lake and spectacular Rocky Mountains. Wildlife is abundant and it's not uncommon to see deer and bighorn sheep frequent the Townsite.

I spent a delightful summer working in a bakery in this dream setting. One of my favorite jobs was making pies. I also prepared pies for a neighboring Lodge. One memorable day the Lodge ran out of Saskatoon pies and panic ensued. An errand boy was sent with a stack of pie plates and a 5-gallon bucket of Saskatoon pie filling. I was to quickly mix the crust and complete the pies for baking.

The friendly young man peered into my bowl of crust and remarked, "So this is the elusive pie crust!" He fell to one knee in a comical pretense of begging. "Your pies are awesome… wonderful… and the cooks are raving about this crust. I was hoping you would have the recipe pinned up so I could copy it!"

"Are you serious?" I asked, greatly amused.

"I sure am!" he answered.

There are no secret ingredients in my pie crust. Here is the recipe.

Perfect Pie Pastry

Pastry for a 9 or 10-inch two-crust pie

2 2/3 cups all-purpose flour
1/2 tsp. baking powder
1/2 tsp. salt
3/4 cup cold butter or margarine,
   cut into pieces
1/4 cup shortening

7 to 8 tbsp. ice water
1 tsp. vinegar

Blend dry ingredients; cut in butter and shortening until mixture is crumbly using your hands or a food processor. Mix water and vinegar; add to butter mixture a little at a time. Toss gently with a fork until mixture is moistened and dough holds together. Press into two discs; wrap in plastic wrap and chill 30 minutes.

On a lightly floured surface, roll one disc to a 13-inch round. Fold in half; turn into a 9 or 10-inch pie plate with folded edge along center of plate. Unfold to cover other side of pie plate; gently press pastry against sides and bottom of plate. Trim edges; roll out second disc. Use as directed in two-crust pie recipe.

To seal pastry: Moisten edge of bottom pastry with water before adding top pastry.

NOTE
For advance preparation, I like to double this recipe to the crumb stage and refrigerate in a tightly covered container. To make one pie, take out half the crumbs and add the liquid.

Fresh Rhubarb Pie

A sure and welcome sign of Spring is the emergence
of the classic pie plant also known as rhubarb.
This recipe is all-rhubarb but feel free to substitute a cup or two
of sliced strawberries for an equal amount of sliced rhubarb.

Pastry for 9 or 10-inch two-crust pie,
   page 178

Prepare pastry and line pan.

1 to 1¼ cups sugar
¼ cup quick-cooking tapioca
¼ tsp. cinnamon
4 cups cut-up fresh rhubarb
2 tbsp. butter or margarine
   (optional)

Stir together sugar, tapioca and cinnamon. Turn half the rhubarb into pastry-lined pan. Sprinkle with half the sugar mixture. Repeat with remaining rhubarb and sugar; dot with butter. Prepare top crust; cut slits in desired pattern. Place over rhubarb in pan. Trim edges, seal and flute.

1 to 2 tsp. cream

Brush pie crust with cream.

Bake at 375° for 50 to 55 minutes or until crust is golden brown.

YIELD   8 TO 10 SERVINGS

Rhubarb Custard Pie

A custard makes a nice change and takes away a bit of the usual rhubarb tang.
My favorite way to eat this pie is barely warm.

Pastry for 10-inch one-crust pie,
   page 177

Prepare pasty and line a 10-inch pie pan or 9-inch deep dish pie pan.

4 cups cut-up fresh rhubarb
   (¼ to ½-inch pieces)
3 eggs
1½ cups sugar
½ cup all-purpose flour
¼ cup whipping cream
½ tsp. nutmeg
¼ tsp. cinnamon
¼ tsp. salt

Turn rhubarb into pastry lined pan. Beat eggs slightly with rotary beater; stir in remaining ingredients. Pour mixture evenly over rhubarb.

Bake at 400° for 15 minutes. Reduce oven temperature to 350° and bake 35 minutes longer.

YIELD   8 TO 10 SERVINGS

Saskatoon berries are a native wild berry slightly smaller than a blueberry. When I was young we would take to the coulees where the steep hills sprouted some vegetation. In amongst the thorny wild rose bushes and other tangled growth we hunted for the elusive purplish-blue berries to fill our pails.

It was difficult and strenuous work and the yield was dependent on the seasonal rainfall. Now they are commercially cultivated and I need only drive a couple miles to a neighboring u-pick berry farm. On cool summer evenings in July while standing on a carpet of grass with only mosquitoes to bother me, I happily pick the choicest clumps. As I gather this wildly wonderful fruit, I can picture pies, desserts, pastries, jam – so on I pick.

I sort, rinse and quick-freeze the berries on cookie sheets lined with clean tea towels to soak up any residual moisture. After they are frozen, I put them in freezer bags in 4-cup increments. And so begin many marvelous culinary delights.

Saskatoon Berry Pie

I served a slice of this pie to my brother's friend and he said,
'It can't get any better than this.' I couldn't agree more; not because I made it
but because tamed saskatoon berries grown in the pristine Canadian fresh air
with open sky and clean water during long sunny days are an unsurpassable treat.

Pastry for 9-inch two-crust pie, page 178

Prepare pastry and line pan.

3/4 cup sugar
3 tbsp. cornstarch or Clearjel
1 cup water
1 tsp. lemon juice
4 cups fresh or
  frozen saskatoon berries

In a large saucepan, blend together sugar and cornstarch. Add water, lemon juice and half of the berries. Cook until thickened, stirring constantly. Stir in remaining berries. Pour into pastry-lined pie pan.

1 to 2 tsp. cream

Prepare top crust; cut slits in desired pattern. Place over fruit in pan. Trim edges, seal and flute. Brush crust with cream. Bake at 375° for 50 to 55 minutes or until crust is golden brown.

Pictured on page 181.

YIELD   6 TO 8 SERVINGS

Blueberry Pie

Substitute fresh or frozen blueberries in place of saskatoon berries.

In a pasture of native grassland that has never been disturbed, an extraordinary view meets the eye. The St. Mary River slowly winds through the prairie river valley known as a coulee. Along the steep incline, dark areas indicate vegetation, which is home to the elusive wild saskatoon berry.

1. Saskatoon Berry Pie, page 180

2. Saskatoon Cream Tarts, page 193

3. Saskatoon Custard Kuchen, page 257

Bumble Berry Pie

Incredibly delicious, bumble berry pie is made with a jumble of berries that typically arrive in the summer when fresh ones are irresistibly in season. There are no boundaries outside of your own choices. I suggest a balance of fresh saskatoons, blueberries, raspberries, strawberries and blackberries. Mixtures are also available in the frozen section of grocery stores.

Pastry for 9-inch two-crust pie, page 178

Prepare pastry and line pan.

1 cup sugar
4 tbsp. quick cooking tapioca
1 tsp. lemon juice
4 cups mixed fresh or frozen berries
1 tbsp. butter or margarine (optional)

Stir together sugar, tapioca and lemon juice. Turn half the berry mixture into pastry-lined pie pan. Sprinkle with half the sugar mixture. Repeat with remaining berries and sugar mixture; dot with butter.

1 to 2 tsp. cream

Prepare top crust; cut slits in desired pattern. Place over berries in pan. Trim edges, seal and flute. Brush top crust with cream.

Bake at 375° for 50 to 55 minutes or until crust is golden brown.

YIELD   6 TO 8 SERVINGS

NOTE
Brushing top crust with light cream before baking turns the crust a beautiful golden color.

French Strawberry Glacé Pie

Make this eye-catching dessert in the summer to celebrate strawberry season.
Garnished with whipped cream, it looks glamorous and tastes luscious,
all in the colors of 'O Canada.'
If you want to get carried away, a little ice cream will do.

Pastry for 9-inch one-crust pie, page 177	*Prepare and prebake pie shell as directed.*
6 cups strawberries	*Wash, drain and hull strawberries.*
1 cup water, divided 3/4 cup sugar 3 tbsp. cornstarch 1/2 tsp. lemon juice	*Mash enough berries to measure 1 cup. Simmer mashed strawberries and 3/4 cup water for 3 minutes. Strain mixture through sieve and discard strawberry pulp. In small saucepan, blend sugar, cornstarch, lemon juice and remaining 1/4 cup water. Add strawberry juice and bring to boil. Boil for 1 minute stirring constantly. Cool.*
1 pkg. (3 oz.) cream cheese, softened 1/4 cup powdered sugar 1 tsp. vanilla	*Beat cream cheese, powdered sugar and vanilla together. Spread over bottom of cooled baked pie shell.*
	If desired, save several choice berries for garnish. Fill shell with remaining berries (whole or halved). Pour cooled berry glaze evenly over top. Chill at least 3 hours or until set. Garnish with whole berries and whipped cream.

YIELD   6 TO 8 SERVINGS

Sweetened Whipped Cream

1 cup chilled whipping cream 1/4 cup powdered sugar 1/2 tsp. vanilla	*Place all ingredients in chilled bowl and beat together until stiff. Don't overbeat or it will get grainy.*

Cherry Empanadas

Empanadas are like Amish half-moon pies or like anyone else's half-moon shaped pies. They can be deep fried but I prefer them baked for health reasons. These pies are portable but still delicate, so pack them carefully if you're taking them on an outing.

3 cups all-purpose flour
2 tsp. baking powder
1/2 tsp. salt
1/2 cup butter or shortening

In a medium mixing bowl, stir together flour, baking powder and salt. Cut in butter until mixture is crumbly using your hands or a food processor.

2 eggs
1/2 cup milk

In a small bowl, beat eggs and milk together. Add to flour mixture, stirring until combined. Form dough into a ball; cover and chill 1 hour.

1 can (19 oz.) cherry pie filling

Divide dough into 16 pieces. Working with one piece of chilled dough at a time, roll each piece into a 6-inch circle on a sheet of lightly floured parchment paper. Spoon about 3 tablespoons filling over half dough, leaving a 1/2 inch border along the edge. Moisten edges; fold empty half over filling, pressing with a fork to seal. When you fold the dough over the filling, lift and fold the parchment paper with the dough on it for ease of handling.

Place on greased baking sheet. Refrigerate while you make remaining pies, putting each on sheet as you finish.

Milk or half-and half
Powdered sugar

Brush each pie with milk or half-and-half. Make vents with a fork to allow steam to escape. Bake at 400° for 15 minutes or until golden brown. Transfer to wire rack to cool slightly. While warm, dust with powdered sugar if desired.

YIELD   16 EMPANADAS

> **NOTE**
> *These pies freeze well. Place on baking sheet after preparation and freeze for 1 hour. Wrap each in foil and return to freezer. To bake, place pies on greased baking sheet and let stand at room temperature for 10 minutes. Bake as directed above, adding 5 to 8 minutes.*

VARIATIONS
In place of cherry pie filling, prepare your favorite berry pie filling such as blueberry, apple or saskatoon.

Country Apple Pie

Over the years my girls have been involved in various capacities with a prison ministry in Indiana. The staff at the home office often gets together for birthdays and other celebrations. My contribution on one occasion was apple pie. The old-fashioned simplicity of this pie is homey and almost nostalgic. Perhaps that is why one of the guests made this comment, 'All apple pie should taste like this'.

Pastry for 9-inch two-crust pie,
   page 178

Prepare pastry and line pan.

6 cups pared tart apples, thinly sliced
3/4 cup sugar
1/4 cup all-purpose flour
1/2 teaspoon cinnamon
1/4 tsp. salt

In a large bowl, stir together sugar, flour, cinnamon and salt. Stir in apples. Turn apple mixture into pastry lined pan.

1 tbsp. butter or margarine (optional)

Cut butter into small pieces; sprinkle over apples if desired. Prepare top crust; cut slits in desired pattern. Place over apples in pan. Trim edges, seal and flute.

1 to 2 tsp. cream

Brush top crust with cream.

Bake at 375° for 50 to 55 minutes or until crust is golden brown.
Serve warm with a scoop of good vanilla ice cream. It's hard to beat!

YIELD   6 TO 8 SERVINGS

Apple Strudel Slab Pie

I was delighted to add this pie recipe to my collection, thanks to my cousin Marie.
The crust is notably light and tender and since it is baked in a large pan,
can be enjoyed by more people.

2 cups all-purpose flour
1 cup butter or margarine
2 egg yolks
1/2 cup sour cream

Measure flour into bowl. Cut in butter until crumbly. Blend egg yolks and sour cream. Add to flour mixture, stirring until blended. Gather dough into ball and chill in refrigerator while preparing apple filling.

Apple Filling

1/2 cup sugar
3 tbsp. flour
1/4 tsp. cinnamon
6 cups pared tart apples, thinly sliced

Stir together sugar, flour and cinnamon; mix with apples.

TO ASSEMBLE

Divide dough in half. Roll bottom pastry directly in 10 x 15 - inch rimmed baking sheet. Spread apple mixture on pastry leaving 1/2 inch pastry exposed on sides.

For top crust, outline 10 x 15 - inch rectangle on sheet of waxed paper. Turn paper over, dust lightly with flour and roll pastry to fit outline. Cut slits in uniform diagonal pattern. Carefully turn pastry over apple layer and remove waxed paper. Seal edges with a fork.

1 egg white

Brush with 1 beaten egg white. Bake at 375° for 30 to 35 minutes or until golden brown. While still warm, drizzle with glaze.

YIELD   15 SERVINGS

Vanilla Glaze

1 cup powdered sugar
2 tbsp. milk
1/2 tsp. vanilla

Blend until smooth and of drizzling consistency, adding more milk if necessary.

VARIATIONS
Substitute fresh thinly sliced peaches in season.
Substitute 4 cups fresh chopped rhubarb in season; increase sugar to 3/4 cup.

Baked Apple Dumplings

These flaky bundles covered with caramel sauce couldn't be more delicious together, unless of course, you add a bit of ice cream.

Pastry for 9-inch two-crust pie,
   page 178

Prepare pastry as directed. On lightly floured surface, roll dough to a 12 x 18 - inch rectangle. Cut into six 6-inch squares.

6 medium tart juicy apples,
   such as Granny Smith
1/2 cup sugar
1 1/2 tsp. cinnamon
2 tbsp. butter or margarine, melted

Peel and core apples; place an apple in the center of each square. In a small bowl, combine sugar, cinnamon and butter; spoon mixture into cored apples. Bring opposite points of pastry up over the apple. Overlap, moisten and seal. (Trim pastry if necessary) Place a little apart, seam side down on a shallow greased baking pan.

1 egg, beaten

Brush dough with beaten egg; prick with a fork. Bake at 375° for 40 to 50 minutes or until crust is golden brown and apple tests done when pierced with a fork.

Pictured on page 127.

Caramel Sauce

1/2 cup brown sugar, firmly packed
2 tbsp. butter
1/2 cup whipping cream
2 tsp. vanilla
1/2 tsp. cinnamon

In a medium saucepan, combine all ingredients. Cook over medium heat until mixture comes to a boil; reduce heat and simmer for 1 minute. Serve sauce over warm dumplings.

YIELD   6 SERVINGS

Southern Pecan Pie

Many pecan pies are too sweet for my liking; this is a lighter version.
Although delectable alone, this nut-filled pie is even better
with a dollop of softly whipped cream flavored with vanilla.

Pastry for 9-inch one-crust pie,
 page 177

Prepare pastry and line pan.

1/4 cup butter or margarine
1/3 cup brown sugar, lightly packed
3 eggs

In mixing bowl, cream butter and sugar. Add eggs one at a time, beating thoroughly after each addition.

1 tbsp. all-purpose flour
1 cup coarsely chopped pecans
1 cup light corn syrup
 OR 1 cup pancake syrup
1 tsp. vanilla
1/4 tsp. salt

Add flour, chopped pecans, syrup, vanilla and salt, stirring until well blended. Pour into pastry-lined pie pan.

Pecan halves, about 1 cup

Arrange the pecan halves decoratively on top of the mixture. Cover edge of pastry with strip of foil to prevent excessive browning; remove foil during last 15 minutes of baking.

Bake at 375° for 35 to 40 minutes until center is set and crust is golden. Cool on a wire rack.

Pictured on cover and page 149.

YIELD 6 TO 8 SERVINGS

Old-Fashioned Autumn Pumpkin Pie

One of the most popular pies of all is a Thanksgiving Pumpkin Pie.
I don't know how the Pilgrims made theirs, but this is my version.
It is spicy, easy to make and can be enjoyed all year round.

Pastry for 9-inch one-crust pie,
page 177

Prepare pastry and line pan.
Trim pastry to 1/2 inch beyond edge of
plate. Build up fluted edge; do not
prick pastry.

2 cups cooked and mashed
   or canned pumpkin
3/4 cup sugar
1 tbsp. cornstarch
1 tsp. cinnamon
1/2 tsp. salt
1/2 tsp. ground ginger
1/2 tsp. ground nutmeg
1/8 tsp. ground cloves
3 eggs
2/3 cup evaporated milk
1/4 cup milk

Combine pumpkin, sugar, cornstarch
and spices. Add eggs, evaporated milk
and milk; beat together with electric
mixer. Pour into pastry-lined pan.

Bake in preheated 425° oven for 10
minutes. (A hot oven for the first 10
minutes should avoid a soggy crust.)
Reduce heat to 350° for about 45
minutes or until a knife inserted in the
center of the pie comes out clean. The
center may still look soft but will set
later. Cool on a wire rack. Garnish with
Sweetened Whipped Cream, page
184, if desired.

YIELD   6 TO 8 SERVINGS

Garnish Option

Roll out remaining pastry scraps and
cut with leaf-shaped cookie cutter or
cut out leaf shapes with sharp knife.
Arrange on a cookie sheet. Brush with
beaten egg and sprinkle with
cinnamon-sugar. Bake until golden,
about 15 minutes. Transfer to a wire
rack to cool before arranging on top of
cooled pie.

NOTE
Butternut or other flavorful winter
squash varieties can be used in
place of pumpkin. Some would
claim the taste is superior to their
pumpkin relative.

Vanilla Flapper Pie

This is the classic vanilla cream pie topped with meringue
or slathered with whipped cream.
Someone suggested this pie should be in every cook's collection.

1 1/2 cups graham cracker crumbs
1/4 cup butter or margarine
3 tbsp. sugar

In a small saucepan, melt butter over medium heat. Stir in crumbs and sugar. Press firmly and evenly over bottom and sides of a 9-inch pie plate. Bake at 350° for 8 minutes; set aside to cool.

Vanilla Cream Filling

1/2 cup sugar
3 tbsp. cornstarch
2 tsp. flour
1/4 tsp. salt

In a medium saucepan, combine sugar, cornstarch, flour and salt.

2 cups milk
3 egg yolks, slightly beaten

Blend milk and egg yolks together with fork. Strain through a sieve into sugar mixture and stir to blend. Cook over medium heat, stirring constantly, until mixture thickens and boils. Boil and stir 1 minute; remove from heat.

1 tbsp. butter or margarine
1 tsp. vanilla

Blend in butter and vanilla. Place plastic wrap directly onto surface of cooked mixture and cool about 15 minutes. Pour into baked pie shell.

3 egg whites
1/4 tsp. cream of tartar
3 tbsp. sugar

Beat egg whites and cream of tartar until foamy. Beat in sugar gradually until stiff, glossy peaks form. Spread meringue over the filling, carefully sealing to edge of pastry to prevent shrinking and weeping.

Bake at 350° for 10 to 15 minutes or until lightly browned. Cool before serving.

NOTE
If you prefer a whipped cream topping, use recipe on page 184.

YIELD   6 TO 8 SERVINGS

Raspberry Cream Tart

A smooth custard is topped with lovely colorful raspberries in this delectable open-faced tart. Prepare tart well ahead of time so it has plenty of time to chill.

1 1/4 cups all-purpose flour
1/2 cup margarine,
  cut into small pieces
1/3 cup powdered sugar

In a medium bowl, combine flour, margarine and sugar. Using a food processor or hands, combine mixture until crumbly. Pat pastry onto bottom and up side of 10-inch tart pan with removable bottom. Bake in preheated 350° oven for 20 minutes or until golden.

1 egg white

Beat egg white; brush thin layer into hot pastry shell, discard remainder. Cool on wire rack.

1/2 cup sugar
2 tbsp. all-purpose flour
1 envelope unflavored gelatin
1/4 tsp. salt
1 egg
1 egg yolk
1 1/4 cups milk
1/4 tsp. almond extract

In a heavy 2-quart saucepan, stir together sugar, flour, gelatin and salt. In a medium bowl, beat together egg, egg yolk and milk; stir into sugar mixture. Cook over medium-low heat, stirring until gelatin is completely dissolved. Continue cooking until mixture thickens and coats a spoon, about 5 to 7 minutes. (Do not boil, or custard may curdle.) Remove from heat; stir in almond flavoring. Strain into bowl through sieve. Cover and refrigerate until mixture mounds slightly when dropped from a spoon, about 1 hour.

1/2 cup whipping cream

In small bowl, beat whipping cream until soft peaks form; fold into custard. Spoon mixture into cooled pastry shell. Refrigerate 1 hour or longer until custard is set.

Raspberry Glaze

2/3 cup sugar
3 tbsp. cornstarch
1/2 tsp. lemon juice
1 1/3 cups raspberry juice

In small saucepan, blend sugar, cornstarch and lemon juice. Add raspberry juice and bring to boil. Boil for 1 minute, stirring constantly; cool.

Raspberry Cream Tart (continued)

2 cups fresh raspberries

Remove side from pan and place tart on serving platter. Arrange raspberries on custard. Pour cooled glaze evenly over whole berries. Chill until set, 3 hours or longer.

NOTE
If you do not need a whole tart at once, this recipe has a wonderful option. The tart can be prepared to the point where the custard is added and chilled. It will keep very well for 2 to 3 days in the refrigerator. Serve up individual slices topped with berries and glaze as needed.

YIELD   10 SERVINGS

Pictured on page 149.

Strawberry Cream Tarts

Prepare pastry as for Raspberry Cream Tart. Divide crumbs evenly and press onto bottom and up side of eight 3-inch tart pans with removable bottoms. Set on cookie sheet. Bake in preheated 350° oven for 15 to 18 minutes or until lightly golden. Cool.

4 oz. cream cheese, softened
1/3 cup powdered sugar
1/2 tsp. vanilla

Beat cream cheese, powdered sugar and vanilla together.

1/2 cup whipping cream

Whip cream in chilled bowl until stiff. Add to cream cheese mixture and beat until smooth. Spoon into cooled tart shells.

Fresh strawberries, halved or sliced
Raspberry glaze, page 192

Arrange strawberries on pastry cream. Spoon glaze over strawberries.

Pictured on page 211.

YIELD   8 TARTS

Saskatoon or Blueberry Cream Tarts
Make as above.
In place of strawberries, top tarts with Blueberrry or Saskatoon Filling, page 50.

Pictured on page 181.

Kiwi-Lime Pie

The color and tang of lime is set off beautifully in this light refreshing dessert. Because it has three distinct layers, it's a bit of work to assemble, but certainly easy to do, a step at a time. It can be made simpler, but I like the three-part blend of taste and texture. Pastry may be prepared and baked a day ahead.

Pastry for 9-inch two-crust pie, page 178

Divide pastry in half. On floured surface roll one half to 1/8 inch thickness. Line a 9-inch pie plate with pastry. Trim 1/2 inch beyond edge. Flute edge; prick pastry. Line pastry with a double thickness of foil; bake at 450° for 8 minutes. Remove foil and bake an additional 5 to 6 minutes or until pastry is golden. Cool.

Divide remaining pastry in half. Roll each half to 1/8 inch thickness. Cut an 8 1/2-inch circle out of one portion. Cut an 8 inch circle out of other portion. Place pastry circles on a baking sheet; prick well. Bake at 375° for 10 minutes or until lightly browned. Cool.

Filling

3/4 cup sugar
3 tbsp. cornstarch
2 tbsp. all-purpose flour
1/8 tsp. salt
1 3/4 cups milk
3 eggs, beaten

In a saucepan combine sugar, cornstarch, flour and salt. Stir in milk and eggs. Cook over medium heat, stirring constantly until thickened and bubbly. Remove from heat.

1/4 cup butter or margarine
2 tsp. finely grated lime peel
1/4 cup lime juice
1 tsp. lemon juice
1 cup plain yogurt
Few drops green food coloring

Stir butter, lime peel, lime and lemon juice into cooked mixture. Fold in yogurt. Tint with food coloring, if desired. Place plastic wrap directly onto surface of cooked mixture. Refrigerate about 1 hour or until chilled.

194

Kiwi-Lime Pie (continued)

TO ASSEMBLE PIE

3 tbsp. apple or apricot jelly

Brush pastry shell with 1 tablespoon jelly. Spoon 1 cup lime filling into shell.

Cover with 8-inch pastry; brush with 1 tablespoon jelly. Spread with 1 1/4 cups lime filling. Top with 8 1/2-inch pastry; brush with remaining jelly. Top with remaining filling. Cover the pie and chill thoroughly, several hours or longer.

Sweetened whipped cream, page 184
Kiwi fruit, peeled and sliced

Before serving, pipe whipped cream around edge. Arrange slices of kiwi in the cream circle.

YIELD   8 TO 10 SERVINGS

NOTE
To simplify this pie, prepare pastry for 9-inch one-crust pie, page 177. Prebake as directed. When shell is cool, pour cooked mixture into pie shell and continue with cooling and garnish steps.

Hawaiian Cream Pie

One taste of this summery pie transports your thoughts to the tropics.
Make it as a special treat when you are entertaining outside in the evening.
If you live in southern Alberta, perhaps you can watch a spectacular
sunset over the Rocky Mountains in place of the sun setting over the ocean.

1½ cups graham wafer crumbs
2 tbsp. brown sugar, firmly packed
¼ cup margarine, melted

Combine crumbs, sugar and margarine. Press onto bottom and sides of a 9-inch pie plate. Bake at 350° for 8 minutes. Cool.

½ cup sugar
2 tbsp. cornstarch or Clearjel
1 tbsp. all-purpose flour
¼ tsp. salt
1½ cups milk
2 egg yolks
1 can (14 oz.) crushed pineapple, drained
½ cup flaked coconut
¼ tsp. ground ginger

In a medium saucepan, stir together sugar, cornstarch, flour and salt. Beat ½ cup milk and egg yolks together with a fork; strain through sieve into saucepan. Add remaining milk and stir to blend. Cook over medium heat, whisking constantly, until mixture thickens and boils. Boil and stir one minute. Remove from heat; stir in pineapple, coconut and ginger. Place plastic wrap directly onto surface; chill until cool.

1½ cups mini marshmallows
½ cup whipping cream, whipped

Fold marshmallows and whipped cream into pudding mixture. Pour into crumb crust. Chill several hours or overnight.

⅓ cup flaked coconut

Toast coconut and sprinkle on top.

Maraschino cherries (optional)
Macadamia nuts (optional)

If desired, garnish with maraschino cherries and toasted macadamia nuts before serving.

YIELD   8 SERVINGS

NOTE
There is a loss of homestyle flavor, but you can create this pie more quickly if you need to. Cook a 4 serving size vanilla pie filling mix, (not instant) according to package directions using 1 ½ cups milk. Use in place of the cooked pudding in recipe.

Banana Cream Pie

I am blessed to have family do things for me that I am unable to do.
As tokens of my appreciation, I love giving gifts of food
which include this favorite pie – banana cream.

Pastry for 9-inch one-crust pie, page 177

Prepare pastry and line pan, prebake as directed until lightly golden.

1/2 cup sugar
3 tbsp. cornstarch
1 tbsp. all-purpose flour
1/4 tsp. salt
2 1/2 cups milk
3 egg yolks

In medium saucepan, stir together sugar, cornstarch, flour and salt. Beat 1 cup milk and egg yolks together with a fork; strain through sieve into saucepan. Add remaining milk and stir to blend. Cook over medium heat, whisking constantly, until mixture thickens and boils. Boil and stir 1 minute.

1 tsp. vanilla
2 tbsp. butter or margarine

Remove from heat; blend in vanilla and butter. Place plastic wrap directly onto surface of cooked mixture to prevent skin from forming. Cool to room temperature.

2 to 3 ripe bananas

Pour half the filling into chilled pie shell, smoothing top. Slice or chunk bananas, letting them fall over the pie. Arrange in a single layer, then spread with remaining filling. Gently press plastic wrap over filling; refrigerate for up to 5 hours.

1 cup whipping cream
1/4 cup powdered sugar

When ready to finish assembling pie, whip cream and sugar together until stiff but not grainy. Mound and swirl or pipe over the top.

Butterfinger candy bar, optional

Sprinkle with chopped candy bar, if desired.

YIELD   6 TO 8 SERVINGS

Coconut Cream Pie

Follow recipe above; omit bananas.
Stir in 3/4 cup flaked coconut. Sprinkle 1/4 cup flaked coconut, toasted, over whipped cream on pie.

Praline Delight Pie

Once you have made the pastry, the crunchy praline
and vanilla filling can be put together quickly.

**Pastry for 9-inch one-crust pie,
page 177**

*Prepare pastry and line pan, prebake
as directed until lightly golden.*

**¼ cup butter or margarine
⅓ cup brown sugar
½ cup chopped pecans**

*Measure butter, sugar and pecans into
saucepan. Heat and stir until butter is
melted and sugar is dissolved. Spread
on bottom of prepared pie shell. Bake
at 400° for 5 minutes or until bubbly.
Cool.*

**1 pkg. vanilla instant pudding
(4 serving size)
2½ cups milk**

*Beat pudding and milk together for 2
minutes. Measure 1 cup filling and set
aside. Spread remaining pudding into
pie shell.*

**1 carton (8 oz.) frozen whipped topping,
thawed
Pecans, whole for garnish**

*Reserve ½ cup whipped topping for
garnish. Fold remaining topping into 1
cup reserved pudding. Spoon over
filling in pie shell. Pipe or dab reserved
whipped topping around outside edge.
Garnish with pecans. Chill 3 to 4
hours.*

YIELD   6 TO 8 SERVINGS

Peanut Butter Cream Pie

'A little slice of bliss' is how I would describe this melt-in-your-mouth pie. The silky filling is topped by a swirl of whipped cream and a scattering of peanut butter crumbs. Thanks to Erma, we have been enjoying this pie for over 3 decades.

Pastry for 9-inch one-crust pie, page 177

Prepare pastry and line pan; prebake as directed.

3/4 cup powdered sugar
1/2 cup peanut butter

Blend powdered sugar and peanut butter together until crumbly. Reserve 1/3 cup and spread remaining crumbs into baked crust.

2/3 cup sugar
3 tbsp. cornstarch
1 1/2 tbsp. all-purpose flour
1/2 tsp. salt
3 cups milk
3 egg yolks

In medium saucepan, stir together sugar, cornstarch, flour and salt. Beat 1 cup milk and egg yolks together with a fork; strain through a sieve. (This strains out any remaining egg white residue.) Add to sugar mixture with remaining 2 cups milk. Cook over medium heat, stirring constantly, until mixture thickens and boils. Boil and stir 1 minute.

1 tsp. vanilla

Remove from heat; blend in vanilla. Pour into medium bowl; place plastic wrap directly onto surface of cooked mixture. Refrigerate about 1 hour or until chilled.

Spoon cooled pudding over peanut butter crumbs in pie shell. Chill pie thoroughly, at least 2 hours.

1 cup whipping cream
2 tbsp. powdered sugar
1 tsp. vanilla

Whip cream, sugar and vanilla until stiff but not grainy. Mound and swirl over cream filling. Sprinkle reserved crumbs on top.

YIELD   6 TO 8 SERVINGS

Erma Yoder
Millersburg, IN

Pictured on page 211.

199

Lemon-Lime Chiffon Tart

Cool and light, this airy pastel and slightly tart dessert
is a refreshing contrast after a heavy meal.

1 cup vanilla wafer crumbs
1/2 cup finely chopped pecans
2 tbsp. sugar
3 tbsp. margarine, melted

*Combine crumbs, nuts, sugar and
margarine; press into bottom of 9-inch
springform pan.*

1 envelope unflavored gelatin
1/4 cup cold water

*In a medium saucepan, soften gelatin
in water; stir over low heat until
dissolved.*

2 egg yolks
1/3 cup milk
1/2 cup frozen lemonade concentrate
1/3 cup lime juice
1/4 cup sugar
1 tsp. finely grated lime peel

*Beat egg yolks and milk with a fork;
strain through sieve into dissolved
gelatin. Add lemonade, lime juice,
sugar and lime peel. Cook over
medium heat, stirring constantly, just
until mixture boils. Set in ice water and
chill until mixture starts to mound
when spooned.*

2 egg whites
1/4 cup sugar
Several drops green food coloring
   (optional)

*Beat egg whites until foamy. Add
sugar gradually, beating well after each
addition. Continue beating until stiff
peaks form. Fold into lemon-lime
mixture.*

1 cup whipping cream

*Whip cream and fold into gelatin
mixture. Transfer filling to pan; cover
loosely and chill for 3 to 4 hours or
until firm.*

*Run thin metal spatula around inside
edge to loosen chiffon. Loosen spring
fastener on side of pan; lift off. Place
on serving platter and garnish as
desired.*

*Garnish options: sweetened whipped
cream, slices of kiwi or chocolate
filigree.*

YIELD   8 TO 10 SERVINGS

CHOCOLATE FILIGREE SHAPES
*To make chocolate filigree shapes:
Cut a small hole in the bottom
corner of a resealable plastic bag
OR fit a small plain tip onto a
piping bag. Fill bag with melted
chocolate. (Chocolate wafers used
to coat candy works well.)
Pipe patterns or shapes onto
parchment or waxed paper. Let
stand until set. Carefully lift
chocolate designs off paper with a
thin metal spatula. You can make
these ahead and store in airtight
container. Pictured on page 287*

Chocolate Marble Chiffon Pie

Chocolate and vanilla are complements in this light-as-a cloud chiffon pie. It involves a few bowls and a bit of time, but it is not difficult. The hard part is waiting for it to chill. It is the ideal summer pie to make in the morning and serve in the evening.

Pastry for 10-inch one-crust pie,
  page 177

Prepare pastry and line pan; prebake as directed.

1/2 cup sugar
1 envelope unflavored gelatin
1/4 tsp. salt
1 1/3 cups milk
3 eggs, separated
1 tsp. vanilla

Combine sugar, gelatin and salt in medium saucepan. Beat milk and egg yolks together lightly with a fork. Strain through a small sieve and stir into gelatin mixture. (This eliminates any white of the egg that may curdle.) Cook over moderate heat, stirring constantly, just until mixture boils. Place pan in bowl of ice water, stirring occasionally, until mixture mounds slightly when dropped from spoon. Stir in vanilla.

1 square (1 oz.) unsweetened
  chocolate, melted and cooled
1/4 tsp. almond extract

Divide gelatin mixture into two equal parts. Add melted chocolate to one part. Add almond extract to second part.

3 egg whites
1/4 tsp. cream of tartar
1/2 cup sugar

Beat egg whites and cream of tartar until foamy. Beat in sugar, 1 tablespoon at a time; continue beating until stiff and glossy. Divide egg white mixture into two equal parts. Fold one part into each of the gelatin mixtures.

1/2 cup chilled whipping cream

Beat cream until stiff. Fold half into each of the gelatin mixtures. With a large spoon, pile into baked pie shell, alternating light and chocolate mixtures. Cut through the mixtures with knife In a circular pattern for a marbled swirl effect. Chill at least 3 hours until set. Garnish with additional whipped cream and chocolate shavings if desired.

YIELD   6 TO 8 SERVINGS

Notes

Cakes

Cakes

Special occasions are wonderful opportunites to create a great-tasting cake from scratch. It is only slightly more difficult than baking one from a mix and far more superior in taste. A homemade cake may not look perfect but has flavor most mixes cannot match. For me, baking a cake has significant rewards. There is the pleasure of creativity, the delight in eating as well as the enjoyment of sharing.

Poppy Seed Charm Cake

The crunch of poppy seeds adds an interesting texture to this tender crumb cake. It has been in our tradition for as long as I can remember and its goodness lives on.

1 cup milk
1/2 cup poppy seeds

Combine milk and poppy seeds; set aside.

3/4 cup butter or margarine, softened
1 1/2 cups sugar
3 eggs, separated
1 tsp. vanilla

In a mixing bowl, cream butter and sugar together until light and fluffy. Add 3 egg yolks, one at a time, beating after each addition. Add vanilla.

2 1/3 cups cake flour
    OR 2 cups all-purpose flour
3 tsp. baking powder
1 tsp. salt

Blend flour, baking powder and salt. Add to creamed mixture alternately with milk and poppy seed mixture. Beat 3 egg whites until stiff but not dry; gently fold into batter.

Line 3 greased 9-inch round layer pans with parchment or waxed paper. OR grease and flour a 9 x 13 - inch baking pan. Transfer batter into prepared pans. Bake round pans in 350° oven for 30 to 35 minutes or until wooden pick inserted in center comes out clean. Bake 9 x 13 - inch pan for 40 to 45 minutes or until wooden pick inserted in center comes out clean.

To make your own cake flour when you have only all-purpose flour, substitute 2 tablespoons cornstarch for 2 tablespoons flour in each cup.

Cool in pan for 10 minutes. Remove from pans to wire rack. Cool completely, about 1 hour.

Fill and frost layers with Cream Cheese Frosting, page 215.

YIELD   12 TO 15 SERVINGS

Luscious Lemon Layer Cake

I selected this exceptional cake for the birthday of an aunt I dearly loved.
It is soft as velvet and marvelous for those occasions that warrant special attention.

1 1/2 cups butter or margarine
3 cups sugar
2 tsp. vanilla
1 tsp. almond extract

In a large mixing bowl, cream butter, sugar and flavorings together until light and fluffy.

4 1/2 cups cake flour
6 tsp. baking powder
1 1/2 tsp. salt

Sift flour once, measure. Blend flour, baking powder and salt.

1 cup milk
1 cup water

Add flour mixture to creamed mixture alternately with milk and water. Beat after each addition until smooth.

9 egg whites, stiffly beaten

Fold in beaten egg whites.

Line 3 greased 9-inch round layer pans with waxed paper. Turn batter into prepared layer pans. Bake at 350° for 30 to 35 minutes or until wooden pick inserted in center comes out clean. Cool on wire rack for 5 minutes. Remove from pans and cool completely.

Lemon Filling

1 1/2 cups sugar
6 tbsp. cornstarch
1/2 tsp. salt
2 1/2 cups water
1/2 cup lemon juice
9 egg yolks

In a medium saucepan, mix sugar, cornstarch and salt. Whisk together water, lemon juice and egg yolks. Strain through a sieve into sugar mixture and stir to blend. Cook over medium heat, stirring constantly, until mixture thickens and boils. Boil and stir 1 minute. Remove from heat; press plastic wrap on filling to prevent skin from forming on top. Chill until cold.

Luscious Lemon Layer Cake (continued)

Lemon Butter Icing

3 cups powdered sugar
6 tbsp. butter or margarine, softened
2 tsp. lemon rind, grated
1 tsp. vanilla

Beat powdered sugar, butter, rind and vanilla together until creamy.

Assemble the cake in layers with the lemon filling. Frost with the lemon butter icing.

2 cups flaked coconut, toasted

Press coconut around the side, if desired.

YIELD   12 GENEROUS SERVINGS

Bakery Frosting

This smooth, fluffy frosting is ideal for
decorating birthday or other celebration cakes.

1/4 cup all-purpose flour
1/4 cup sugar
1 cup milk

In a small saucepan, blend flour and sugar; stir in milk. Cook over medium heat, stirring constantly until mixture thickens and boils. Cool.

1 cup shortening
1 cup powdered sugar
1 tsp. vanilla
1/4 tsp. salt

In a medium mixing bowl, cream together shortening, sugar, vanilla and salt. Add the cooled flour mixture, 1 tablespoon at a time, beating constantly.

If desired add food coloring. Store in refrigerator for up to 3 months or freeze. Bring to room temperature and whip before spreading on cake.

YIELD   ABOUT 4 CUPS

German Chocolate Cake

This superb chocolate classic is presented with an intensely rich coconut-pecan filling and topping. Although the name implies a German origin, the cake is named for Sam German, an American, who developed German's sweet baking chocolate.

Grease 3 round 9-inch layer pans. Line bottoms of pans with waxed paper.

1 bar (4 oz.) sweet cooking chocolate, chopped
1/2 cup boiling water

In a small bowl, combine chocolate and boiling water, stirring until chocolate is melted. Set aside to cool until tepid.

1 cup butter or margarine, softened
2 cups sugar
4 egg yolks
1 tsp. vanilla

In a mixing bowl, cream butter and sugar until light and fluffy. Add egg yolks, one at a time, beating after each addition. Stir in chocolate and vanilla.

2 cups all-purpose flour
  OR 2 1/2 cups cake flour
1 tsp. baking soda
1/2 tsp. salt
1 cup buttermilk

Blend flour, soda and salt. Add alternately to creamed mixture with buttermilk, beating after each addition until batter is smooth.

4 egg whites

Beat egg whites until stiff peaks form; gently fold into batter. Pour evenly into prepared pans.

Bake at 350° for 30 to 35 minutes or until pick inserted into centers comes out clean. Transfer to rack and cool 15 minutes. Remove from pans and remove wax paper; cool completely.

Spread Coconut-Pecan Frosting between layers and onto top of cake.

YIELD   12 GENEROUS SERVINGS

German Chocolate Cake (Continued)

Coconut-Pecan Frosting

1 cup evaporated milk
1 cup sugar
3 egg yolks
½ cup butter or margarine

Combine evaporated milk, sugar, egg yolks and butter in medium saucepan. Cook and stir over medium heat until mixture thickens and bubbles, about 12 minutes.

1 tsp. vanilla
1⅓ cups flaked coconut
1 cup coarsely chopped pecans, toasted

Stir in vanilla, coconut and pecans. Cool for about 1 hour, or until mixture is thick enough to spread.

NOTE
May be stored in an airtight container in the refrigerator for up to 2 weeks; let soften at room temperature before using.

Poppy Seed Sheet Cake

I seldom use a mix because I prefer to use healthy natural products without additives. On occasion I make this and it is very good.

1 (18 oz.) white cake mix
1 tbsp. mayonnaise
1 tbsp. all-purpose flour
⅓ cup poppy seeds

Prepare cake mix according to directions. Add mayonnaise, flour and poppy seeds; mix well. Spread batter evenly in greased 11 x 17 - inch rimmed baking sheet. Bake at 350° for 20 minutes or until wooden pick inserted in center comes out clean. Let stand in baking sheet on wire rack until cooled completely. Ice with Cream Cheese Frosting, page 215.

YIELD   15 SERVINGS

Banana Cake

Here's a cake to use up those overripe bananas. I have family members
who are unabashedly delighted when I show up with this
dense yet moist version frosted with delicious caramel flavored icing.

½ cup butter or margarine, softened
1 cup brown sugar
2 eggs
1 tsp. vanilla

In a mixing bowl, cream butter and sugar until light and fluffy. Add eggs and vanilla; continue beating until smooth.

2 cups all-purpose flour
1 tsp. baking soda
1 tsp. baking powder
½ tsp. salt
¾ cup buttermilk
1¼ cups mashed ripe bananas
  (about 3 medium)

Combine dry ingredients and add to creamed mixture alternately with buttermilk, beating well after each addition. Add mashed bananas and mix well.

Pour into greased and floured 9 x 13 - inch baking pan. Bake at 350° for 35 minutes or until wooden pick in center comes out clean. Cool on wire rack. Spread with Creamy Nut Icing.

YIELD   15 SERVINGS

Creamy Nut Icing

½ cup butter or margarine
2½ tbsp. all-purpose flour
¼ tsp. salt
½ cup milk

Melt butter in a saucepan over low heat. Remove from heat and blend in flour and salt. Gradually stir in milk. Cook over low heat, stirring constantly until mixture thickens and boils. Boil and stir about 30 seconds. Mixture may separate but that is normal.

½ cup brown sugar

Remove from heat; stir in brown sugar until smooth. Cool to lukewarm.

2 cups powdered sugar
½ tsp. vanilla
½ cup chopped walnuts (optional)

Stir in powdered sugar, vanilla and nuts, mixing thoroughly.

**YIELD   ENOUGH TO GENEROUSLY COVER
9 X 13 - INCH CAKE OR 9-INCH
ROUND TWO-LAYER CAKE.**

Maraschino Cherry Cake

Flavor, color and ease of preparation have kept this tender cake
in my collection as well as a wonderful way to use leftover egg whites.
It is a perfect accompaniment to a cup of tea.

2 1/4 cups cake flour
1 1/3 cup sugar
3 tsp. baking powder
1 tsp. salt

In a large mixing bowl, blend flour, sugar, baking powder and salt.

1/2 cup soft shortening
1/2 cup milk
1/4 cup maraschino cherry juice

Add shortening, milk and juice to dry ingredients. With electric mixer, beat vigorously for 2 minutes.

2/3 cup egg whites, unbeaten

Add egg whites and beat 2 more minutes.

16 maraschino cherries, cut into pieces
1/2 cup chopped walnuts

Fold in cherries and nuts.

Line 2 greased 9-inch layer pans with waxed paper; grease again. Or grease and flour a 9 x 13 - inch baking pan. Pour batter into prepared pans. Bake layers in preheated 350° oven for 30 to 35 minutes or until a wooden pick in center comes out clean. Bake oblong pan for 35 to 40 minutes.

Cool in pans for 10 minutes. Remove from layer pans to wire rack. Cool completely, about 1 hour. Fill and frost with Cream Cheese Frosting, page 215.

YIELD   12 TO 15 SERVINGS

Pineapple Layer Cake

This light layer cake is spread with a creamy pineapple filling.
Other fillings and a variety of frostings would do as well.

1/2 cup butter or margarine, softened 1/2 cup vegetable shortening 2 cups sugar 5 egg yolks 1 1/2 tsp. vanilla extract	In a large mixing bowl, cream butter, shortening and sugar until light and fluffy. Add egg yolks, one at a time, beating well after each addition. Beat in vanilla.
2 cups all-purpose flour 1 tsp. baking soda 1/4 tsp. salt 1 cup buttermilk	Blend dry ingredients; add to creamed mixture alternately with buttermilk, beating well after each additon.
5 egg whites 1/2 tsp. cream of tartar	In another mixing bowl, beat egg whites and cream of tartar until stiff peaks form. Fold into cake batter.
	Line 3 greased 9-inch round layer pans with waxed paper; grease again. Pour batter into prepared pans. Bake at 350° for 25 to 30 minutes or until wooden pick inserted in center comes out clean. Cool for 10 minutes before removing from pans to wire racks to cool completely.

Pineapple Filling

1/4 cup sugar 1 1/2 tbsp. cornstarch 1/8 tsp. salt 2 egg yolks 1 cup milk	In a medium saucepan, mix sugar, cornstarch and salt. Beat egg yolks and milk together with a fork. Strain through a sieve into sugar mixture and stir to blend. Cook over medium heat, stirring constantly, until mixture thickens and boils.
1/2 cup crushed pineapple, drained 1/2 tsp. vanilla 1 tsp. butter	Blend in crushed pineapple; boil and stir until thick. Remove from heat; stir in vanilla and butter. Press plastic wrap on filling to prevent skin from forming on top. Chill.
	To assemble cake, spread pineapple filling between layers. Frost with Cream Cheese Frosting, page 215 or White Mountain Frosting, page 227.

YIELD   12 SERVINGS

Tropical Carrot Cake

After a turnover of favorite carrot cake recipes, I was hopeful when
I tried this one with a reduced amount of oil. I was not disappointed.
It is moist, nutritious and simply delicious.

3 eggs
2 cups sugar
3/4 cup vegetable oil
2 tsp. vanilla

In a large mixing bowl, beat eggs until frothy. Add sugar, oil and vanilla and continue beating until mixture is thick and creamy.

2 cups + 2 tbsp. all-purpose flour
2 tsp. baking soda
1/2 tsp. salt
1/2 tsp. cinnamon
3/4 cup buttermilk

Combine dry ingredients and add to egg mixture with buttermilk; beat well.

1 cup crushed pineapple, undrained
2 cups finely shredded carrots
1 cup raisins
   OR dried cranberries (optional)
1 cup pecans, coarsely chopped
3/4 cup flaked coconut

Stir in pineapple, carrots, raisins, nuts and coconut; mix well. Pour into a greased and floured 11 x 17 - inch baking pan, OR line pan with parchment paper.

Bake at 350° for 40 to 45 minutes until wooden pick inserted in center comes out clean. Cool and spread with Cream Cheese Frosting.

Cake may also be baked in a 9 x 13 - inch pan, if preferred. Increase baking time for 50 to 55 minutes.

Pictured on page 69.

YIELD   12 TO 15 SERVINGS

Cream Cheese Frosting

This is the perfect frosting for carrot cake. Store frosted cake or any remaining
frosting covered in refrigerator as cream cheese will spoil if left at room temperature.

1 pkg. (8 oz.) cream cheese, softened
1/4 cup butter or margarine, softened
1 tbsp. milk
1 tsp. vanilla
4 cups powdered sugar

Beat cream cheese, butter, milk and vanilla in large bowl until fluffy. Gradually beat in powdered sugar until smooth. Spread on cooled cake.

YIELD   ABOUT 2 1/2 CUPS

Crunchy Top Oatmeal Cake

Many recipes in my collection are from friends who have shared favorite recipes with my family. Lorene shared this cake and recipe with my daughters who passed it on to me. This cake has a marvelous texture, keeps well and is ideal for picnics. A broiled topping makes it extra special.

1 1/4 cups boiling water
1 cup quick-cooking oats

Pour boiling water over oats and let stand for 20 minutes.

1/2 cup butter or margarine
1 cup brown sugar
1 cup white sugar
1 tsp. vanilla
2 eggs

Cream butter, sugars and vanilla together until fluffy. Add unbeaten eggs, one at a time, beating well after each addition. Blend in oatmeal mixture.

1 1/2 cups all-purpose flour
1 tsp. cinnamon
1 tsp. baking soda
1/2 tsp. salt

Measure dry ingredients and stir together. Fold into oatmeal mixture. Pour into greased and floured 9 x 13 - inch baking pan. Bake at 350° for 30 to 35 minutes.

Prepare topping while cake is baking.

Topping

2/3 cup brown sugar
1 cup chopped nuts
1 cup flaked coconut
6 tbsp. melted butter
1/4 cup heavy cream
   OR evaporated milk
1 tsp. vanilla

Mix all ingredients together thoroughly. Spread mixture evenly over hot cake. Set oven control at broil or 550° degrees. Place cake 5 inches from heat; broil about 2 minutes or until topping bubbles and browns slightly. (Watch carefully – mixture burns easily.)

YIELD   15 SERVINGS

Lorene Petersheim
Catlett, VA

Pumpkin Sheet Cake

An inviting spiced pumpkin flavor is the essence of this moist cake.
It can be an alternative to pumpkin pie at Thanksgiving.

4 eggs, beaten
2 cups sugar
3/4 cup vegetable oil

In a mixing bowl, combine eggs, sugar and oil; beat together thoroughly.

2 cups all-purpose flour
2 tsp. baking soda
1 tsp. baking powder
1 tsp. cinnamon
1/2 tsp. salt
1/4 tsp. ground nutmeg
1/4 tsp. ground cloves
2 cups canned pumpkin

Blend dry ingredients together and add to creamed mixture alternately with pumpkin. Pour batter into a greased 11 x 17 - inch baking pan or two 9 x 9 - inch baking pans. Bake at 350° for 20 to 25 minutes or until wooden pick inserted in center comes out clean.

1/3 cup chopped pecans, toasted

Frost with Cream Cheese Frosting, page 215. Sprinkle with pecans if desired.

YIELD   24 SERVINGS

Beth Hershberger
Goshen, IN

Texas Sheet Cake

Very chocolate with a tender crumb, this sheet cake is also referred to as
Texas Brownies. The first time I tried it was a disaster because
I did not follow the instructions. It is very important that the boiled mixture
is added to the flour mixture while it is still very hot.

2 cups sugar
2 cups all-purpose flour

Blend sugar and flour in a large mixing bowl.

1 cup butter or margarine
1 cup water
4 tbsp. cocoa

In medium saucepan, combine butter, water and cocoa. Cook over medium heat until mixture comes to a boil. Immediately pour over flour mixture and beat well.

1/2 cup buttermilk
2 eggs
1 tsp. baking soda
1 tsp. cinnamon
1 tsp. vanilla

Add remaining ingredients to flour mixture and beat thoroughly. Pour into a greased 11 x 17 - inch baking pan. OR bake in two 9 x 9 - inch cake pans. Bake at 375° for 20 to 25 minutes or until wooden pick inserted in center comes out clean.

While cake is baking, prepare icing.

Chocolate Icing

1/2 cup butter or margarine
4 tbsp. cocoa
6 tbsp. milk
1 tsp. vanilla
3 1/2 to 4 cups powdered sugar

In medium saucepan melt butter; add cocoa and milk and heat to a boil. Remove from heat and cool until tepid. Add remaining ingredients; beat until smooth. Spread on cake while the cake is still warm. If desired, sprinkle 1 cup chopped toasted pecans on top.

YIELD   24 SERVINGS

VARIATION
WHITE CHOCOLATE SHEET CAKE
Mix cake as above; omit cinnamon, substitute 1/3 cup white chocolate chips for the cocoa in cake and 1/3 cup white chocolate chips for the cocoa in the icing. If desired sprinkle toasted coconuts or nuts on top.

Spicy Raisin Nut Cake

My mother often made this dense, yet moist cake, and it became one of my favorites.
I remember taking one across the continent to savor and share with my
roommate in our College dorm. This egg-less, milk-less wonder didn't need
refrigeration during transit and the short time it sat on the shelf.

2 cups raisins
2 cups water
1 1/2 cups sugar
3/4 cup butter or margarine

In medium saucepan, combine
raisins, water, sugar and butter. Cook
over medium heat until mixture
begins to boil. Boil for 5 minutes,
stirring occasionally. Cool.

2 cups all-purpose flour
2 tsp. baking soda
2 tsp. cinnamon
1 tsp. nutmeg
1/2 tsp. ground cloves
1 1/2 cups walnuts, coarsely chopped

Blend dry ingredients and nuts. Add
to raisin mixture, stirring to mix well.
Turn into a greased and floured 9 x
13 - inch cake pan. Bake at 350° for
40 to 50 minutes or until wooden pick
inserted in center comes out clean.
Cool.

Needs no icing, but if you wish, dust
with powdered sugar or frost with
Brown-Sugar Caramel Icing.

YIELD   *15 SERVINGS*

Brown-Sugar Caramel Icing

The strong caramel flavor is perfect on date or spice cakes.

1/2 cup butter
1 cup brown sugar, packed

Melt butter in medium saucepan; stir
in brown sugar. Boil and stir over low
heat for 2 minutes.

1/4 cup milk or heavy cream
1 3/4 to 2 cups powdered sugar

Stir in milk; bring to boil, stirring
constantly. Cool to lukewarm.
Gradually stir in powdered sugar.
Place pan in ice water and stir until
thick enough to spread.

YIELD   *ENOUGH FOR TWO 8 OR 9-INCH*
        LAYERS OR 9 X 13 - INCH CAKE

Angel Food Cake

Light, tender and not overly sweet, this cake is a perfect fat-free dessert. Food writers attribute its invention to thrifty Pennsylvania Dutch bakers who developed the recipe to use leftover egg whites. When I recall all the egg yolks that went into homemade noodles in our kitchen, I can believe that is the case.

1 1/4 cups cake flour
1/3 cup sugar
1/4 tsp. salt

Measure flour, sugar and salt; sift onto a sheet of waxed paper. Sift together 3 more times, working back and forth over 2 sheets waxed paper. Set aside.

1 1/2 cups egg whites,
   (at room temperature)
1 1/2 tsp. cream of tartar
1 tsp. vanilla
1/2 tsp. almond extract

In a large mixing bowl, beat egg whites with electric mixer until foamy. Add cream of tartar, vanilla and almond flavorings. Continue beating until soft peaks form.

1 cup sugar

Gradually add sugar, 2 tablespoons at a time, beating on high speed until the whites are glossy and smooth and form stiff peaks.

Sprinkle flour-sugar mixture, 1/4 cup at a time, over egg white mixture, folding in gently with rubber spatula just until sugar-flour mixture disappears. Scrape batter into an ungreased, 10-inch tube pan. Cut gently through batter with metal spatula or knife to break air pockets.

Bake for 40 to 45 minutes or until cracks feel dry and top springs back when touched lightly. Immediately turn pan upside down onto heat-proof funnel or bottle. Let hang about 2 hours or until cake is completely cool. Loosen side of cake with knife or long metal spatula, making sure to press the knife against the side of pan to avoid marring the cake. Lift up to remove from pan, and slide knife under the cake to detach it from the pan bottom. Invert onto a serving plate dusted with powdered sugar.

Delicious served with fresh berries and softly whipped cream.

YIELD   12 TO 14 SERVINGS

Mango Angel Food Cake

Turn a tender angel food cake into a lovely and luscious torte with the cool flavor of mango and whipped cream. A perfect summer dessert!

Bake angel food cake, page 220
  OR use a mix.

Cut cake horizontally to make 3 layers. (Mark side of cake with wooden picks and cut with long, thin serrated knife) Fill layers and frost side and top of cake with Mango Topping. Store loosely covered in refrigerator.

YIELD   12 TO 14 SERVINGS

Mango Topping

1 envelope unflavored gelatin
1/4 cup cold water

Sprinkle gelatin over cold water; let stand 5 minutes.

1 cup frozen mango concentrate
1/4 cup sugar

In a saucepan, combine mango concentrate, sugar and gelatin. Cook and stir over low heat until gelatin is dissolved. Chill until slightly thickened.

2 oz. cream cheese softened
2 tbsp. powdered sugar

Beat cream cheese and powdered sugar together until smooth. Add to mango mixture and beat together until well blended.

1 1/2 cups whipping cream

Whip cream in chilled bowl until stiff. Fold into mango mixture. Chill until spreading consistency.

Cool Lemon Chiffon Cake

Tall, moist and airy, this simple cake is an ideal base to serve with fresh berries.
If you feel indulgent add ice cream or sweetened whipped cream.
Or frost with the lemon topping.

2 cups all-purpose flour
1½ cups sugar
3 tsp. baking powder
½ tsp. baking soda
1 tsp. salt

Blend flour, sugar, baking powder, soda and salt in large mixing bowl.

½ cup vegetable oil
7 egg yolks
Juice of one lemon
  + enough water to make ⅔ cup
2 tsp. vanilla
2 tsp. grated lemon rind

Make a well or large indention in flour mixture and add in order: oil, yolks, juice, vanilla and rind. Beat together until batter is smooth.

1 cup egg whites (7 or 8)
½ tsp. cream of tartar

Measure egg whites and cream of tartar into large mixing bowl. Beat until whites form very stiff, straight peaks. Gradually pour batter mixture over beaten egg whites, gently folding just until blended. Pour into ungreased 10-inch tube pan.

Bake at 325° for about 70 to 75 minutes or until top springs back lightly when touched. Invert tube pan onto heatproof funnel or bottle. Let hang about 2 hours or until cake is completely cool.

Loosen side of cake with knife or long metal spatula. Lift up to remove from pan, and slide knife under the cake to detach it from the pan bottom. Invert onto a serving platter dusted with powdered sugar.

Frost side and top of cake with Lemon Topping if desired. Store loosely covered in refrigerator.

YIELD   12 TO 14 SERVINGS

Cool Lemon Chiffon Cake (continued)
Lemon Topping

3/4 cup sugar
4 egg yolks
2 tsp. finely grated lemon rind
1/3 cup freshly squeezed lemon juice
1/2 cup butter
1 tbsp. cornstarch
2 tbsp. cold water

In a heavy saucepan or double boiler, whisk together sugar and egg yolks until blended. Stir in lemon zest, juice and butter. Dissolve cornstarch in water and add. Cook over medium heat, whisking constantly, until the mixture thickens, 7 to 10 minutes. (Do not let the custard boil, or it will curdle).

Strain the mixture through a fine-mesh sieve into a bowl. Set bowl in ice water for about 15 minutes, stirring frequently. Cover with plastic wrap and press against the surface. Refrigerate until completely cold.

1 cup whipping cream

Beat whipping cream until stiff. Fold into lemon custard.

Orange Chiffon Cake

This exceptionally light cake has a fresh orange flavor.
Serve with fresh fruit and sweetened whipped cream or ice cream.

Make cake, page 222, except omit soda, vanilla, lemon juice and lemon rind. Use juice from one orange plus cold water to make 3/4 cup and 3 tablespoons grated orange rind. Frost with Orange Butter Icing.

YIELD   12 TO 14 SERVINGS

Orange Butter Icing

1/3 cup butter or margarine, softened
3 cups powdered sugar
1 1/2 tbsp. grated orange rind
3 tbsp. orange juice

Blend butter, sugar, orange rind and juice until smooth enough to spread.

Maple Pecan Chiffon Cake

Henry Baker is credited for developing the original chiffon cake in 1927.
He was an insurance salesman who made and sold cakes on the side.
One day he discovered that adding vegetable oil to sponge cake batter made a very
moist and tender cake. Twenty years later he sold his coveted recipe. With an
amazing number of variations, it seemed to be the cake of the day when I was
growing up. After the cake is frosted, it looks impressive and tastes wonderful.

2 cups all-purpose flour
3/4 cup white sugar
3/4 cup brown sugar, packed
3 tsp. baking powder
1 tsp. salt

In a mixing bowl, stir together flour, sugars, baking powder and salt.

1/2 cup vegetable oil
7 egg yolks
3/4 cup water
1 tsp. vanilla
1 tsp. maple extract

Make a well or large indention in flour mixture and add in order: oil, yolks, water and flavorings. Beat together until batter is smooth.

1 cup egg whites (about 8),
   at room temperature
1/2 tsp. cream of tartar
1 cup chopped pecans

Measure egg whites and cream of tartar into large mixer bowl. Beat until whites form very stiff, straight peaks. Gradually pour egg yolk mixture over beaten whites, gently folding just until blended. Gently fold in 1 cup very finely chopped pecans. Pour into ungreased 10 x 4 - inch tube pan.

Bake on bottom rack at 325° for about 70 to 75 minutes or until top springs back lightly when touched. Immediately turn upside down onto heatproof funnel or bottle. Let hang about two hours or until cake is completely cool.

Loosen side of cake with knife or long metal spatula. Lift up to remove from pan, and slide knife under the cake to detach it from the pan bottom. Invert onto a serving platter dusted with powdered sugar and cake will slip out.

Spread with Creamy Nut Icing, page 210.

YIELD   12 TO 14 SERVINGS

Mocha Nut Chiffon Cake

Beautiful high layers of rich sponge cake is flavored
as well as frosted with coffee and chocolate.

*Make cake as previous page except:
add 1 tablespoon instant coffee
granules and 1/4 teaspoon cinnamon to
dry ingredients. Omit maple flavoring;
add 2 teaspoons vanilla. Grate 3
squares unsweetened chocolate and
gently fold into batter with nuts just
before pouring into pan.*

*Frost with Mocha Creole Frosting or
drizzle with Chocolate Ganache,
page 227.*

YIELD   12 TO 14 SERVINGS

Mocha Creole Frosting

1/3 cup butter or margarine, softened
4 cups sifted powdered sugar, divided

*In a medium mixing bowl, cream butter
until light. Gradually add 2 cups
powdered sugar, beating after each
addition.*

1/2 tsp. vanilla
1/4 tsp. salt
2 squares bakers chocolate, melted

*Add vanilla, salt and chocolate;
continue beating until well mixed.*

1/3 cup strong coffee

*Add remaining 2 cups powdered sugar
alternately with coffee, until mixture is
the right consistency to spread. Beat
after each addition until smooth.*

*YIELD   ENOUGH FROSTING TO COVER TOP
AND SIDES OF ONE 9 - INCH TWO-
LAYER CAKE OR ONE CHIFFON CAKE*

Fluffy Custard Buttercream

A satiny texture is the beauty of this filling that can also be used as the frosting.
Prepare up to a week in advance and refrigerate, or freeze.
Bring to room temperature and whip before spreading on cake.

1 cup butter, softened
(no substitute)

In a bowl, beat butter until light and smooth, set aside.

2/3 cup sugar
4 tbsp. cornstarch
1 1/4 cups milk

In a medium saucepan, blend sugar and cornstarch; stir in milk. Cook over medium heat, stirring constantly until mixture thickens and boils. Boil 30 seconds to eliminate the taste of uncooked starch.

2 tsp. vanilla

Remove from heat and whisk vigorously until custard is smooth and glossy. Add vanilla. Transfer to clean metal bowl and stir over ice water until completely cooled.

Beat custard with electric mixer for a few seconds. With mixer running, beat in butter, 1 tablespoon at a time, beating after each addition. After all butter is incorporated, whip an additional 30 seconds. Use at once or cover and refrigerate.

VARIATION
COFFEE BUTTERCREAM
Omit vanilla and add 1 tablespoon instant coffee granules dissolved in the milk.

CHOCOLATE BUTTERCREAM
Add 3 or 4 oz. semisweet chocolate, melted and cooled, to buttercream with vanilla.

**YIELD   3 CUPS, TO FILL AND FROST
3-LAYER CAKE**

White Mountain Frosting

This fluffy white frosting holds its large white peaks long after it's beaten.

2 large egg whites

In a medium bowl, beat egg whites with electric mixer just until stiff peaks form.

1/2 cup sugar
1/4 cup light corn syrup
2 tbsp. water
1 tsp. vanilla

In a medium saucepan, stir sugar, corn syrup and water until well mixed. Cover and heat to a rolling boil over medium heat. Uncover and boil 4 to 8 minutes, without stirring to 242°F on a candy thermometer or until syrup spins a 6 to 8-inch thread. Pour hot syrup very slowly in a thin stream into beaten egg whites, beating constantly. Blend in vanilla; beat on high speed about 10 minutes or until stiff peaks form.

YIELD   FROSTS 9 X 13 - INCH CAKE GENEROUSLY, OR 9-INCH LAYER CAKE

Chocolate Ganache

This elegant glaze or frosting is smooth as satin and perfect on a chocolate cake.

1 cup semi-sweet chocolate chips
2/3 cup whipping cream
1 tsp. vanilla

In a heavy saucepan, melt chocolate chips with cream over low heat. Remove from heat and add vanilla; stir gently until mixture is smooth. Cool until mixture is slightly thickened, about 35 minutes. Pour over cake, allowing some to flow down the edges. Chill until set.

If desired, chill until mixture reaches a spreading consistency. Spread over cake and chill until set.

Store in refrigerator.

YIELD   ABOUT 1 1/4 CUPS

Chocolate Cream Cheese Icing

For the chocolate fans, this is even more wonderful than the original.

6 squares semi-sweet chocolate, chopped
  (1 oz. each)
3 tbsp. water

Heat chocolate and water over low heat, stirring until chocolate is completely melted and smooth. Cool to lukewarm.

1 pkg. (8 oz.) cream cheese, softened
1 tsp. vanilla
2½ cups powdered sugar

Add cream cheese and vanilla; beat until well blended. Gradually beat in powdered sugar until well blended and smooth.

YIELD   ABOUT 2 ½ CUPS; ENOUGH TO ICE ONE 9 X 13 - INCH CAKE OR TWO 9-INCH LAYERS

Desserts

Desserts

Mocha Nut Torte

My mother's legacy of recipes included this favored family dessert.
Not overly sweet, the graham cake is ideally suited to the
definitive taste of coffee in the creamy filling.

1/2 cup butter or margarine, softened
1 cup sugar
3 eggs, separated

In a large mixing bowl, cream butter
and sugar. Add egg yolks and beat
until light.

1/2 cup all-purpose flour
2 tsp. baking powder
2 cups fine graham cracker crumbs
1 cup strong cold coffee

Stir together flour and baking powder;
add crumbs. Add dry ingredients
alternately with coffee to creamed
mixture, beating well until smooth.

1 tsp. vanilla
3/4 cup chopped nuts, optional

Stir vanilla and nuts into mixture. In
another bowl, beat egg whites until
stiff; fold into batter.

Pour into two 9-inch round waxed
paper-lined baking pans. Bake at 350°
for 30 to 35 minutes. Cool in pans for
10 minutes, then remove and cool
completely.

Filling

1 pkg. instant vanilla pudding
  (4 serving size)
1 1/2 cups milk
1 tsp. instant coffee granules
1/2 cup heavy cream, whipped

Prepare pudding with milk and coffee
granules. Chill until set and granules
are dissolved, about 1 hour. Fold in
whipped cream.

Chocolate curls or shavings

Split each cake layer and spread
filling between layers and on top.
Garnish with chocolate curls.

VARIATION
MOCHA NUT SHEET CAKE
*Mix as above except bake cake in a
greased and floured 11 x 17 - inch
baking pan. Bake in 350° oven for 18
to 20 minutes. Cool.*

*To serve: cut into squares and top
with mocha filling or make a two layer
serving with filling in between and on
top.*

YIELD   12 TO 14 SERVINGS

Tiramisu

Tiramisu which literally translated means, 'pick-me-up',
can be made with extravagant flair. I put together a simplified version
that is rich yet light and altogether luscious. Layers of coffee-flavored
sponge cake are spread with a silky smooth filling in this dreamy Italian dessert.

Line a 10 x 15 - inch rimmed baking pan with waxed or parchment paper. Lightly grease and flour the paper.

3 egg yolks
1/2 tsp. vanilla
1/8 tsp. salt

In a small bowl, beat egg yolks, vanilla and salt until thick and pale yellow in color.

3 egg whites, at room temperature
1/3 cup sugar
1/3 cup all-purpose flour

Beat egg whites until they form soft peaks. Gradually add sugar, beating until stiff peaks form. Fold egg yolks into egg whites. Gradually fold in flour until well combined, without over-mixing.

Spread batter into pan, gently spreading to the edges. Bake in preheated 375° oven for 12 to 15 minutes or until cake is golden.

Invert cake onto a piece of parchment paper and carefully peel off paper. Cool completely. Cake will shrink.

1/4 cup sugar
2 tbsp. water
1/3 cup strong coffee

In small saucepan, combine sugar and water; boil together to dissolve sugar. Remove from heat and stir in coffee.

3/4 cup whipping cream
1/4 cup powdered sugar
1/2 tsp. vanilla
1 cup mascarpone cheese*

Whip cream, powdered sugar and vanilla together until stiff. Beat in mascarpone cheese.

Cut cake into 3 equal pieces. Place bottom layer on serving plate. Brush 1/3 syrup over cake. Gently top the cake with 1/3 of cream mixture. Repeat with another layer of cake, syrup and cream. For top layer, moisten cake with syrup and spread with remaining cream mixture. Cover and chill for at least 4 hours or overnight.

*Flavor changes, but cream cheese may be substituted, if desired

1 (1 oz) semi-sweet chocolate*
  baking square

*Grate chocolate and sprinkle over
servings. Garnish with fresh
raspberries.*

YIELD   12 SERVINGS

Mandarin Orange Cake

A shallow cake layer with orange sections is topped with a creamy pineapple
pudding to create a lovely dessert that is perfect for any day or a special occasion.

1 can (11 oz.) mandarin oranges
1 pkg. (18 oz.) yellow cake mix
4 eggs
3/4 cup vegetable oil

*Drain oranges and reserve juice. In
mixing bowl, combine dry cake mix,
eggs, oil and juice. Beat with electric
mixer until smooth. Fold in orange
sections. Pour into greased and
floured 11 x 17 - inch baking pan.
Bake at 350° for 18 to 20 minutes or
until lightly browned. Cool.*

Topping

1 can (20 oz.) crushed pineapple in juice
1 pkg. (3 1/2 oz.) instant vanilla pudding
1 carton (8 oz.) frozen whipped topping,
  thawed

*In medium mixing bowl, combine
crushed pineapple and pudding mix.
Stir or whisk together until blended
and mixture is thickened. Fold in
whipped topping; spread over cooled
cake and refrigerate.*

VARIATION
LAYERED MANDARIN ORANGE CAKE
*Mix as above but bake in 3 greased
and floured 9-inch round cake pans.
Cool in pans 10 minutes, then remove
and cool completely. Spread filling
between layers and on top of cake.*

Viola Petersheim
Catlett, VA

233

Chocolate Éclair Cake

Vanilla pudding sandwiched between graham crackers and topped with
a chocolate frosting is a beautiful make-ahead dessert.
It is the perfect ending to a family or company meal.

1 box (1 lb.) whole graham crackers

Line a greased 9 x 13 - inch baking pan with graham crackers.

1 pkg. French vanilla instant pudding
  (4 serving size)
1 pkg. vanilla instant pudding
  (4 serving size)
3 cups milk
2 cups frozen whipped topping, thawed
  (or 1 cup whipping cream, whipped)

In a mixing bowl, combine instant pudding and milk. Whisk or beat together until blended and smooth, about 2 minutes. Fold whipped topping into pudding. Spread half of pudding mixture over crackers. Arrange a second layer or crackers over pudding; spread with remaining pudding. Cover with a third layer of crackers. Refrigerate for 2 hours or longer.

1 ½ cups powdered sugar
5 tbsp. cocoa
3 tbsp. margarine, softened
3 tbsp. milk
2 tbsp. vegetable oil
2 tbsp. light corn syrup
1 tsp. vanilla

In a mixing bowl, combine powdered sugar, cocoa, margarine, milk, oil, syrup and vanilla. Beat thoroughly until it turns very light and fluffy. (Do not underbeat). Spread over top of crackers. Refrigerate for at least 18 hours before serving.

YIELD   10 TO 12 SERVINGS

Karen Yoder
Goshen, IN

Cookies And Cream Cheesecake

A classic pairing of chocolate and cream cheese are delicious in this rich and moist cheesecake. Preparation can be done well ahead of serving.

2 cups (24) crushed cream-filled chocolate cookies (Oreos are excellent)
6 tbsp. margarine, softened

Combine crumbs and margarine; press into bottom and 1½ inches up sides of 9-inch springform pan.

1 envelope unflavored gelatin
¼ cup cold water

In a small saucepan, soften gelatin in water; stir over low heat until dissolved.

1 pkg. (8 oz.) cream cheese, softened
½ cup sugar
¾ cup milk
1 cup whipping cream, whipped

In a mixing bowl, combine cream cheese and sugar; beat together until well blended. Gradually add gelatin and milk, mixing until smooth. Chill until mixture is thickened but not set. Fold in whipped cream. Reserve 1½ cups cream cheese mixture. Pour remaining cream cheese mixture over crust.

1¼ cups (15) chopped cream-filled chocolate cookies

Top with chopped cookies and reserved cream cheese mixture. Chill until firm, 6 hours or overnight. To serve: remove side of pan and place cheesecake on serving plate.

YIELD   8 TO 10 SERVINGS

NOTE
This dessert also looks very nice in a 10-inch shallow glass dish. Cut and serve as you would a pie.

Peaches and Cream Cheesecake

A lush, creamy peach topping is set off by the tasty base in this simple cheesecake.
It is usually served cool but some prefer to enjoy it warm with a scoop of ice cream.

Grease a 9 or 10-inch deep-dish pie pan. (Glass is good to see doneness of crust.)

3/4 cup all-purpose flour
1 pkg. vanilla pudding mix (not instant)
   (4 serving size)
1/2 cup milk
1 egg
3 tbsp. butter or margarine, softened
1 tsp. baking powder
1/2 tsp. salt

In a large mixing bowl, combine flour, pudding mix, milk, egg, butter, baking powder and salt. Beat for 2 minutes with electric mixer until smooth. Pour batter into prepared pie pan.

4 large fresh peaches, peeled and sliced
   OR 1 can (15 to 20 oz.) sliced peaches,
   well drained; reserve juice

Arrange peach slices on top of mixture in pan.

1 pkg. (8 oz.) cream cheese, softened
1/2 cup sugar
3 tbsp. milk
   OR reserved peach juice

In a small bowl, combine cream cheese, sugar and milk; beat for 2 minutes until smooth. Spoon mixture over peaches to within 1 inch of edge of pan.

1 tbsp. sugar
1/2 tsp. cinnamon

Blend sugar and cinnamon; sprinkle evenly over cream cheese layer.

Bake in preheated 350° oven for 30 to 35 minutes or until crust is golden. Cool before serving. Refrigerate leftovers.

YIELD   8 TO 10 SERVINGS

Sun-Sational Cheesecake

A thick lemon glaze adds the perfect finish to this sunny citrus cheesecake.

1 cup graham cracker crumbs
1/4 cup brown sugar, packed
1/4 cup melted butter

Combine crumbs, sugar and butter; press onto bottom of 9-inch springform pan. Bake at 350° for 10 minutes.

4 pkgs. (8 oz.) cream cheese, softened
1 cup sugar
1 tbsp. lemon juice
1 tsp. grated lemon peel
1 tsp. grated orange peel
1 tsp. vanilla
4 eggs

In a large mixing bowl, beat cream cheese, sugar, juice, peel and vanilla just until smooth. Add eggs one at a time, beating just until blended, after each addition. Pour over crust. Bake in preheated 350° oven for 55 to 60 minutes. Remove from oven; loosen cake from rim of pan with a thin knife. Cool completely on wire rack before removing rim of pan. Refrigerate cake at least four hours or overnight until well chilled.

3/4 cup sugar
2 tbsp. cornstarch
1/2 cup cold water
1/4 cup lemon juice
1 egg yolk

In small saucepan, combine sugar and cornstarch; stir in water and juice. Cook, stirring constantly, until clear and thickened. Beat egg yolk in small bowl. Add small amount of hot mixture to yolk. Return to mixture in saucepan; cook 3 minutes, stirring constantly. Cool slightly. Spoon over cheesecake; chill.* Garnish with whipped cream, lemon slices and fresh mint, if desired.

*ALTERNATE GLAZE TOPPING
1 pkg. lemon pudding (not instant)
Cook and cool according to package directions and use in place of the cooked topping in recipe.

YIELD   10 TO 12 SERVINGS

Candied Lemon Slices

1/4 cup sugar
1/4 cup water
Thin slices of lemon
   OR strips of lemon peel

In small frying pan, stir sugar and water over low heat until sugar is dissolved. Add slices of lemon. Boil for 5 minutes, without stirring, until slightly thickened. Remove to wire rack to cool.

White Chocolate Raspberry Swirl Cheesecake

Cheesecakes are a great dessert for entertaining because they can be made ahead. This impressive cheesecake takes some time to complete but the result is a rich and creamy beauty.

28 vanilla wafers
1 1/4 cups sliced almonds (reserve 1 cup)
3 tbsp. butter or margarine, melted
2 tbsp. sugar

In food processor or blender, process vanilla wafers and 1/4 cup almonds until fine. Mix melted butter and sugar into crumb mixture; pack into the bottom of 9-inch springform pan.

2 cups whole raspberries, fresh or frozen
1/3 cup water

In medium saucepan, simmer raspberries in water until soft, about 3 minutes. Press through a fine sieve to remove seeds. Return raspberry juice to saucepan, about 2/3 cup.

1/3 cup water
1 tbsp. cornstarch or Clearjel
1/3 cup sugar

Dissolve cornstarch in water; stir into raspberry juice with sugar. Cook over medium heat, stirring constantly, until mixture boils and thickens. Boil 1 minute; cool.

1 (6 oz.) white chocolate baking bar, chopped
4 pkgs. (8 oz.) cream cheese, softened
3/4 cup sugar
1/2 tsp. almond extract (optional)
4 large eggs

Melt chocolate in microwave or in saucepan over low heat; cool. In large mixing bowl, beat cream cheese and sugar just until smooth. Add melted chocolate and almond flavoring. Add eggs one at a time beating just until blended.

2 tsp. raspberry extract (optional)

Reserve 2 tablespoons raspberry sauce, set aside. Stir 1/2 cup cream cheese mixture and raspberry flavoring into remaining sauce. Spread half plain cream cheese mixture over crust in pan. Drop half raspberry cream cheese by spoonfuls on plain layer; swirl. Repeat with remaining plain and raspberry cream cheese; swirl.

Bake cake in preheated 350° oven for 55 to 60 minutes. Remove from oven; loosen cake from rim of pan with a thin knife.

238

White Chocolate Raspberry Swirl Cheesecake (continued)

Cool completely on wire rack. Refrigerate cake at least four hours or overnight until well chilled.

To serve: remove sides of pan and place on serving plate. Brush 2 tablespoons reserved raspberry sauce on sides of cake.

1 cup sliced almonds, toasted
Whipped cream

Press almonds onto sides. Using decorating bag, garnish with whipped cream or whipped topping on top and around bottom of cake.

NOTE
Almonds tend to soften if not served immediately.

YIELD   12 TO 16 SERVINGS

Lorene Petersheim
Catlett, VA

Cheesecake can be prepared a day or two before, chilled in a springform pan, and unmolded when time to serve. To freeze a cheesecake up to one month, remove from the pan, place on a cardboard circle, and wrap in heavy-duty aluminum foil. Thaw in the refrigerator 24 hours before serving.

Stabilized Whipped Cream

To be sure whipped cream will remain stiff for about 24 hours,
it can be stabilized with gelatin. This stabilized cream will also hold shape
when piped through a pastry bag in fancy shapes.

1 tbsp. cold water
1 tsp. unflavored gelatin

Heat water and gelatin until gelatin is melted. Cool but keep it liquid.

I cup whipping cream
1/3 cup powdered sugar

Whip the cream and powdered sugar until soft peaks form, then slowly add the gelatin while whipping until stiff.

YIELD   ABOUT 2 CUPS

Strawberry Cream Roll

Truly decadent, each slice features a profusion of berries spilling over a luscious cream filling in a soft cake roll. This large-size dessert is ideal for a potluck dinner or other family gathering. Can also be made ahead and frozen.

	Grease 11 x 17-inch baking pan. Line with parchment paper, extending paper 1 inch beyond sides.
6 egg whites, at room temperature 1/2 cup sugar	In a large mixing bowl, beat egg whites until soft peaks form. Gradually add sugar 1 tablespoon at a time, beating well after each addition until meringue is stiff and glossy.
6 egg yolks 3 tbsp. water 1/2 cup sugar 1 1/2 tsp. vanilla	In another mixing bowl, beat egg yolks until light and lemon-colored. Add water, sugar and vanilla; continue beating until thick and fluffy. Gently fold into egg whites.
1 cup + 2 tbsp. all-purpose flour 1 1/2 tsp. baking powder 1/2 tsp. salt	Blend dry ingredients. Sprinkle over egg mixture, folding in with rubber spatula just until blended. Spread into prepared pan; bake in preheated 375° oven for 12 to 15 minutes or until wooden pick inserted in center comes out clean.
	Run knife along sides to loosen. Spread large tea towel on counter. Cover with a sheet of parchment paper. Sprinkle paper with powdered sugar using a small sieve. Invert cake onto powdered sugar. Carefully peel off and discard original parchment paper. Roll up cake from long side with towel. Let stand about 15 to 20 minutes until cooled completely.
	Unroll cake; spread cream filling over cake to within 1 inch of each edge. Roll up cake from long side; place roll, seam-side down on long serving plate. Dust with powdered sugar. Cover loosely with plastic wrap; refrigerate.

Strawberry Cream Roll (continued)

NOTE
A jelly roll is always sliced with a serrated knife, using a sawing motion to prevent compressing the roll and squeezing out the filling.

When ready to serve, cut into 1-inch slices. Top with fresh strawberry sauce.

To freeze, wrap in aluminum foil and place in plastic bag before adding strawberries.

YIELD   ABOUT 15 SERVINGS

Cream Filling

1/2 cup sugar
2 tbsp. + 2 tsp. all-purpose flour
1/2 cup milk
1/2 cup pineapple juice
1 egg, beaten

In medium saucepan, combine sugar and flour. Add milk, juice and egg; stir to mix. Cook over medium heat until thickened, stirring constantly. Chill.

4 oz. cream cheese, softened
1/4 cup powdered sugar

Beat cream cheese and powdered sugar together.

1/2 cup whipping cream
1/2 tsp. vanilla

Whip cream and vanilla together until stiff. Add cream cheese and cooled pudding mixture; beat together until smooth.

Fresh Strawberry Sauce

2 cups strawberries
1 1/3 cups water

Wash, drain and hull strawberries; mash slightly. In a medium saucepan, simmer strawberries and water for 3 minutes. Strain mixture through sieve and discard strawberry pulp.

1 1/2 cups sugar
1/4 cup cornstarch
1 tsp. lemon juice
2/3 cup water

In medium saucepan, blend sugar, cornstarch, lemon juice and water. Add strawberry juice and bring to boil. Boil for 1 minute stirring constantly. Cool.

4 to 5 cups sliced fresh strawberries

Fold sliced strawberries into cooled glaze.

VARIATION
In place of strawberries, use fresh raspberries.

Chocolate Log Roll

For a convenient refreshing dessert, you can have this ready in the freezer.

Line bottom of 10 x 15 - inch rimmed baking sheet with parchment paper.

3/4 cup all-purpose flour
1/4 cup cocoa
1 tsp. baking powder
1/4 tsp. salt

In a bowl, blend flour, cocoa, baking powder and salt.

3 eggs
1 cup sugar
1/3 cup water
1 tsp. vanilla

Beat eggs in small mixing bowl until very thick and lemon-colored, about 10 minutes. Transfer to large mixing bowl; gradually beat in sugar. Blend in water and vanilla on low speed. Slowly mix in dry ingredients just until batter is smooth. Pour into prepared pan, spreading evenly.

Bake at 375° for 12 to 15 minutes or until wooden pick inserted in center comes out clean. Loosen cake from edges of pan; invert on towel sprinkled with powdered sugar. Carefully peel off and discard paper. While hot, roll up from long side, using towel as a guide; cool.

1 quart vanilla or mint chip ice cream

Unroll cake; spread with slices of ice cream. Reroll cake; transfer to sheet of aluminum foil and wrap. Freeze until firm, about 6 hours. To serve, glaze with Chocolate Fudge Sauce, page 17. Cut into slices.

YIELD   10 SERVINGS

Ellen Eigsti
Goshen, IN

Cream Puffs

The possibilities for enhancing these lovely golden puffs are endless.
They can be filled simply with whipped cream. Or they can be turned into an
elegant dessert with a creamy pudding or pie filling and a pretty garnish.

1 cup water
1/2 cup butter or margarine
2 tsp. sugar
1/8 tsp. salt
1 cup all-purpose flour

*In medium saucepan, heat water,
butter, sugar and salt to a rolling boil.
Stir in flour and beat vigorously with a
wooden spoon over low heat until
mixture forms a ball, about 1 minute.
Remove from heat.*

4 eggs

*Let dough cool to lukewarm. Beat in
eggs one at a time with a wooden
spoon or electric mixer, beating well
after each addition. Drop by rounded
spoonfuls, 2 inches apart, onto
greased or parchment-lined baking
sheet. Make about 12 to 15 large
mounds.*

*For tea-size puffs, make 24
small mounds and bake for
20 to 25 minutes.*

*Bake at 400° for 30 to 35 minutes or
until golden brown and dry. Remove to
wire rack. Immediately cut a slit in
each to allow steam to escape; cool.*

1 cup chilled whipping cream
1/4 cup powdered sugar
1/4 tsp. vanilla

*Chill deep bowl and beater. Place all
ingredients in bowl and beat together
until stiff.*

*Cut off tops with a sharp knife; scoop
out soft dough and discard. Fill with
whipped cream; replace tops and dust
with powdered sugar or drizzle with
chocolate sauce. Serve immediately.*

YIELD   12 TO 15 CREAM PUFFS

Filling Options

*Fold 2 cups raspberries or sliced strawberries into sweetened whipped cream
before filling. Drizzle with Chocolate Fudge Sauce, page 17*

Fill puffs with lemon or orange curd and whipped cream; dust with powdered sugar.

Fold 2 cups whipped cream into chilled instant pie pudding; fill puffs.

Use cream puffs in place of tart shells and fill as cream tarts, page 193.

Frozen Strawberry Dream Pie

Karen has this to say: 'Since Lilly shared this recipe with me I have made it numerous times. Some overnight guests enjoyed it so much they requested it for breakfast!'

2½ cups graham cracker crumbs
½ cup melted butter or margarine
¼ cup sugar

Mix graham cracker crumbs, melted butter and sugar together. Press into two 9-inch pie plates.

Blend enough strawberries
  to make 1 cup
1 pkg. (8 oz.) cream cheese

Blend strawberries and cream cheese together until smooth.

1 can (14 oz.) sweetened
  condensed milk
1 container (8 oz.) frozen
  whipped topping, thawed

Stir condensed milk into strawberry mixture. Fold in whipped topping. Spread evenly into two prepared pie shells. Cover with plastic wrap and freeze several hours or overnight.

YIELD   2 PIES, 8 SERVINGS EACH

This dessert can be made in a 9 x 13 - inch baking dish.

Lilly Riegsecker
Goshen, IN

Fudge Cream Roll

This is a little-fuss dessert that is very quick to assemble.
It is great for a picnic or child's birthday party.

2 cups whipping cream
¼ cup powdered sugar
30 crisp round chocolate wafers

In a mixing bowl, whip cream with powdered sugar until stiff. Spread a spoonful on a cookie. Place another cookie on top. Continue until there are 6 piles of 5 cookies with whipped cream in between. Lay piles end to end on serving platter. Cover the roll evenly with remaining whipped cream. Chill for 6 hours or longer. Cut diagonally into slices for serving.

YIELD   10 TO 12 SERVINGS

Toastie Ice Cream Dessert

*This was one of the family favorites from the days when my girls were
still at home. We tried to have one in the freezer at all times during hot weather.*

1 cup flaked coconut
1/2 cup slivered almonds
1 1/2 cups crisp rice cereal
1/4 cup brown sugar
1/4 cup butter or margarine, melted

1 1/2 quarts vanilla ice cream, softened

*Toast coconut and almonds in 300°
oven for 15 minutes. In a mixing bowl,
combine coconut, almonds, cereal and
brown sugar. Stir in melted butter and
mix well. Spread one-half of mixture in
bottom of a 9 x 13 - inch pan.*

*Spoon softened ice cream over
bottom layer. Sprinkle remaining crust
mixture on top; freeze.*

*To serve, cut into squares and garnish
with your choice of topping.*

YIELD   12 TO 15 SERVINGS

TOPPING CHOICES
Saskatoon or Blueberry pie filling,
    page 180

Cherry pie filling

Butterscotch or Chocolate sauce,
    page 17

Fresh sweetened strawberries
    or raspberries

Napoleon or Vanilla Slice

There was one bakery in our city that made a decadent creation called Vanilla Slice or Napoleon. Delicate puff pastry was layered with a rich cream filling. A pastel pink icing with a swirl of chocolate covered the top. For special occasions it was the ultimate treat. This homemade presentation is equally delightful.

1 pkg. (17¼ oz.) frozen
  puff pastry sheets, thawed

Follow instructions on package for thawing pastry. Cut each pastry sheet with sharp knife or cutter into thirds length-wise and fourths cross-wise. Place on ungreased baking sheets. Bake in preheated 400° oven for 15 to 18 minutes or until golden brown and puffed. Cool on wire rack.

½ cup sugar
2 tbsp. cornstarch
2 tsp. all-purpose flour
¼ tsp. salt
3 egg yolks
2 cups milk
1 tbsp. butter
1 tsp. vanilla

In medium saucepan, combine sugar, cornstarch, flour and salt. Blend egg yolks and milk together with whisk. Strain through a sieve into sugar mixture and stir to blend. Cook over medium heat, stirring constantly, until mixture thickens and boils. Boil and stir 1 minute. Remove from heat; whisk in butter and vanilla. Place plastic wrap directly onto surface of cooked mixture and chill thoroughly.

½ cup whipping cream
2 tbsp. powdered sugar

Whip cream and powdered sugar together until stiff. Add to cool cream filling and beat until smooth. Refrigerate until ready to use, up to 2 days.

2 cups powdered sugar
¼ tsp. vanilla
2 to 3 tbsp. boiling water
Pink food coloring, optional

In a mixing bowl, combine powdered sugar and vanilla. Add enough boiling water until mixture is of spreading consistency. Stir in food coloring.

Chocolate wafers, melted

To serve, separate each pastry into 2 layers. Spread cream filling between layers. Gently top the filled Napoleons with a coating of vanilla icing. Drizzle pastries with melted chocolate.

YIELD 24 NAPOLEONS

Baked, unfilled pastry may be frozen in airtight containers for up to 6 weeks.

Baked, filled pastries are best enjoyed the day they are made; and don't refrigerate well.

Fruit Trifle

This scrumptious layered treat looks great on a buffet table.
Use your favorite fruit or any combination you prefer.

3½ cups fruit, such as raspberries and blueberries, strawberries, hulled and quartered

Prepare your choice of fruit.

Cream filling, page 241

Prepare 1 recipe cream filling; refrigerate to chill.

3 eggs, at room temperature
½ cup sugar
½ tsp. vanilla

In medium bowl, beat eggs and sugar together until eggs are light and lemon-colored, about 6 to 8 minutes. Beat in vanilla.

2 tbsp. butter or margarine melted

Stir ½ cup egg mixture into melted butter until combined; set aside.

½ cup all-purpose flour
¼ tsp. salt

Blend flour and salt; sprinkle over egg mixture and gently fold in until mixed. Fold melted butter mixture into batter just until blended.

Grease bottom and sides of 9 x 13 - inch rimmed baking pan; line with parchment paper. Spread batter into pan, gently spreading to the edges. Bake in preheated 350° oven for 20 to 25 minutes or until wooden pick inserted in center comes out clean.
Loosen side of cake with a knife; invert onto a sheet of parchment paper. Let cake cool completely; peel off parchment paper. Cut into 1-inch squares.

TO ASSEMBLE TRIFLE
Layer one third each, cake squares, fruit and cream filling in 8-cup trifle dish or glass bowl. Repeat layering to make a total of 3 layers. Cover with plastic wrap and refrigerate for at least 6 hours and up to 24 hours.

1 cup whipping cream
¼ cup powdered sugar
¼ tsp. vanilla

Place all ingredients in bowl and beat together until stiff. Pipe or spread whipped cream over trifle when ready to serve. Garnish with fruit if desired.

YIELD   6 TO 8 SERVINGS

Summer Fruit Platter

Try a refreshingly cool summer dessert, picture-pretty and simply delicious! This recipe lists choices of fruit but you can create your own rainbow of fresh fruit in season. A small amount of white chocolate in the filling adds flavor and sets the filling as well.

3/4 cup butter, softened
1/2 cup powdered sugar
1 1/2 cups all-purpose flour

In a mixing bowl, cream together butter and sugar. Gradually add flour; mix well.

Press onto bottom and up side of ungreased 11-inch tart pan or a 12-inch pizza pan with sides. Bake in preheated 300° oven for 25 to 30 minutes or until lightly browned.

1 pkg. (8 oz.) cream cheese, softened
1/2 cup whipping cream, whipped
1 square (1 oz.) white chocolate, melted

In a mixing bowl, beat cream cheese until light. Add whipped cream and melted chips; beat until smooth. Spread over crust. Chill for 30 minutes.

1 can (20 oz.) pineapple chunks
1 pint strawberries, halved
1 can (11 oz.) mandarin oranges, drained
3 fresh peaches, peeled and sliced
2 kiwi, peeled and sliced

Drain pineapple, reserving 1/2 cup juice; set juice aside. Arrange strawberry halves and oranges around the edge of pastry shell. Place peaches in a circle next to strawberries. Mound pineapple in the center and then arrange circle of overlapping kiwi slices.

1/2 cup sugar
2 tbsp. cornstarch
1/4 tsp. salt
1 cup orange juice
1/4 cup lemon juice
1/2 cup pineapple juice
1/2 tsp. grated orange rind
1/2 tsp. grated lemon rind

In a saucepan, combine sugar, cornstarch and salt. Stir in orange, lemon and reserved pineapple juice. Cook over medium heat, stirring constantly, until mixture thickens and boils. Boil and stir for 1 minute. Remove from heat and stir in orange and lemon rind. Cool. Spoon sauce over the fruit. Chill 1 hour. Cut into wedges and serve. Store in the refrigerator.

YIELD   12 TO 14 SERVINGS

Spring Fruit Cobbler

This delightful combination was discovered during one of the Springtimes
of my youth and its seasonal goodness has never diminished.
It is chock-full of berries and rhubarb topped with a tender crust.

4 cups cut-up fresh or frozen rhubarb
  (1/2 inch pieces)
1 box (10 oz.) frozen strawberries
  (about 1 1/2 cups including juice)
3/4 cup sugar
2 tbsp. instant cooking tapioca

Heat oven to 350° degrees. Mix
rhubarb, strawberries, sugar and
tapioca together thoroughly. Let stand
for 10 minutes. Pour fruit mixture into
well buttered 9 x 13 - inch glass baking
dish. Heat in oven until bubbly, about
25 to 30 minutes, before adding
topping.

1 1/2 cups all-purpose flour
1/2 cup sugar
2 1/2 tsp. baking powder
1/4 tsp. salt
3/4 cup milk
1/3 cup melted butter or margarine

Measure flour, sugar, baking powder
and salt into bowl. Add milk and
melted butter; mix all together stirring
just until blended. Drop by spoonfuls
onto hot fruit mixture. Continue baking
for 25 to 30 minutes or until golden
brown. Delicious served warm with a
scoop of ice cream.

YIELD   8 TO 10 SERVINGS

Raspberry Peach Cobbler

Warm and saucy fruit cobbler
topped with a dollop of ice cream is nostalgic from way back.
Perfection comes when dumplings are dropped onto hot fruit mixture before baking.
Even when fresh fruit is not in season, you can enjoy a bubbly hot cobbler.

1 cup all-purpose flour
1/2 cup sugar
1 tsp. baking powder
1/4 tsp. salt
1 egg, beaten
3/4 cup sour cream
2 tbsp. butter or margarine, melted

In mixing bowl combine flour, sugar, baking powder and salt. Combine egg, sour cream, and butter; stir into flour mixture blending well. Set mixture aside.

1/3 cup sugar
2 tbsp. cornstarch
dash salt
3 to 4 cups sliced fresh or frozen
   peaches (slightly sweetened)

In saucepan combine sugar, cornstarch, and salt. Stir in peaches. Cook over medium heat, stirring constantly until mixture thickens and bubbles. Pour into ungreased 9 x 13 - inch glass baking dish.

1 cup fresh or frozen red raspberries

Sprinkle raspberries evenly on top of peach mixture.

Drop dough from a tablespoon onto hot fruit mixture, making small even mounds. Bake in preheated 350° oven for 25 to 30 minutes or until biscuit topping is golden brown. Serve warm with ice cream, if desired.

VARIATIONS

YIELD   6 TO 8 SERVINGS

FRESH CHERRY COBBLER:
4 cups pitted fresh red tart cherries, 1 1/4 cups sugar, 3 tbsp. cornstarch, 1/4 tsp. almond extract.
Use method above to prepare filling.

FRESH BLUEBERRY COBBLER:
4 cups fresh blueberries, 1/2 cup sugar, 1 tbsp. cornstarch, 1 tsp. lemon juice.
Use method above to prepare filling.

Graham Cracker Chiffon

Cool, light, and fluffy, this vanilla treat is just the right finish to a rich meal.

1 cup graham cracker crumbs
3 tbsp. melted butter or margarine
2 tbsp. sugar

Combine crumbs, melted butter and sugar. Sprinkle half of crumbs on bottom of 9 x 9 - inch baking pan. Reserve remaining crumbs.

1 cup milk
1/2 cup sugar
2 egg yolks, slightly beaten

In a medium saucepan, blend together milk, sugar and egg yolks. Cook over moderate heat, stirring constantly, until slightly thickened.

1 envelope unflavored gelatin
1/2 cup cold water

Soften gelatin in cold water. Add to hot mixture and stir until smooth. Chill until mixture begins to thicken but not set.

2 egg whites
1 cup whipping cream, whipped
1 tsp. vanilla

Beat egg whites until soft peaks form. Fold whipped cream, vanilla and beaten egg whites into chilled mixture. Spread over crumbs in prepared pan. Sprinkle reserved crumbs over top. Chill in refrigerator for several hours or until set.

YIELD   6 TO 8 SERVINGS

Creamy Vanilla Dessert

The cooked pudding in this dessert sets it apart from the
instant kind and tastes made from scratch.
With a change of flavors, it can be altered to any number of pleasing variations.

1 ½ cups all-purpose flour
½ cup butter or margarine
½ cup chopped pecans

Mix flour, butter and nuts together until crumbly. Press into a 9 x 13 - inch baking pan. Bake in 350° oven for 10 to 15 minutes. Cool.

1 pkg. (8 oz.) cream cheese, softened
¾ cup powdered sugar
1 carton (12 oz.) frozen whipped topping,
  thawed

Beat cream cheese and powdered sugar together until smooth. Blend in 1 cup topping and spread over cooled crust.

2 pkgs. vanilla pudding (not instant)
  (4 serving size)
3 cups milk

Cook pudding as directed on package using 3 cups milk. As pudding cools, press plastic wrap on pudding to prevent skin from forming. When cool, spread over cream cheese layer. Spread remaining whipped topping over pudding layer.

Garnish options: toasted chopped pecans, shaved chocolate, toasted coconut.

VARIATIONS
Substitute your choice of pudding flavor – chocolate, butterscotch, lemon, coconut cream, etc. for the vanilla pudding. Select garnish to complement pudding flavor.

YIELD   15 SERVINGS

Caramel Butterfinger Dessert

A crumb crust with a lightened layer of caramel pudding is a
cool dessert at summer picnics or family get-togethers.
I have made it for countless potluck meals and seldom had any left over.

1 1/2 cups graham cracker crumbs
1/4 cup melted butter or margarine
3 tbsp. sugar

*Combine crumbs, butter and sugar.
Press into ungreased 9 x 13 - inch
baking pan.*

2 pkgs. vanilla instant pudding mix
   (4 serving size)
1 pkg. caramel or butterscotch instant
   pudding mix (4 serving size)
3 cups milk

*Beat pudding mix and milk together on
low speed for 2 minutes.*

3 cups vanilla ice cream, softened

*Add ice cream to pudding mixture and
beat until smooth. Spread over graham
cracker layer. Cover and chill
thoroughly in fridge until set, 6 hours
or overnight.*

1 cup whipping cream
1/4 cup powdered sugar
1/2 tsp. vanilla
   OR 1 carton (8 oz.) frozen whipped
   topping, thawed

*Whip cream, sugar and vanilla until
stiff. Spread over second layer.*

1 Butterfinger candy bar
   OR Skor candy bar

*Grate candy bar and sprinkle over top.
Refrigerate leftovers.*

YIELD   12 TO 15 SERVINGS

When I was growing up, I had the pleasure of relating to a lovely and gracious lady who was a family friend. As homesteaders, she and her family came to Alberta from Missouri and we had the good fortune to be close neighbors. I remember watching with wonder as Mabel prepared a double recipe of angel food cake to be baked in a large round pan with a tumbler secured in the center for the funnel. I was never brave enough to try it. But I often made her plain but intensely flavored lemon loaf. I like it as well now as I did then.

Frosted Lemon Tea Loaf

½ cup butter or margarine, softened
1 cup sugar
2 eggs

In a mixing bowl, cream butter and sugar until fluffy. Add eggs and continue beating until light.

1½ cups all-purpose flour
1 tsp. baking powder
¼ tsp. salt
Grated peel of 1 lemon
½ cup milk

Blend together flour, baking powder, salt and peel. Stir into creamed mixture alternately with milk, beating after each addition until batter is smooth.

Grease bottom only of one 9 x 5 - inch or two 8 x 4 - inch loaf pans. Divide batter evenly between 8-inch pans or pour into 9-inch pan. Bake 8-inch loaves in 350° oven for 45 to 50 minutes, 9-inch loaf for 55 to 60 minutes or until wooden pick inserted in center comes out clean.

Juice of 1 lemon
½ cup sugar

Mix lemon juice and sugar; pour evenly over loaf when taken from hot oven. Cool thoroughly before removing from pan. Loosen sides of loaf from pan; remove from pan and place on wire rack. Cool completely before slicing.

YIELD   10 TO 12 SERVINGS

Berry Coffee Cake

This is an inviting brunch or luncheon treat that can be made with a variety of berry pie fillings. In Alberta, the native Saskatoon berry would be my favorite, naturally!

1½ cups sugar
1 cup butter or margarine, softened
4 eggs
1 tsp. vanilla
½ tsp. almond extract

In large mixing bowl, combine sugar, butter, eggs, and flavorings. Beat with electric mixer at low speed until mixed. Beat at high speed for an additional 3 minutes until smooth.

3 cups all-purpose flour
1½ tsp. baking powder
¼ cup milk
2 cans (19 oz.) cherry pie filling
   OR Saskatoon or Blueberry
   pie filling, page 180

Blend dry ingredients; stir into creamed mixture with milk. Spread 2/3 batter on greased 10 x 15 - inch baking pan. Top with cherry pie filling. Drop remaining batter by teaspoonfuls on top of pie filling.

Bake in preheated 350° oven for 30 to 35 minutes or until lightly golden brown. Cool for 15 minutes and drizzle with icing glaze.

Great on its own, but you can also serve warm, with ice cream or whipped cream.

YIELD   20 SERVINGS

Icing Glaze

1 cup powdered sugar
2 tbsp. milk

Blend until smooth and of drizzling consistency, adding more milk if necessary.

Glazed Pineapple Squares

Many years ago, a dear neighbor lady shared a pan of these
delectable squares with me and the recipe has been in my collection ever since.
The pastry crust includes yeast and a rising period, yet they are
not difficult to make. Wonderful with a cup of coffee or tea!

Filling

3/4 cup sugar
1/4 cup cornstarch
1 can (20 oz.) crushed pineapple,
   undrained

*Mix sugar and cornstarch in heavy
saucepan. Stir in crushed pineapple.
Cook over medium heat, stirring
constantly until thickened. Cool.*

Crust

1 pkg. dry yeast (1 tbsp.)
1/4 cup lukewarm water
1 tsp. sugar

*Measure water and sugar into bowl;
sprinkle with yeast. Let stand until
bubbly.*

4 cups all-purpose flour
1/4 tsp. salt
1 cup butter or margarine
2/3 cup warm milk
4 egg yolks

*Mix flour and salt; cut in butter using
pastry blender or food processor. Add
yeast, milk and egg yolks. Mix together
until dough is formed. Divide dough in
half. Roll bottom pastry directly in
10 x 15 - inch rimmed baking pan.
Spread with pineapple filling.*

*For top crust, outline 10 x 15 - inch
rectangle on sheet of waxed paper.
Turn paper over, dust lightly with flour
and roll pastry to fit outline. Cut slits in
uniform diagonal pattern. Carefully turn
pastry over pineapple layer and
remove waxed paper. Press lightly to
seal edges around pan.*

1 egg white
1/2 cup chopped pecans

*Brush top with slightly beaten egg
white; sprinkle with nuts. Cover and let
rise in warm place for 1 1/2 hours.*

*Bake in preheated 350° oven for 30
minutes or until golden brown. While
still warm drizzle with a glaze.*

1 cup powdered sugar
2 tbsp. milk

*Blend powdered sugar and milk until
smooth and of drizzling consistency.*

YIELD   24 SERVINGS

Saskatoon Custard Kuchen

This scrumptious German treat or 'Kuchen' has a shortbread crust topped with a berry-infused custard. Simple to prepare using your favorite berries, it is ideal for a brunch or special dessert.

1 1/4 cups all-purpose flour
1/2 tsp. salt
1/2 cup butter or margarine
2 tbsp. whipping cream

1/2 cup sugar
1/2 cup all-purpose flour
3 cups fresh or frozen saskatoons

1/2 cup sugar
1 tbsp. all-purpose flour
2 eggs, beaten
1 cup whipping cream
1 tsp. vanilla

Pictured on page 181.

VARIATIONS
Use fresh or frozen raspberries or blueberries in place of saskatoon berries.

In a mixing bowl, combine flour and salt. Cut in butter with pastry blender or food processor until mixture is crumbly. Stir in cream; pat into greased 9 x 13 - inch baking pan.

Combine sugar and flour; sprinkle over crust. Arrange berries over flour mixture.

Combine sugar and flour. Stir in eggs, cream and vanilla; pour over berries. Bake at 350° for 45 to 50 minutes or until lightly browned. Serve warm or chilled. Store in refrigerator.

YIELD   10 TO 12 SERVINGS

White Chocolate Mousse

The French word 'mousse' means foam, which describes its
smooth and spongy quality. Layered with fruit in tall stemmed glasses,
it is a beautiful and light dessert or parfait.

1 square (1 oz.) white chocolate, melted
1 pkg. (3 oz.) cream cheese, softened

*Blend chocolate and cream cheese
together until well blended.*

1 cup whipping cream
2 tbsp. powdered sugar
1/2 tsp. vanilla

*Place whipping cream, powdered
sugar and vanilla in small mixing bowl.
Set bowl and beater into freezer until
thoroughly chilled. Beat until stiff; add
chocolate mixture and beat together.*

Fresh fruit

*Layer mousse into clear bowls or tall
glasses with fresh fruit ... raspberries,
strawberries, blueberries...
Serve immediately.*

Karen Hochstetler
Napanee, IN

Cookies

Cookies

Christmas

Almond Apricot Toasties

My love for apricots prompted me to adapt a recipe to my liking and it became an instant favorite. Whenever I sent a special 'care' package to my girls after they moved away, these were the pick. A batch of this snappy cookie is always in the freezer when they come home to visit.

1 cup butter or margarine, softened
1/2 cup brown sugar, packed
1/2 cup white sugar
1 egg, beaten
1 tsp. vanilla
1/4 tsp. almond extract

In mixing bowl, cream butter and sugars together. Add egg and flavorings and continue to beat until fluffy.

2 cups all-purpose flour
2 tsp. baking powder
1/2 tsp. salt
1 1/2 cups coconut
1 cup dried apricots, chopped
(see note)

Blend dry ingredients and stir into creamed mixture. Add coconut and apricots; mix well. Form into 1-inch balls and place 2 inches apart on greased cookie sheets. Flatten balls slightly with a fork.

Whole almonds, toasted

Top each cookie with whole toasted almond. Bake at 350° for 12 to 15 minutes or until lightly golden.

YIELD   ABOUT 4 DOZEN COOKIES

NOTE
Chop apricots in food processor together with a spoonful of the measured flour to keep the fruit from sticking to the blade.

Cookie Grandmother

Any child who does not have a country grandmother who keeps a cookie jar is as much to be pitied as one who grows up without a pet. If it is impossible for a grandmother to live in or move to the country, solely to insure the proper spiritual start for coming generations, at least it is possible to have a cookie jar.

Marjorie Kinnan Rawlings, Cross Creek Cookery, 1942

Amish Church Cookies

It was a wonderful day in our tasting experience when 'Grandma Minnie' served these cookies during a visit to Indiana. These soft cookies are traditionally served to children during the lengthy Amish church services, hence the name. Over the years I have offered them to many guests who in turn have shared their appreciation for one of our family's favorite cookies. One of my recipients declares they are "the best cookie" she has ever eaten. My grandson, Brendan, adores them as he does any cookie with icing.

1 cup butter or margarine, softened
1 2/3 cups granulated sugar
2 eggs, beaten
1 tsp. vanilla

In a mixing bowl, cream butter and sugar together thoroughly. Add beaten eggs and vanilla; continue beating until fluffy.

5 cups all-purpose flour
2 tsp. baking powder
1 tsp. baking soda
1 cup milk

Blend dry ingredients and add to creamed mixture alternately with milk. Chill until firm or overnight.

Divide dough in half and roll out on lightly floured surface to 3/8 inch thickness. Cut with a 3-inch round cookie cutter. Place on lightly greased baking sheet. Bake at 350° for 10 to 12 minutes or until edge is slightly golden. The tops should not be browned or cookies will be dry. Ice cookies with a glaze.

Glaze

2 1/2 cups powdered sugar
2 to 3 tbsp. milk

Blend powdered sugar with milk until spreading consistency. If icing is too stiff, stir in a few drops of milk.

YIELD   ABOUT 2 1/2 DOZEN 3-INCH COOKIES

Minnie Yoder
Goshen, IN

NOTE
These cookies freeze well; however it is best to freeze them in single layers on a cookie sheet before stacking in freezer container. This prevents iced cookies from sticking together.

Pictured on page 91.

White Chocolate Macadamia Cookies

White chocolate and macadamia nuts are a delightful combination in these buttery morsels.

1 cup butter or margarine, softened
2 tbsp. milk
3/4 cup brown sugar, packed
1/2 cup granulated sugar
1 egg
1 1/2 tsp. vanilla

Cream butter and milk together until well blended. Add sugars, egg and vanilla; continue beating until fluffy.

2 cups all-purpose flour
1 tsp. baking soda
1/2 tsp. salt
1 white chocolate bar,
   cut into chunks (6 oz.)
1 cup macadamia nuts, coarsely
   chopped and toasted

Combine flour, soda and salt; add to creamed mixture; mix well. Stir in white chocolate and nuts. Drop the dough by rounded teaspoonfuls 2 inches apart onto ungreased cookie sheet.

Bake at 375° for 8 to 10 minutes or until edges are lightly browned. Cool one minute on baking sheet; remove to wire rack.

YIELD   ABOUT 4 DOZEN 2-INCH COOKIES

VARIATION
Add 1/2 cup dried cranberries and 1/2 cup shredded coconut to the dough. Use pecans for the nuts.

Soft Ginger Cookies

Crisp on the outside and chewy on the inside,
these cookies are wonderfully flavored with ginger.
Beverly makes these as a special treat for her husband Marcus.

2 cups sugar
1⅓ cups vegetable oil
2 eggs
½ cup molasses

In mixing bowl, beat together sugar, oil, eggs and molasses.

4 cups all-purpose flour
4 tsp. baking soda
1 tbsp. ground ginger
2 tsp. cinnamon
1 tsp. salt
Additional sugar

Combine flour, soda, ginger, cinnamon and salt. Add to the creamed mixture; mix well.

Roll into 1 inch balls, then roll in sugar. Place 2 inches apart on ungreased or parchment-lined baking sheets. Flatten slightly with a glass tumbler.

Bake at 350° for 10 to 12 minutes or until puffy and lightly browned. Cool in pan for 1 to 2 minutes. Remove to wire racks to cool.

YIELD   ABOUT 4 DOZEN COOKIES

DIPPED GINGER COOKIES
1 pkg. (12 oz.) vanilla baking chips
1 tbsp. vegetable oil

Melt vanilla chips with oil in a saucepan over low heat. Dip one third of cookie into chocolate; shake off excess. Place on waxed paper to harden.

Ultimate Chocolate Chip Cookies

This outstanding chocolate chip cookie is deliciously soft and chewy.
Together with a glass of cold milk,
my granddaughter Kyrie thinks this is the ultimate cookie experience.

1 cup butter or margarine, softened
1 cup brown sugar
1 cup white sugar
2 eggs
1 tsp. vanilla

In a mixing bowl, cream butter and sugars together until fluffy. Add eggs and vanilla; beat until creamy.

3 cups all-purpose flour
1 tsp. salt
1 tsp. baking soda
2 tbsp. hot water

Blend flour and salt; dissolve soda in hot water. Add to creamed mixture; mix well.

2 cups milk chocolate chips
1 cup coarsely chopped pecans

Stir in chocolate chips and nuts. Drop by teaspoonfuls 2 inches apart onto lightly greased baking sheets. Flatten slightly with a glass tumbler.

Bake at 350° for 10 to 12 minutes for chewy cookies. They will look light and moist - DO NOT OVERBAKE. Cool on baking sheet for 2 minutes. Remove to wire racks to cool completely.

YIELD   ABOUT 5 DOZEN COOKIES

Chocolate Toffee Munchie

The delightful mix of chocolate, toffee and pecans
turns out a stunningly good cookie.

Make cookie dough as above except replace the 2 cups chocolate chips with the following:

1 cup milk chocolate chips
2 cups white chocolate chips
1/2 cup English toffee bits

Rana's Sugar Cookies

Cut with a heart-shaped cookie cutter, these are my special treat on Valentine's Day. After they are iced, each one is topped with a cinnamon heart for color and to add some zing. I have also made these cookies in the shape of an oval and decorated them with pastel-colored butter icing using my smallest flower and leaf tips.

1 cup butter or margarine, softened
1½ cups powdered sugar
1 egg
1 tsp. vanilla
½ tsp. almond extract

In a mixing bowl, combine butter, sugar, egg and flavorings; beat together thoroughly.

2½ cups all-purpose flour
1 tsp. baking soda
1 tsp. cream of tartar

Blend dry ingredients and add to creamed mixture until well blended. Cover and chill 2 to 3 hours.

Divide dough in half. Roll each half ¼ inch thick on lightly floured surface or parchment paper. Cut into desired shapes and place on lightly greased baking sheet. Bake at 375° for 7 to 8 minutes or until light brown on edge.

When cool spread with a quick white icing.

2 cups powdered sugar
2 to 3 tbsp. milk

Measure powdered sugar into bowl; moisten with milk to spreading consistency.

*YIELD   ABOUT 5 DOZEN
2 TO 2½-INCH COOKIES*

Cookie cutters come in a wonderful array of shapes and sizes.
You can find one to suit almost any occasion.
At my niece's wedding, heart-shaped cookies served as the placecards.
A fun group of ladies gathered to form a decorating bee after I baked them.
When the icing was dry, my friend Eva and I wrote the names using
paintbrushes and food coloring. I packed them in
single layers in new shallow boxes and froze them until the big day.

Cinnamon Nut Rugelach

Tender cream cheese pastry is the base for these rolled and stuffed cookies.
Their tight curls can contain a variety of sweet fillings.

1 cup butter, softened
1 pkg. (8 oz.) cream cheese, softened
2 cups all-purpose flour
1/4 cup sugar

In a mixing bowl or food processor, beat butter and cream cheese together until well blended. Add flour and sugar; combine with your hands or pulse in food processor to form a dough.

Divide dough into four portions. Shape each portion into a 1-inch-thick circle. Wrap tightly in plastic wrap and refrigerate for 4 hours or overnight.

1/2 cup sugar
1 tbsp. cinnamon
3/4 cup finely chopped walnuts or pecans
1/4 cup melted butter

Mix together sugar, cinnamon and nuts; set aside. On a lightly floured surface, roll one portion of dough into a 10-inch circle. Brush with 1 tablespoon melted butter; sprinkle evenly with 1/4 of the walnut mixture. Cut circle into 12 pie-shaped wedges. Beginning at the wide edge, roll up tightly, finishing with the point in the middle.

Place point side down, on parchment-lined cookie sheet; curve roll slightly to form a crescent. Repeat with remaining dough.

VARIATIONS

RASPBERRY HAZELNUT RUGELACH
In a small bowl, mix together 1/2 cup raspberry jam and 1/2 cup finely chopped toasted hazelnuts. Spread over circle after brushing with butter. Sprinkle lightly with sugar. Proceed as above.

APRICOT ALMOND RUGELACH
In a small bowl, mix together 1/2 cup finely chopped slivered toasted almonds, 1/2 cup shredded coconut and 1/4 cup sugar. Brush each circle of dough with 2 tablespoons apricot jam. Sprinkle with 1/4 of the almond mixture. Proceed as above.

Bake in preheated 350° oven for 25 to 30 minutes or until delicately browned. Remove from cookie sheet and cool on wire rack.

YIELD   4 DOZEN COOKIES

Pictured on page 287.

Apricot Cream Cheese Drops

Apricot jam gives these cookies just the right amount of flavor and sweetness.
They are soft and taste like little cakes while still warm from the oven.

1/2 cup butter or margarine
1 pkg. (3 oz.) cream cheese, softened
1 tbsp. milk
1/4 cup firmly packed brown sugar
1/2 cup apricot jam
   OR apricot compote, page 272

In medium mixing bowl, cream butter, cream cheese and milk until well blended. Add brown sugar and apricot jam; continue beating until smooth.

1 1/4 cups all-purpose flour
1 1/2 tsp. baking powder
1/4 tsp. salt
1/4 tsp. almond extract
1/2 cup coarsely chopped pecans, toasted

Blend flour, baking powder and salt. Add to creamed mixture with flavoring and mix until well blended. Stir in nuts. Drop dough by rounded tablespoonfuls 2 inches apart onto greased baking sheet.

Bake at 350° for 14 minutes. Cool on baking sheet one minute. Remove to cooling rack. Cool completely before frosting.

Frosting

2 oz. cream cheese, softened
2 tbsp. butter or margarine, softened
1/4 cup apricot jam
1 cup powdered sugar
Finely chopped pecans, toasted

In small mixing bowl, beat cream cheese and butter until smooth. Beat in apricot jam. Gradually add powdered sugar beating until smooth. Spread frosting over cooled cookies. Sprinkle finely chopped pecans over frosting, if desired.

VARIATIONS
Try peach or pineapple jam in place of apricot. Use flaked coconut in place of chopped pecans or a combination of both. Substitute toasted macadamia nuts in place of pecans.

YIELD   ABOUT 24 COOKIES

Oatmeal Macaroons

My father loved cookies and coffee. Fellow farmers and sales persons often made their way to the kitchen with him where cookies were always in good supply. Oatmeal cookies were among the preferred.

2 cups brown sugar
2 eggs
1 tsp. vanilla

In a mixing bowl, beat sugar, eggs and vanilla together until creamy.

1/2 cup margarine
1/2 cup shortening

Melt margarine and shortening; add to the creamed mixture. Beat together until fluffy.

2 cups all-purpose flour
2 1/2 tsp. baking powder
1 tsp. baking soda
1/4 tsp. salt

Blend dry ingredients and add to creamed mixture; mix well.

3 cups quick-cooking oats
1 cup shredded coconut

Stir in oats and coconut. Roll into balls and place on greased or parchment-lined cookie sheet. Flatten slightly with a fork.

Bake at 350° for 10 to 12 minutes. Cool on a wire rack.

YIELD   ABOUT 4 DOZEN COOKIES

Crispy Oat Drops

Loaded with a variety of tasty ingredients,
these cookies are energy-packed crunchers.

½ cup butter or margarine, softened
½ cup vegetable oil
½ cup granulated sugar
½ cup light brown sugar, packed
1 tsp. vanilla

In a large mixing bowl, cream butter, oil, sugars and vanilla together until fluffy.

2 eggs

Add eggs and beat well.

2 cups all-purpose flour
1 tsp. cream of tartar
½ tsp. baking soda
¼ tsp. salt

Blend dry ingredients and add to creamed mixture; mix well.

1 cup crisp rice cereal
½ cup quick-cooking oats
½ cup flaked coconut
½ cup milk chocolate chips
½ cup coarsely chopped pecans

Stir in cereal, oats, coconut, chips and pecans. Drop by heaping tablespoonfuls about 2 inches apart onto ungreased or parchment-lined cookie sheets.

Bake at 350° for 10 to 13 minutes or until lightly browned. Cool completely on wire racks.

YIELD   ABOUT 36 COOKIES

NOTE
For best results, do not refrigerate dough as rice cereal becomes soggy.

Crunchy Oatmeal Cookies

With so many choices, I find it impossible to have one favorite cookie.
For my mother, however, this was the only cookie to bake
and that loyalty remained to the last crumb. It is a great cookie!

1 cup butter or margarine, softened
1 cup white sugar
1 cup brown sugar
1 tsp. vanilla
2 eggs, well beaten

Cream butter, sugars and vanilla together until fluffy. Add eggs and beat well.

2 1/2 cups all-purpose flour
1 tsp. baking powder
1/2 tsp. baking soda
1/4 tsp. salt

Blend dry ingredients and add to creamed mixture. Mix well.

1 cup quick-cooking oats
1 cup crushed cornflakes
1 cup shredded coconut (optional)

Stir in oats, cornflakes and coconut. Form into balls and place on greased or parchment lined cookie sheet. Flatten slightly with a fork or glass. Bake at 350° for 10 to 12 minutes.

YIELD   ABOUT 4 DOZEN COOKIES

Frosted Viennese Drops

These dainty cookies are delicate, slightly sweet and topped with crisp meringue...
pretty enough for a party.

½ cup butter or margarine, softened
¼ cup sugar
1 egg yolk

In a mixing bowl, cream butter and sugar together. Beat the egg yolk until thick. Add to the creamed mixture, beating until fluffy.

1 ½ cups sifted cake flour
¼ tsp. salt
Apricot compote
  OR thick jam or jelly, any flavor

Blend flour and salt and gradually add to creamed mixture. Roll dough into 1-inch balls. Place on a greased or parchment-lined baking sheet about 1 inch apart. Make a deep indention in the center of each cookie.
Fill indention with jam or jelly.

1 egg white
2 tbsp. sugar
¼ cup chopped pecans (optional)

Beat egg white until glossy peaks form. Gradually add sugar and continue beating until stiff. Drop a spoonful of meringue over jam and sprinkle with nuts if desired. Bake at 325° for 15 minutes or until delicately browned.

YIELD   ABOUT 30 COOKIES

Dried Apricot Compote

This beautiful golden orange compote gives intense flavor to pastries
and can be used in any recipe calling for apricot jam.

1 cup dried apricots, coarsely chopped
½ tsp. grated lemon rind
2 cups water
1 cup sugar

In a heavy saucepan, combine apricots, lemon and water; bring to a boil. Add sugar and stir until dissolved. Reduce heat and simmer gently for 1½ hours.

Compote may be mashed lightly or processed to a smooth sauce. Store well covered in fridge or freezer for several months.

Whoopie Pies

These cake-like chocolate cookies are sandwiched together with a creamy filling.
Pop them frozen into a bag lunch for a perfect snack later on.
Try both filling suggestions and pick a favorite.

1 cup butter or margarine, softened
2 1/4 cups sugar
2 eggs
2 tsp. vanilla

Cream butter and sugar together until light and fluffy. Add eggs and vanilla and continue beating until smooth.

4 cups all-purpose flour
2/3 cup cocoa
1/2 tsp. salt
1 cup hot water
2 tsp. baking soda
1 cup buttermilk

Combine flour, cocoa and salt. Dissolve soda in hot water. Add dry ingredients to mixture alternately with water and buttermilk. Drop by large spoonfuls onto greased baking sheet.

Bake at 375° for 8 to 10 minutes or until almost no imprint remains when touched with finger. Remove to wire rack; cool completely.

Put cookies together in pairs with Creamy Filling OR Fluffy Custard Buttercream, page 226. Wrap each whoopie pie individually in plastic wrap. Refrigerate or freeze.

YIELD   ABOUT 3 DOZEN PIES

Creamy Filling

2 egg whites
1/4 cup all-purpose flour
1/4 cup milk
2 tsp. vanilla

In a mixing bowl, combine egg whites, flour, milk and vanilla; beat together thoroughly.

1 cup shortening (Crisco)
3 cups powdered sugar

Add to egg white mixture, beating until fluffy.

Kathy Yoder
Goshen, IN

Brownies

It is nice to have a trusted quick brownie recipe like this when you are in a hurry.

2 squares unsweetened chocolate, chopped (1 oz. each) OR 1/3 cup cocoa 1/3 cup butter or margarine	*In a small saucepan over low heat, melt chocolate and butter.*
1 cup sugar 2 eggs 1 tsp. vanilla	*In a mixing bowl, combine chocolate, sugar, eggs and vanilla; beat together thoroughly.*
2/3 cup all-purpose flour 1/2 tsp. baking powder 1/4 tsp. salt	*Blend dry ingredients and add to chocolate mixture.*
1 cup coarsely chopped pecans, toasted	*Stir in nuts.*
	Transfer batter into a greased 9 x 9 - inch baking pan. Bake in 350° oven for 20 to 25 minutes or until slight imprint remains when touched lightly with finger. Cool slightly and cut into squares. If desired, spread with Chocolate Icing before cutting.

YIELD   16 SQUARES

Chocolate Icing

1 square unsweetened chocolate OR 2 1/2 tbsp. cocoa 1 tbsp. butter or margarine 1 tbsp. milk	*In a small saucepan, melt chocolate and butter; add milk and stir to blend.*
1 cup powdered sugar	*Beat in about 1 cup powdered sugar, until icing is spreading consistency.*

Lemon Almond Bars

A pan of squares glistening with a fresh, tangy lemon filling is hard to resist.
Perfect to have on hand in the freezer.

2 cups all-purpose flour
1/3 cup powdered sugar
1/2 cup ground almonds
1 cup butter or margarine

In a mixing bowl, combine flour, sugar and almonds. Cut in butter until mixture is crumbly using a pastry blender or food processor. Press evenly into the bottom of greased 9 x 13 - inch pan. Bake in 350° oven for 15 minutes.

4 eggs
2 cups sugar
1/3 cup lemon juice, freshly squeezed
1/4 cup all-purpose flour
1 tsp. baking powder
1/4 tsp. salt

In mixing bowl, beat eggs until frothy. Add sugar and lemon juice, beating well. Blend flour, baking powder and salt; stir into eggs. Pour over baked crust.

Bake an additional 20 to 25 minutes or just until set. Cool completely, then cut into squares. Sprinkle with powdered sugar before serving. Squares keep well; covered and refrigerated up to 3 days or in freezer up to 1 month.

VARIATION
LIME ALMOND BARS
Substitute lime juice for lemon juice.

YIELD   24 TO 30 BARS

Citrus Almond Bars

Prepare crust and bake as Lemon Almond Bars above.

4 eggs
1 cup + 2 tbsp. sugar
1/3 cup fresh lemon juice
1/3 cup fresh orange juice
1 tsp. finely grated orange rind
1/4 cup all-purpose flour
1 tsp. baking powder
1/4 tsp. salt

Prepare citrus layer ingredients using method in above recipe. Pour over baked crust and continue with baking instructions in above recipe.

YIELD   24 TO 30 BARS

Deluxe Apricot Chews

Chewy and smooth layers combine to make this bar exceptional.
After the first taste it is hard to resist a second.

½ cup butter or margarine
1¼ cups all-purpose flour
½ cup brown sugar, packed

Mix butter, flour and brown sugar together until crumbly. Press into ungreased 9 x 9 - inch baking pan. Bake at 350° for 15 minutes.

2 eggs
¼ tsp. almond extract
⅓ cup all-purpose flour
1¼ cups sweetened condensed milk
½ cups slivered almonds
1⅓ cups flaked coconut
1 cup dried apricots, finely chopped*
  *see note, page 261

In small mixing bowl, beat eggs and flavoring until frothy. Add flour, condensed milk, almonds, coconut and apricots; stir well to mix. Spread over first layer. Bake at 350° for 30 minutes or until golden brown. Cool.

2 oz. cream cheese, softened
2 tbsp. butter or margarine, softened
1¼ cups powdered sugar

In small mixing bowl, beat cream cheese and butter until fluffy. Gradually add powdered sugar beating until smooth. Spread over cooled bars.

Slivered almonds, toasted (optional)

Sprinkle with toasted almonds if desired. Bars freeze well.

YIELD   *36 BARS (ABOUT 1½-INCH)*

Cheesecake Cream Squares

My daughter Karen and I made these lovely squares to serve at her wedding.
They could also celebrate a lesser occasion.
Top each piece with a piped rosette of pastel tinted cream cheese icing.
Or cut into squares and garnish with fresh strawberry halves.

1/3 cup butter or margarine, softened
1/3 cup brown sugar, packed
1 cup all-purpose flour
1/2 cup chopped pecans

Cream butter and sugar until fluffy. Add flour and nuts; blend until crumbly. Reserve 3/4 cup crumbs. Press remaining crumbs into 8 x 8 - inch lightly greased baking pan. Bake at 350° for 10 minutes.

1 pkg. (8 oz.) cream cheese, softened
1/4 cup + 2 tbsp. sugar
1 egg, beaten
2 tbsp. milk
1 tbsp. lemon juice
1/2 tsp. vanilla

Combine cream cheese and sugar; beat until smooth. Add remaining ingredients and mix well. Pour evenly over crust. Sprinkle with reserved crumbs. Continue baking for an additional 20 minutes or just until set. Cool and cut into squares. Keep refrigerated.

YIELD   25 SQUARES (ABOUT 1 1/2-INCH)

Ruth Ann Stelfox
Raymond, Alberta

Nanaimo Bars

There is a lot of speculation surrounding the origin of the famous
Nanaimo Bar treat, although little solid evidence exists.
The city of Nanaimo on Vancouver Island shares its namesake and offers a theory.
It is alleged that these homemade bars were sent to miners by their families as a
sweet treat to brighten their day. Whatever the case, Nanaimo bars are
offered in most restaurants and cafes throughout the city.

My first sampling happened during a high school home economics class.
It was Peggy's turn to bring a confection to have with tea. After the first bite,
I knew I had never tasted anything more wonderful. This is truly a Canadian classic.

½ cup butter or margarine ¼ cup sugar 5 tbsp. cocoa	*In a heavy saucepan, cook and stir butter, sugar and cocoa until melted.*
1 egg, beaten 1 tsp. vanilla	*Add beaten egg and vanilla; cook and stir until thickened.*
1¾ cups graham cracker crumbs ¾ cup flaked coconut ½ cup chopped walnuts	*Combine cooked mixture, crumbs, coconut and nuts. Press firmly into greased 9-inch square pan.*
¼ cup butter or margarine, softened 3 tbsp. milk 3 tbsp. vanilla instant pudding powder 2 cups powdered sugar 1 tsp. vanilla	*In a small mixing bowl, cream together butter, milk, pudding powder, powdered sugar and vanilla. Beat until light, spread over first layer in pan. Chill until firm.*
⅔ cup semi-sweet chocolate chips (or 4 squares semi-sweet chocolate) 2 tbsp. butter or margarine	*Melt chips and butter over low heat; cool. When cool but not set, spread evenly over second layer. Chill in refrigerator. Use a sharp knife to cut into squares.*

Pictured on page 211.

YIELD   36 BARS (ABOUT 1½-INCH)

Gala Apricot Cheesecake Squares

These squares require a block of time but they are not difficult to make.
I am very fond of apricots and almonds so I adapted these to a
cheesecake recipe and came up with an irresistible combination.

1 pkg. dry yeast (1 tbsp.)
1/4 cup warm water
1 tbsp. sugar

Dissolve yeast and sugar in warm water.

1 cup butter or margarine
2 1/2 cups all-purpose flour
1/2 tsp. salt
4 egg yolks, slightly beaten

In a large mixing bowl, cut butter into flour and salt using a pastry blender or food processor. Add yolks and yeast mixture; mix thoroughly. Divide dough in half. Roll out each half to fit a 9 x 13 - inch baking pan.

1 egg yolk
2 pkgs. (8 oz. each) cream cheese, softened
1 cup sugar
1 tsp. vanilla
1/4 tsp. almond extract

In small mixing bowl, beat egg yolk, cream cheese, sugar and flavorings until smooth.

1/3 to 1/2 cup apricot jam
   OR apricot compote, page 272

Line baking pan with bottom pastry. In small saucepan, over low heat, melt jam to spreading consistency. Brush jam over bottom pastry using pastry brush. Spread cream cheese filling over jam layer. Place top pastry over filling; press lightly to seal edges around pan.

1 egg white
1/2 cup sliced almonds, toasted

Brush top with slightly beaten egg white; sprinkle with nuts.

Cover and let rise in a warm place 1 1/2 hours. Bake at 350° for 30 to 35 minutes or until lightly browned. Cool.

3/4 cup powdered sugar
1 tbsp. milk

Blend until smooth and of drizzling consistency adding more milk if necessary. Drizzle over pastry and cut into squares. Keep refrigerated.

YIELD   24 SERVINGS

Chunky Pecan Pie Bars

These simple delicious bars have a tender shortbread crust
and capture the flavor of pecan pie.

Crust

1 ¼ cups all-purpose flour
3 tbsp. brown sugar
½ cup butter or margarine

Combine flour and sugar; cut in butter using a pastry blender or food processor until crumbly. Press into the bottom of a greased 9 x 9 - inch baking pan. Bake at 375° for 15 minutes.

Pecan Topping

2 eggs
½ cup brown sugar, packed
½ cup golden corn syrup
2 tbsp. butter or margarine, melted
1 tsp. vanilla
1 cup coarsely chopped pecans

In a medium mixing bowl, beat eggs lightly. Whisk in sugar, corn syrup, butter and vanilla; stir in pecans. Spread pecan mixture evenly on crust layer.

Bake an additional 15 to 20 minutes or until set and top is golden brown. Cool slightly in pan on wire rack; cut into bars. Cool completely. Cover and store in refrigerator.

VARIATION
Omit vanilla,
substitute 1 teaspoon rum extract

YIELD   25 BARS

Full O' Goodness Granola Bars

My daughter Beverly has this to say:
"When I first made these bars for my family, the smell of orange zest instantly took me back to my mother's kitchen. Mother discovered the recipe in a farm magazine and made the bars often because they were so good. My husband and boys love them and I try to always have some on hand or in the freezer for a quick snack."

1 3/4 cups all-purpose flour
1/2 cup skim milk powder
1 tsp. salt
1 tsp. baking soda

Stir together flour, skim milk powder, salt and soda.

1 1/2 cups brown sugar
3/4 cup butter or margarine
1/2 cup vegetable oil
2 eggs
1/4 cup corn syrup
1 1/2 tsp. grated orange rind
1 tsp. vanilla

In a mixing bowl, cream sugar, butter and oil together until fluffy. Beat in eggs, corn syrup, orange rind and vanilla. Mix in dry ingredients until well blended.

1/2 cup wheat germ
1 1/2 cups quick-cooking oats
3/4 cup shredded coconut
3/4 cup chopped nuts
1/3 cup sesame seeds

Stir together wheat germ, oats, coconut, nuts and sesame seeds. Stir into batter until well mixed. Spread mixture in greased 11 x 17-inch baking pan.

Bake at 350° for 20 to 25 minutes or until golden brown. Cut into bars while still slightly warm.

YIELD   35 BARS

NOTE
This is a large recipe and if you do not have a 11 x 17-inch pan, use two 9 x 13-inch pans. These bars freeze well.

Sesame Snap Wafers

Brimming with toasted seeds, these wafers have a crunchy snap
like the ones you buy. The fact they are homemade has a distinct appeal.

1/2 cup butter or margarine, softened 1 cup brown sugar, lightly packed 1 egg 1 tsp. vanilla	In a mixing bowl, cream butter and sugar together until fluffy. Add egg and vanilla; beat until creamy.
2/3 cup plus 2 tbsp. all-purpose flour 1/4 tsp. baking powder	Blend flour and baking powder. Add to creamed mixture until combined.
1 1/4 cups sesame seeds, toasted	Stir in seeds.
	Drop by teaspoonfuls 2 inches apart onto cookie sheet lined with parchment paper. Bake at 350° for 6 to 9 minutes or until lightly browned. Cool for 5 minutes on sheet, then transfer to rack and cool completely. Store in airtight container.

YIELD   ABOUT 36 WAFERS

NOTE
To toast sesame seeds, place in large ungreased shallow pan. Bake at 300° for 5 to 10 minutes, stirring often, until lightly golden. Watch carefully.

Pictured on page 91.

No~Bake Granola Bars

These sweet bars are a perfect picnic dessert or a quick snack anytime.
My daughter sent them with a youth group on a mission trip to Africa. One recipient
was quick to note quality and goodness were not compromised by distance.

4 1/2 cups crisp rice cereal
2 1/2 cups quick-cooking oats
1/2 cup graham cracker crumbs

Blend cereal, oats and graham crumbs. Turn into well-greased large mixing bowl.

3 tbsp. butter or margarine
1 pkg. (1 lb.) marshmallows
1/4 cup peanut butter
2 tbsp. vegetable oil
2 tbsp. honey
2 tbsp. corn syrup

In large saucepan melt butter, marshmallows, peanut butter, oil, honey and syrup.

1/2 cup chocolate chips
3/4 cup raisins
1/2 cup flaked coconut

Stir in chips, raisins and coconut. Pour over cereal mixture and mix until well blended. Grease 9 x 13 - inch baking pan or line with parchment paper. Transfer granola mixture into pan and pack lightly. Cool and cut into bars.

YIELD   15 TO 18 BARS

Reba Rhodes
Bridgewater, VA

NOTE
Since these bars freeze well, recipe can be doubled if desired. Press into a 13 x 17 - inch rimmed baking sheet.

Maple Granola Bars

Make as above except:
Omit corn syrup; substitute 2 tbsp. maple syrup.
Omit chocolate chips and raisins; substitute 3/4 cup dried cranberries and 1/2 cup slivered toasted almonds.

Chocolate Marshmallow Bars

These bars travel well and disappear quickly at potlucks and picnics.
Children especially enjoy this chewy snack.

½ cup butter or margarine, softened
¾ cup sugar
2 eggs
1 tsp. vanilla

In a mixing bowl, cream together butter and sugar. Add eggs and vanilla; continue to beat until fluffy.

¾ cup all-purpose flour
2 tbsp. cocoa powder
¼ tsp. baking powder
¼ tsp. salt
½ cup chopped pecans

Blend dry ingredients and add to creamed mixture; mix well. Stir in nuts. Spread into bottom of greased 9 x 13 - inch baking pan.

Bake at 350° for 15 to 20 minutes or until bars test done.

2 cups miniature marshmallows

Sprinkle marshmallows evenly over chocolate layer. Return to oven and bake an additional 3 minutes to melt. Cool.

1 cup milk chocolate chips
2 tbsp. butter or margarine
¾ cup peanut butter
2 cups crisp rice cereal

In a small saucepan, combine chocolate chips, butter and peanut butter. Cook and stir over low heat until chocolate is melted; remove from heat. Stir in rice cereal. Spread over bars. Chill; cut into bars.

YIELD   24 BARS

Rosettes

A teacher in grade school introduced me to these crisp, whimsically shaped
delicacies from Scandinavia. It was another of those defining moments in
my life when I tasted something totally out of the ordinary.
Surprisingly, they are not hard to make but you will need a rosette iron,
which is a metal mold attached to a rod and handle.

1 egg
1 tbsp. sugar
1/2 cup all-purpose flour
1/2 cup milk
1 tsp. vanilla

*In a mixing bowl, whisk together egg
and sugar. Add flour, milk and vanilla;
beat with an electric mixer until batter
is smooth.*

Oil for frying
  (use an oil that will not smoke at high
  temperatures, such as corn or peanut
  oil)

*Heat a rosette iron in preheated oil
(375°) for 30 seconds. Remove iron
from oil and briefly drain on paper
towels.*

*Dip the hot iron into batter, being
careful not to let the batter go over
the top edge. Immediately dip iron
into hot oil. Fry for 15 to 20 seconds
or till golden. Lift iron out of oil,
tipping slightly to drain.*

*Push rosette off with fork onto paper
towel on wire rack. Repeat with
remaining batter, reheating iron about
10 seconds each time. Sift powdered
sugar over cooled rosettes.*

YIELD   20 TO 25 ROSETTES

Pfefferneusse or Peppernuts

Peppernuts are traditional Christmas fare in Germany and wherever else in the
world there's a German community. Over 30 years ago a German friend introduced
me to these crisp, aromatic treats that pack a powerful flavor in a small size.
I knew instantly they would become my tradition as well.
Once a year I happily share this spicy love offering with family and friends.

1 cup butter or margarine, softened
1/2 cup sugar
1 cup corn syrup
1/2 cup molasses
1/2 cup boiling water
11/2 tsp. baking soda

Cream butter, sugar, syrup and
molasses. Add water and soda; mix
well.

6¼ cups all-purpose flour
1/2 tsp. ground ginger
1/2 tsp. ground cloves
1/2 tsp. cinnamon
1/2 tsp. ground anise
  (or 3 drops oil of anise)
1/4 tsp. salt

Blend flour and spices; add to
creamed mixture and mix thoroughly.
Shape about 1/2 cup of dough at a
time into rope the diameter of a
penny rolling back and forth on a
sheet of waxed paper. Roll each rope
onto 4-inch strip waxed paper, wrap
and place on a cookie sheet; freeze.
Continue with remaining dough;
freeze.

Sugar

When ready to bake, remove one
rope at a time from freezer and slice
into pennies. Toss 'penny cookies' in
sugar until coated. Place 1/2 inch
apart on slightly greased baking
sheet.

Bake at 350° for 10 to 12 minutes or
until golden brown. Remove and
spread on paper towels or heavy
brown paper to cool and crisp up.
When completely cool, store in
airtight container or freeze.

Pictured on page 287.

YIELD   ABOUT 8 CUPS PEPPERNUTS

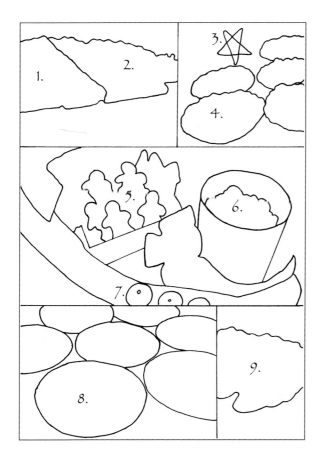

1. Coconut Cranberry Squares, page 292

2. Cherry Almond Squares, page 292

3. Chocolate Filigree Star, page 200

4. Raisin Butter Tarts, page 297

5. Gingerbread Children, page 291

6. Pfefferneusse or Peppernuts, page 286

7. Whipped Shortbread, page 290

8. Holly Berry Christmas Cookies, page 290

9. Apricot Almond Rugelach, page 267

Smor Krans (Butter Wreath)

This delicious buttery cookie recipe originates from a Norwegian friend
who made these festive little wreaths each Christmas season.

2 cups all-purpose flour
1 cup sugar
1 tsp. baking powder
1/8 tsp. salt
1 cup butter
1 large egg, beaten
1 tsp. vanilla

Measure flour, sugar, baking powder,
and salt into mixing bowl. Cut in
butter thoroughly using pastry blender
or a food processor. Add egg and
vanilla; mix thoroughly.

Fill cookie press and form into 2 1/4 -
inch wreaths on ungreased baking
sheet.

Red and green candied cherries

Decorate with red and green candied
cherries to resemble holly.

Bake at 375° for 6 to 9 minutes or
until set but not brown.

YIELD   ABOUT 3 DOZEN SMALL WREATHS

Jewish Shortbread

This petite portion of a cookie melts in your mouth
leaving a lingering hint of cinnamon.

1 cup butter (no substitute)
1/3 cup sugar
1 tsp. vanilla

Cream butter, sugar and vanilla
together until fluffy.

1 2/3 cups all-purpose flour
1/2 cup finely ground pecans
2 tsp. cinnamon
1/8 tsp. salt

Blend flour, nuts, cinnamon and salt.
Add to butter mixture and beat well.
Take a heaping teaspoon-sized
portion of dough and form it with
your hands to make a roll about 3
inches long. Curve it to make a
crescent and place on ungreased
baking sheet. Repeat with rest of
dough, spacing crescents well apart.
Bake at 325° for 15 to 18 minutes or

Powdered sugar

until firm. While still warm dredge in
powdered sugar.

YIELD   ABOUT 2 1/2 DOZEN COOKIES

Whipped Shortbread

There's nothing more inviting at holiday time
than a plate of handmade buttery shortbread cookies.

1 lb. butter (no substitute)	Beat butter until very light and fluffy.
1 cup powdered sugar 3 cups all-purposed flour	Gradually add sugar and flour and continue beating for 10 minutes. Chill dough until firm enough to handle.
Sliver balls (optional)	Roll dough into 1-inch balls and place on ungreased cookie sheet. Place silver ball in center of each cookie. Bake at 350° for 10 to 12 minutes or until set.

Pictured on page 287.

YIELD   ABOUT 3 DOZEN COOKIES

Holly Berry Christmas Cookies

These cookies received raves at a Christmas gathering.
They looked so festive and creative, guests thought the cook would also need to
be an artist. Not so; follow the simple directions and favor your guests with a little
masterpiece. Personalize them with a paintbrush and use them for place cards.

1 recipe Rana's Sugar Cookies, recipe page 266	Divide dough in half. On a lightly floured surface, roll out dough to 1/4 inch thickness. Cut with a 2-inch round cookie cutter. Place on lightly greased baking sheets. Bake at 375° for 7 to 8 minutes or until edges are lightly browned. Cool.
2 cups powdered sugar 2 tbsp. milk	In small mixing bowl, stir sugar and milk until smooth and spreading consistency. Ice cookies and decorate with red-hots before glaze is set. Allow to dry.
Green food coloring	Paint green holly leaves around the 'berries' using a small new paintbrush and food coloring.

Pictured on page 287.

Gingerbread Children

My grandsons love the great taste and novelty of eating cutout gingerbread boys.
My granddaughter Jodie orders gingerbread girls far in advance.
The dough is exceptionally easy to work with.

1 cup butter or margarine, softened
1 cup sugar

Cream butter and sugar together until fluffy.

1 cup molasses
1 tbsp. white vinegar

Heat molasses to almost boiling. Pour over butter mixture. Add vinegar, mixing well. Cool to lukewarm.

1 egg, beaten

Stir in beaten egg.

4 3/4 cups all-purpose flour
2 tsp. baking soda
1 tsp. cinnamon
1 tsp. ginger
1/2 tsp. salt

Blend dry ingredients together; stir into molasses mixture to form a soft dough. Chill dough several hours or overnight.

On a lightly floured surface, roll out dough to about 1/4 inch thickness. Cut with a floured gingerbread child cookie cutter. Place on greased baking sheets.

Bake at 350° for 8 to 10 minutes or until edges are firm. Do not overbake. Remove to wire racks to cool. Decorate as desired.

Pictured on page 287.

YIELD   ABOUT 40 FOUR-INCH TALL GINGER
CHILDREN

Royal Icing

1 tbsp. meringue powder
2 tbsp. cold water
1 cup powdered sugar

In medium bowl, beat meringue powder and cold water with electric mixer on medium speed until peaks form. Gradually beat in powdered sugar until soft peaks form, about 1 minute.

Spoon icing into decorating bag fitted with medium round tip, and pipe over cookies. Or place in small resealable food-storage plastic bag; cut a small hole in bottom of bag. Decorate cookies. Let stand about 5 minutes or until icing is set.

Cherry Almond Squares

Red and green cherries peek out of the golden caramel-like
topping in these showy squares.

2 cups all-purpose flour
1/2 cup brown sugar, packed
1 cup butter or margarine

In a mixing bowl, combine flour and brown sugar; cut in butter until crumbly. A food processor works well for this step. Press into ungreased 10 x 15 - inch rimmed baking sheet.

1 cup raisins or currants
1 cup chopped red and green
  maraschino cherries
2/3 cup sliced almonds
1 can (14 oz.) sweetened condensed milk
  (not evaporated)

Sprinkle with raisins, cherries, and almonds. Drizzle sweetened condensed milk over all. Bake in 325° oven for 25 to 30 minutes or until caramelized and browned. Cool and cut into squares.

YIELD   35 SQUARES (ABOUT 2-INCH)

Pictured on page 287.

Coconut Cranberry Squares

These rich and attractive squares are so delicious
you would guess they were made in a gourmet bakery.

2 cups all-purpose flour
1/2 cup brown sugar, packed
1 cup butter or margarine

In a mixing bowl, combine flour and brown sugar; cut in butter until crumbly. A food processor works well for this step. Press into ungreased 10 x 15 - inch rimmed baking sheet.

1 1/2 cups dried cranberries
1 1/2 cups white chocolate chunks
  (Callebaut is good)
1 cup flaked coconut
1 cup pecans halves
1 can (14 oz.) sweetened condensed milk
  (not evaporated)

In mixing bowl, combine cranberries, chocolate, coconut and pecans. Sprinkle over crust; drizzle with sweetened condensed milk. Bake in 325° oven for 25 to 30 minutes or until golden brown. Cool on a wire rack. Cut into squares.

Pictured on page 287.

YIELD   35 SQUARES (ABOUT 2-INCH)

Fruit and Nut Refrigerator Cookies

Jewelled with candied fruit, these festive cookies are tasty and slightly chewy.
My daughter Beverly is particularly fond of them.

½ cup butter or margarine
½ cup shortening
1 cup sugar
1 tsp. vanilla

Cream butter, shortening, sugar and vanilla until light and fluffy.

2 eggs

Add eggs and beat well.

2½ cups all-purpose flour
1 tsp. baking powder
½ tsp. baking soda
¼ tsp. salt
½ cup walnuts, coarsely chopped
1½ cups chopped candied fruit

Blend flour, baking powder, soda and salt; stir into creamed mixture with nuts and fruit.

Shape dough into 2 smooth rolls about 1¼ inches in diameter. Wrap in waxed or parchment paper and chill at least 4 hours or overnight.

When ready to bake, slice with sharp thin knife into ¼-inch slices. Place 2 inches apart on ungreased baking sheet. Bake in preheated 350° oven for 8 to 10 minutes or until golden.

Cool for 5 minutes on baking sheet, then transfer to rack and cool completely. These cookies freeze well.

YIELD   ABOUT 4 DOZEN COOKIES

Trilbys

A hearty oatmeal sandwich cookie with a date filling can be
enjoyed any time but especially during the holidays.

1 cup butter or margarine, softened
1 1/2 cups brown sugar
1 tsp. vanilla

In a mixing bowl, cream butter, sugar and vanilla together until fluffy.

3 cups all-purpose flour
2 cups quick-cooking oats
1 tsp. baking soda
1/2 tsp. salt
1/2 cup buttermilk

Blend dry ingredients; add to creamed mixture alternately with buttermilk. Mix thoroughly. Chill in refrigerator for 2 hours or until easy to handle.

On lightly floured surface or parchment paper, roll out to 1/4 inch thickness. Cut with 2 1/2-inch round cookie cutter and place 1 inch apart on lightly greased baking sheet.

Bake at 375° for 8 to 9 minutes or until golden brown. Cool on wire rack.

When cookies are cold, put together in pairs with the following filling:

1 1/2 cups finely chopped dates
3/4 cup sugar
3/4 cup water
1 tbsp. flour

In a medium saucepan, combine dates, sugar, water and flour. Cook and stir until thick; cool. Spread on cooled cookie; top with another cookie.

YIELD   30 SANDWICH COOKIES

Chocolate Caramel Candy

This treat rivals a commercial confection but has a wonderful homemade flavor.
The four layers may be time consuming but don't let that stop you.
Family and friends will bless you for sharing.

Line 9 x 9 - inch pan with foil; butter foil and set aside.

1 cup milk chocolate chips
1/4 cup butterscotch chips
1/4 cup creamy peanut butter

In a small saucepan, combine chips and peanut butter. Cook and stir over low heat until melted and smooth. Spread into prepared pan; chill until firm but still tacky.

1/4 cup butter or margarine
1 cup sugar
1/4 cup evaporated milk
1 1/2 cups marshmallow crème
1/4 cup creamy peanut butter
1 tsp. vanilla
1 1/2 cups chopped salted peanuts

In a heavy saucepan, melt butter over medium heat; add sugar and milk. Bring to a gentle boil; boil and stir on low heat for 5 minutes. Remove from heat; stir in marshmallow crème, peanut butter and vanilla. Add peanuts and stir to mix. Spread over chocolate layer in pan; chill until firm but still tacky.

1 pkg. (14 oz.) caramels
1/4 cup whipping cream

In a small saucepan, combine caramels and cream. Stir over low heat until melted and smooth; cook and stir 4 minutes longer. Spread over peanut layer; chill until firm but still tacky.

1 cup milk chocolate chips
1/4 cup butterscotch chips
1/4 cup creamy peanut butter

In a small saucepan, combine chips and peanut butter; stir over low heat until melted and smooth. Pour over caramel layer; chill for at least 4 hours. Remove from refrigerator 20 minutes before cutting. Lift foil and candy out of pan; cut into 1-inch squares. Store in refrigerator.

YIELD   ABOUT 8 DOZEN

Karen Yoder
Goshen, IN

Cherry Walnut Bars

Attractive, festive and flavorful, these bars are perfect for holiday entertaining.
They appeared at every special event when I was growing up.

1/4 cup butter or margarine, softened
1 cup brown sugar, packed
2 egg yolks
1 tsp. vanilla
1 1/2 cups all-purpose flour
1 tsp. baking powder
1/2 tsp. salt

Cream butter, sugar, egg yolks and vanilla until fluffy. Blend flour, baking powder and salt; stir into creamed mixture. Mix until crumbly. Pat mixture into lightly greased 9 x 9 - inch pan. Bake at 350° for 15 minutes.

2 egg whites
1 cup brown sugar, packed
3/4 cup flaked coconut
3/4 cup walnuts, coarsely chopped
1/2 cup maraschino cherries, cut in half

Beat egg whites until stiff; add brown sugar and mix well. Stir in coconut, walnuts and cherries. Spread evenly over crust layer. Bake at 350° for 25 to 30 minutes or until golden brown. Cool and cut into bars.

YIELD   36 BARS (ABOUT 1 1/2-INCH)

Snowballs

These cookies also go by the name of Russian Teacakes or Mexican Wedding
Cakes. Whatever the name, these little balls of nutty goodness will melt in your mouth.
A simple favorite to make at Christmas.

1 cup butter (no substitute)
1/2 cup powdered sugar
1 tsp. vanilla
1 3/4 cups all-purpose flour
1/4 tsp. salt
1 cup finely chopped pecans

Cream butter, sugar and vanilla together until fluffy. Mix in flour, salt and nuts until dough holds together. Shape dough into 1-inch balls; place on ungreased baking sheet.

Bake at 350° for 10 to 12 minutes or until set but not brown. While warm, roll in powdered sugar. Cool; roll in powdered sugar again.

VARIATION
ALMOND CRESCENTS
Omit pecans.
Add 1 cup finely chopped almonds.
Roll into ropes as thick as your finger.
Cut into 2 inch lengths. Pinch ends to taper. Shape into crescents.

OR alternately, dip warm cookies in Quick White Icing, page 46.

YIELD   ABOUT 4 DOZEN COOKIES

Raisin Butter Tarts

To my surprise, I learned that butter tarts are a completely Canadian food.
This wonderful creation unites quality pastry with tender raisin butter filling.
The recipe merits sharing.

Pastry to line 12-tart pan or 2-mini tart
  pans, page 178

1 cup sugar
1 cup seedless raisins
1/3 cup butter or margarine
2 eggs, beaten
1/4 cup whipping cream
1 tsp. vanilla

1/2 cup walnut pieces, toasted

Pictured on page 287.

*Prepare pastry and line tart pans; set
aside.*

*In medium saucepan, combine sugar,
raisins, butter, beaten eggs, cream
and vanilla. Bring to a boil over
medium heat; boil for 3 minutes.
Add walnuts and stir to mix. Fill
unbaked tart shells about 2/3 full.
Bake in 375° oven for 15 to 20
minutes or until lightly browned.*

YIELD   12 TARTS

Pecan Tarts

Mini muffin pans are used to create these dainty gems.

1/3 cup butter or margarine
1/4 cup sugar
1 tsp. vanilla
1 egg yolk
1 cup all-purpose flour
1/4 tsp. salt

1/2 cup sugar
1/4 cup butter or margarine, melted
2/3 cup finely chopped pecans
1 egg, beaten
1/2 tsp. vanilla

*In a medium mixing bowl, beat butter,
sugar and vanilla together until fluffy.
Add egg yolk; mix well. Stir in flour
and salt. Press dough into twenty-
four 13/4-inch muffin cups.*

*In a small bowl, stir together sugar,
melted butter, pecans, egg and
vanilla. Place 1 rounded teaspoonful
in each muffin cup. Bake at 350° for
18 to 20 minutes or until crust is
golden. Cool in pans on rack for 15
minutes; remove from pans.*

YIELD   24 MINI TARTS

NOTE
*If you don't have 24 muffin cups,
keep remaining dough chilled
while you bake the first batch.*

Chocolate Fudge

A grandmother's legacy needs to include memories created with small but sweet indulgences. On one of my visits, I made this creamy melt-in-your-mouth fudge for my grandsons. Once a day I rationed a half-inch square to them as well as myself.

2 cups sugar
2 tbsp. light corn syrup
3/4 cup evaporated milk
2 squares baking chocolate
   (1 oz. each)

In a medium saucepan, cook sugar, syrup, milk and chocolate to soft ball stage.

> **NOTE**
> *Soft ball is reached when a small amount of mixture dropped into cup of very cold water forms a soft ball that flattens when removed from water.*

2 tbsp. butter

Remove from heat and add butter. Cool until you can hold your hand on the pan bottom.

1 tsp. vanilla
1 cup chopped pecans

Add vanilla and beat until creamy. Stir in nuts. Pour into buttered 4 x 8 - inch pan. Cool and cut into squares.

YIELD   32 DELICIOUS 1-INCH MORSELS

Equivalent Measures

Measures

3 teaspoons	= 1 tablespoon
4 tablespoons	= 1/4 cup
5 tablespoons + 1 teaspoon	= 1/3 cup
8 tablespoons	= 1/2 cup
12 tablespoons	= 3/4 cup
16 tablespoons	= 1 cup (8 ounces)
2 cups	= 1 pint (16 ounces)
4 cups	= 1 quart (32 ounces)
4 quarts	= 1 gallon (128 ounces)

Weight

U.S. Units	Canadian Metric
1 ounce	30 grams
2 ounces	55 grams
3 ounces	85 grams
4 ounces (1/4 pound)	115 grams
8 ounces (1/2 pound)	225 grams
16 ounces (1 pound)	455 grams

Volume

U.S. Units	Canadian Metric
1/4 teaspoon	1 ml
1/2 teaspoon	2 ml
1 teaspoon	5 ml
1 tablespoon	15 ml
1/4 cup	50 ml
1/3 cup	75 ml
1/2 cup	125 ml
2/3 cup	150 ml
3/4 cup	175 ml
1 cup	250 ml
1 quart	1 liter
1 1/2 quarts	1.5 liters
2 quarts	2 liters

Ingredient Substitutions

Instead of	Use
1 cup all-purpose flour	1 cup plus 2 tbsp. cake flour
1 cup cake flour	1 cup minus 2 tbsp. all-purpose flour
1 cup self-rising flour	1 cup all-purpose flour + 1 1/2 tsp. baking powder and 1/2 tsp. salt
1 tsp. baking powder	1/2 tsp. cream of tartar + 1/4 tsp. baking soda
1 tbsp. cornstarch	2 tbsp. all-purpose flour
1 cup brown sugar, packed	1 cup granulated sugar + 2 tbsp. molasses OR dark corn syrup
1 cup dark corn syrup	3/4 cup light corn syrup + 1/4 cup molasses
1 oz. unsweetened baking chocolate	3 tbsp. cocoa + 1 tbsp. melted butter or margarine
1 cup semi-sweet chocolate chips	6 oz. semi-sweet baking chocolate, chopped
1 cup buttermilk	1 cup plain yogurt OR 1 tbsp. white vinegar + 1 cup milk; let stand 5 min. before using
1 cup dairy sour cream	1 cup plain yogurt
1 whole egg	2 egg whites OR 2 egg yolks (for custards or puddings) OR 2 egg yolks + 1 tbsp. water (for cookies or bars)
1 cup beef or chicken broth	1 tsp. beef or chicken bouillon granules OR 1 cube + 1 cup hot water
1/4 cup dry bread crumbs	1/4 cup finely crushed cracker crumbs, corn flakes OR quick-cooking oats
1 tbsp. fresh chopped herbs	3/4 to 1 tsp. dried herbs
1 tsp. dried herb	1/2 tsp. ground herb
1 tsp. poultry seasoning	3/4 tsp. ground sage + 1/4 tsp. ground thyme
1 tsp. dry mustard	1 tbsp. prepared mustard
1 garlic clove	1/8 tsp. garlic powder
1/3 cup chopped onion	1 tsp. onion powder OR 1 tbsp. minced dried onion
1 cup tomato juice	1/2 cup tomato sauce + 1/2 cup water

General Index

C

Order Additional Books

FROM:

At Home in the Kitchen
PO Box 22033
Lethbridge, Alberta T1K 6X5

—Canadian Mail Orders—

Name _____

Address_____

City_____

Province _____

Postal Code_____

Yes! Please send me _____ copies of *At Home in the Kitchen*

at only $19.95 per copy *(Canadian Funds)*

plus $10.50 Shipping & Handling.

Make check or money order payable to:
At Home in the Kitchen

For Gift Giving:
Enclose a personal card or note and we will gladly include it with your gift order.

Order Additional Books

FROM:

At Home in the Kitchen
62915 Planeville Ave.
Goshen, IN 46528

—US Mail Orders—

Name _____

Address _____

City _____

State _____

Zip _____

Yes! Please send me _____ copies of *At Home in the Kitchen*

at only $17.95 per copy *(US Funds)*

plus $5.00 Shipping & Handling.

Indiana residents please add 7% sales tax per book

Make check or money order payable to:
At Home in the Kitchen

For Gift Giving:
Enclose a personal card or note and we will gladly include it with your gift order.

Visit us at: www.athomeinthekitchen.ca